Twayne's English Authors Series

Sylvia E. Bowman, *Editor*

INDIANA UNIVERSITY

Colley Cibber

 17

Colley Cibber

By LEONARD R. N. ASHLEY

Brooklyn College, The City University of New York

Twayne Publishers, Inc. :: New York

ANNE CONSTANCE NELLIGAN ASHLEY

Matri carissimæ meæ
sine cuius auxilio
hoc libellum scribi non potuisset
dono atque dedico

```
I give & dedicate
this booklet to
my very dear
mother without
whose help it w'd
not have been
able to be
written .
```

Preface

Even the Gospel of St. John begins with a preface, and scholarly works apparently cannot dispense with positioning introductions. This study of Colley Cibber needs one more than most, for Cibber wrote his own *Apology for the Life of Mr. Colley Cibber, Comedian* in 1740 and wrote it so well that Dean Swift stayed up all night to read it. Even Dr. Johnson, who treated Cibber with such condescension as to arouse Samuel Richardson's wonder, conceded to his ever-attentive Boswell years after the *Apology's* publication that it was "very entertaining and very well done, to be sure, Sir."

Anyone who writes after the *Apology* must indeed offer some apology of his own, for Walpole was right: Cibber's autobiography is undeniably "inimitable." I am all the more called upon to explain my book in that I am not the first to write about Cibber in modern times. In 1928 Dorothy Senior accepted the challenge of retelling Cibber's story with verve. Her *Life and Times of Colley Cibber* was unquestionably "entertaining." In 1939 Richard Hindry Barker published *Mr. Cibber of Drury Lane*, a definitive and comprehensive study.

In the face of these and shorter studies, such as those by Croissant and Habbema, what can I hope to add? I cannot undertake to challenge Miss Senior's charm or Professor Barker's scholarship. So much sound work has been done on this limited subject in books and articles that there must necessarily be substantial agreement between my conclusions and those of scholars who have preceded me: I should be concerned if there were not. But my researches in manuscripts of the period have permitted me to present some material about The Theatre-Royal under Cibber which has not previously appeared in print, and I have views of my own about Cibber's work and importance. These opinions, where they occur, have been adequately identified, and for them I must accept full responsibility. Otherwise "I have gathered a posie of other men's flowers, and nothing but the thread that binds them is mine own." I borrow even that explanation: it is from Montaigne.

What I have tried to do is to avoid offering a feast of crumbs and to present a unified, coherent, entertaining, and informative combination of critical biography and literary analysis. This is not a book for Cibber specialists, but neither is it designed for Miss Senior's slightly unsophisticated circulating-library audience, though I hope that I have not achieved accuracy and completeness at the expense of vivacity and readableness. Here is a critical and analytical study of Cibber's works, the biography of the man who wrote them, and sufficient theatrical and literary history to make those works understandable to the modern reader. Perhaps I may tempt the adventurous to take an interest in a few of Cibber's better plays and to investigate the *Apology* for themselves with increased judiciousness and appreciation.

I have attempted to keep the Notes and References to a minimum, but the reader will find in this section full bibliographical details, ancillary information, and the important sources of each chapter. I have done a rather pedantic thing: whenever I quote Cibber's *Apology*, I use the first edition (1740) and have not modernized the spelling and punctuation of that more lavish age, hoping that something of Cibber's personal manner of expression will come through.

I take sincere pleasure in acknowledging my debt to the many who have enabled me to offer this study. Professor Alan S. Downer of Princeton University first interested me in Cibber and directed the doctoral dissertation I wrote there on the management of The Theatre-Royal in Drury Lane under Cibber, Booth, and Wilks. Others who assisted me in that original study were Dr. Louis B. Wright and Dr. James J. MacManaway, of the Folger Shakespeare Library; the late Dr. William van Lennep, curator of the Harvard College Library Theatre Collection; Dr. George Feedley, curator of the Theatre Collection in the New York Public Library; Tyrus G. Harmson, of the Henry E. Huntington Library; Miss Sybil Rosenfeld, of the Society of Theatre Research, London; G. W. Nash, for information on the holdings of the Gabrielle Enthoven Collection in the Victoria and Albert Museum; David G. Mearns, of the Library of Congress; Sir St. Vincent Troubridge, for a report on the manuscript holdings in the Garrick Club, London; and others, too numerous to mention, all of whom, insofar as some of the information in this book comes from studies which they encouraged and from more than 500 unedited manuscripts which they helped me to collect, it is fitting to thank here.

Preface

My debt is greater to Miss Senior and all the subsequent scholars who appear in my bibliography. Chief among these is Professor Richard Hindry Barker, my colleague at Brooklyn College, on whose work all recent Cibber critics have leaned. He very graciously read my manuscript and helpfully made many useful suggestions. I have also had the assistance of the New York Public Library, the British Museum, the Public Records Office, and the libraries of Brooklyn College, Princeton University, and the University of Utah. I make reference in this book for the first time in print to some unpublished manuscript material through the kind permission of the Harvard Theatre Collection and the Folger Shakespeare Library.

Nonetheless, I am aware that "No book is complete until *Error* has crept in and affixed his sly Imprimatur," so I must accept reponsibility for any mistakes. Having had the opportunity of working closely with Professor Sylvia Bowman, the editor of this series, I cannot believe that the errors are many.

The manuscript was prepared and proofread with the help of Harold Hollingsworth, Dennis Williams, and Stuart Richard Townsend.

L. R. N. ASHLEY

Brooklyn College,
The City University of New York
September, 1964

Contents

Chronology

1671   November 6: Colley Cibber born in London. November 29: Christened at St.-Giles-in-the-Fields, London.

1682   Sent to the free school at Grantham, Lincolnshire.

1687   Unsuccessfully stood for election to Winchester College. Spent a few months in London, attracted by the theaters. Summoned by his father to Chatsworth. Met him at Nottingham as the Revolution broke out and took arms in the cause of William of Orange.

1688   Failed to receive a commission. Left the army. In the service of the Earl of Devonshire at Chatsworth and in London. Frequented the play-houses. Friend of Downes, the prompter at Drury Lane.

1690   Joined Drury Lane as an unpaid probationer. Unless otherwise noted below, all performances at Drury Lane.

1691   Theatrical debut as a servant in Southerne's *Sir Anthony Love*. Also in *Alphonso, King of Naples* and *Bussy d'Ambois*.

1692   Played bit parts in *The Rape, The Marriage-Hater Match'd, The Traitor,* and *The Orphan*.

1693   May 6: Married Katherine Shore. Their ten children included the eldest daughter (born 1694), the eldest son Theophilus (born 1703), and the youngest daughter Charlotte (born 1710). Played Aminadab in *The Very Good Wife*.

1694   Played Lord Touchwood in *The Double Dealer;* and in both parts of *Don Quixote*.

1695   March 25: The Theatre-Royal reopened and Cibber wrote and recited a Prologue. April: Prologue to Mrs. Aphra Behn's *Abdelazer*. June: A *Poem on the Death of Our Late Soveraign Lady Queen Mary*. Played Pharamond in *Philaster* and Fondlewife in *The Old Bachelor*.

1696   January: Starred as Sir Novelty Fashion in his *Love's Last Shift*, published in February. Played Lorenzo in *Agnes de Castro*, Smyrna in *The Lost Lover*, Artabazus in *Pausanius*.

1697 March: Published *Womans Wit,* played Longville. April:
Starred as Lord Foppington in *The Relapse* and Praiseall
in *Female Wits,* Antonio in *The Triumphs of Virtue,* Bull
Junior in *Plot and No Plot,* the title role in *Aesop,* De-
metrius in *The Humourous Lieutenant,* and Careless in
The Sham Lawyer.

1698 Played Bertram in *The Campaigners* and Bond in *Imposture Defeated.*

1699 Cibber's tragedy *Xerxes* produced at Lincoln's Inn Fields.
Published in April. Played Ulysses and Calchas in *Iphi-
genia in Aulis.*

1700 Played two parts in *The Pilgrim,* Parmenio in *Love's
Paradise,* and the lead in his *Richard III,* published March
16. Became adviser to Christopher Rich in the management of Drury Lane. Played Clodio in *Love Makes a Man,*
his new comedy, premièred in December.

1701 January 22: Published *Love Makes a Man.* Played the
Marquis in *Sir Harry Wildair* and Crab in *The Bath.*

1702 Played Malespine in *The Generous Conqueror,* Lord Pro-
mise in *The Modish Husband,* Don John in *The False
Friend,* Lord Hardy in *The Funeral,* Young Benjamin
Wou'be in *The Twin-Rivals.* Created Don Manuel in
She Wou'd and She Wou'd Not (his new comedy, first
acted November 26, published December) and as *The
School-Boy* (announced for October 24 and not perform-
ed, first recorded performance April 30, 1703).

1703 Played Tom Pistole in *The Old Mode and the New,*
Spring Love in *The Fair Example,* First Alderman's
Lady in *City Customs.*

1704 November: Signed a five-year contract for acting and
managing at Drury Lane. December 7: Première of his
comedy *The Careless Husband,* published December 14.

1705 Played Howdee in *The Northern Lass,* Doctor Ref-
ugee in *The Quacks,* Wimble in *Squire Trelooby,* Lampoon in *Hampstead Heath,* and (December 3) Pacuvius
in his new tragedy *Perolla and Izadora.*

1706 January 3: *Perolla and Izadora* published. Played Captain Brazen in *The Recruiting Officer,* Sir Fopling Flutter
in *The Man of Mode,* Sharper in *The Platonick Lady,*
Corvino in *Volpone,* Humphry Gubbin in *The Tender
Husband,* Sir John Daw in *Epicœne.* Acted 1706-1707 at
the Haymarket. Sued by Rich for breach of contract.

1707 *The School-Boy* published. February 4: played Celadon

in his comedy *The Comical Lovers,* Haymarket. November 1: Played Atall in his comedy *The Double Gallant,* Haymarket. November 8: *The Double Gallant* published. December 5: *The Comical Lovers* published. December 13: played Lord George Brilliant in his comedy *The Lady's Last Stake,* Haymarket, published December 30. Also played: Surrey in *Henry VIII,* Gibbet in *The Beaux' Stratagem,* Renault in *Venice Preserv'd,* Zeal-of-the-Land Busy in *Batholomew Fair,* Worcester in *Henry IV, Part I.*

1708 January: Brett united the Drury Lane and Haymarket companies and in March delegated the management of Drury Lane to Wilks, Cibber, and Estcourt. Trouble with Christopher Rich. October 26—December 14: Drury Lane temporarily closed "by reason of Prince George's illness and death." Cibber played Hilliard in *The Jovial Crew,* Osric in *Hamlet,* Sir Roger in *The Scornful Lady,* Trim in *Bury Fair,* Young Reveller in *Greenwich Park,* Frederick in *The Rover.*

1709 January 11: Cibber played Samuel Simple in his comedy *The Rival Fools,* published January 26. December 12: Epilogue by Cibber to Mrs. Centlivre's *The Man's Bewitch'd.* Played Prince Volscius in *The Rehearsal,* Gloucester in *King Lear,* Cranmer in *Henry VIII,* Owen Glendower in *Henry IV, Part I,* Subtle in *The Alchemist,* Nicknack in *A Fine Lady's Airs,* Count Codgie in *The Gamester,* Iago in *Othello,* Sparkish in *The Country Wife,* Tiresias in *Oedipus.* Rich opposed the actors and on March 10 they secretly entered partnership with Swiney and planned to move to the Haymarket in the fall. June 6: Drury Lane closed, silencing Christopher Rich.

1710 Played Tattle in *Love for Love,* Burleigh in *The Unhappy Favourite,* Manage in *The Man's Bewitch'd.*

1711 Played Kick in *Epsom Wells* and Captain Cruise in *Injured Love.*

1712 William Collier reopened Drury Lane and Wilks, Doggett, and Cibber returned. The Haymarket left to Swiney and the opera. Cibber played Riot in *The Wife's Relief* and Wolsey in *Virtue Betrayed.*

1713 Played Syphax in *Cato,* starring Booth. November 11: Booth's success parlayed into a share in the management. Thomas Doggett opposed this. Cibber played Major Outside in *The Humours of the Army.*

1714 January 5: Epilogue by Cibber to Johnson's *The Victim.* Cibber played Gloster in *Jane Shore.* August 1: Queen

Anne died. Theaters closed. September 21: Drury Lane reopened. October 18: new license issued to Steele, Wilks, Doggett, Cibber, Booth. Suits and countersuits between Doggett and the management, *re* Barton Booth.

1715 January 19: Steele exchanged the license for a royal patent and assigned it to Cibber, Wilks, and Booth. Doggett sued. March 5: the managers countersued. Cibber played the Bishop of Winchester in *Lady Jane Grey*. March 12: première of *Venus and Adonis*. November 5: première of *Myrtillo*. December 2: Cibber's *Bulls and Bears* first performed. Apparently never published.

1716 Cibber played Tinsel in *The Drummer*.

1717 March: Booth allowed to buy into Drury Lane partnership for £600. Doggett, defeated, left the partnership. December 6: Cibber's comedy *The Non-Juror* a great success. Cibber played Dr. Wolf in *The Non-Juror* and acted Barnaby Brittle in *The Amorous Widow*, Bayes in *The Rehearsal*, and Plotwell in *Three Hours after Marriage*. Quarreled with Pope over this last play.

1718 Three editions of *The Non-Juror* in the first week of January. Cibber played Witwoud in *The Way of the World* and Peter Pirate in *The Play's the Plot*.

1719 Played Alexas in *All for Love*, Alamode in *Chit Chat*, two parts in *The Masquerade*, and Don Alvarez in his *Ximena*. October 24: *Ximena*, first acted seven years before, published. Preface angered the Lord Chamberlain. December 19: the Lord Chamberlain suspended Cibber from acting at Drury Lane, quarreled with Steele. Cibber's son Theophilus began his theatrical career. Cibber's only new piece: an Epilogue (November 11) to Dennis' *The Invader of His Country*.

1720 January 23: The Lord Chamberlain closed Drury Lane, revoking the patent. January 27: Drury Lane reopened. Cibber, Booth, and Wilks accepted a rescindable license which excluded Steele and continued despite financial difficulties. Played Crites in *The Spartan Dame*.

1721 Drury Lane patent restored. Steele reinstated as a silent partner. February 14: first performance of Cibber's comedy *The Refusal*, published the same year. Also published: collected plays, *Plays Written by Mr. Cibber*. Played Dufoy in *The Comical Revenge*, Abel Drugger in *The Committee*, Justice Shallow in *Henry IV, Part II*, and Wilding in *The Refusal*.

1722 Cibber assisted Steele with *The Conscious Lovers.*

1723 Played Tom in *The Conscious Lovers,* Jaques in *Love in a Forest,* Cardinal Beaufort in *Humphrey, Duke of Gloucester,* Tryphon in *Fatal Constancy,* and Novel in *The Plain Dealer.*

1724 Played Cardinal Wolsey in *Henry VIII.* December 8: première of *Caesar in Aegypt,* published December 15.

1725 Played Achoreus in his *Caesar in Aegypt.*

1726 Played Trueman in *The Twin-Rivals* and Sir John Brute in *The Provok'd Wife.*

1727 Played the Earl of Late-Airs in *The Rival Modes.* Booth retired.

1728 January 10: première of *The Provok'd Husband,* published January 31. Cibber acted Sir Francis Wronghead. Played Rattle in Fielding's *Love in Several Masques.* Cibber mentioned five times in Pope's first *Dunciad.*

1729 January 7: Première of his *Love in a Riddle.* (Cibber played Philautus.) Published with a title page misprinted 1719. August 16: *Damon and Phillida* at The New Theatre in the Haymarket. Published 1729.

1730 September 27: Eusden, Poet Laureate, died. December 3: Cibber named Poet Laureate; fiercely attacked. Cibber played Apeall in *The Humours of Oxford* and Scipio in *Sophonisba.*

1731 *An Ode . . . For the New Year,* Cibber's first work as Poet Laureate. January 20: Epilogue to Theophilus Cibber's *The Lover.* June 22: Epilogue to Lillo's *The London Merchant.* October 30: *An Ode for His Majesty's Birthday.* Similar occasional poems as Laureate for the rest of his life. Played no new character. Poetry satirized in the press.

1732 Robert Wilks died. Cibber sold his share in Drury Lane to John Highmore. February 14: Epilogue by Cibber to Fielding's *The Modern Husband,* in which Cibber played Lord Richley. Played Grinley in *The Modish Couple.*

1733 Cibber's last regular season at Drury Lane. February 17: Epilogue by Cibber to Fielding's *The Miser.* No new character. Officially retired as an actor in May.

1734 Cibber trained Susannah Maria Cibber, his daughter-in-law, as an actress. Contracted with Charles Fleetwood to appear in his favorite parts: six performances 1734-1735. Occasional verse published in *The Scarborough Miscellany for the Year 1734.* February 2: Cibber's libretto for

Polypheme first performed, Haymarket.

1735   Cibber insulted in Pope's *Epistle to Dr. Arbuthnot.* Cibber's son Theophilus ruined Highmore (who sold out to Fleetwood). Published *The Blind Boy,* a poem in broadside. Played no new character but appeared in galas for Fleetwood as in 1734.

1736   January 12: Prologue by Cibber to Hill's *Zara.* Appeared in *Love's Last Shift* ("Not Acted these Six Years") and as *The Man of Taste.*

1739   Still returning from retirement to play occasional special performances and benefits.

1740   April 7: First edition of *An Apology for the Life of Mr. Colley Cibber.* Great success—reprinted, pirated, satirized.

1741   Cibber in *The Old Bachelor,* a benefit for William Chetwood. Repeated it twice by popular demand, for his own benefit.

1742   Fielding satirized Cibber in *Joseph Andrews.* July 27: Pope's attacks, renewed in *The New Dunciad,* answered by Cibber in *A Letter from Mr. Cibber to Mr. Pope.*

1743   January: *The Egotist* in the pamphlet war with Pope and others. February 15: *A Second Letter from Mr. Cibber to Mr. Pope* on attacks in *The Dunciad* revision not yet published. October 29: *The Dunciad* reissued by Pope, with Cibber as "hero."

1744   January: *Another Occasional Letter from Mr. Cibber to Mr. Pope.* May 30: The controversy ended by the death of Pope. Cibber suppressed attacks on Pope during his last illness and published an epitaph on his death.

1745   February 15: Cibber as Cardinal Pandulph in his *Papal Tyranny in the Reign of King John,* Covent Garden, for ten performances. Last appearance on the stage. Play published the same year.

1747   *The Character and Conduct of Cicero.* Cibber a friend of Samuel Richardson and prominent in society.

1748   *The Lady's Lecture, a Theatrical Dialogue.*

1750   Cibber seriously ill. Recommended Henry Jones for the laureateship. Recovered.

1751   *A Rhapsody upon the Marvellous.*

1754   *Verses to the Memory of Mr. Pelham.* Cibber troubled by his two incorrigible children, Theophilus Cibber and Charlotte Charke. Living in Berkeley Square.

1757   December 11: Cibber died. Buried in the Cibber vault of the Danish Church, Wellclose Square, London.

CHAPTER 1

Youth

COLLEY CIBBER, actor and theater manager, Poet Laureate and prose polemicist, autobiographer and dramatist, was the eldest child of Caius Gabriel Cibber and his second wife, Jane Colley.[1] Caius Gabriel was the son of a cabinetmaker to Frederick II of Denmark, and his surname was originally something like Sibert; but, when the King of Denmark sent him to study art in Italy, Caius Gabriel changed his name to resemble that of the famous Cibò family; he also borrowed its coat of arms (Gules, a fesse checky Azure and Argent).[2] Later, in England, the name was apparently pronounced sometimes with a hard "C," for Fielding lampooned Colley Cibber as "Conny Keyber" and Pope made much of the alliteration in "King Colley" Cibber; but the sibilant "C" seems preferable.

After study in Rome and the Netherlands, Caius Gabriel was apprenticed to the London sculptor John Stone in his Long Acre studio.[3] When Stone died in 1667, Caius Gabriel became his own master and was soon claiming to be sculptor to the court of Denmark. It is doubtful if he ever held that appointment (and characteristic that he appropriated the title), but he did become "Sculptor in Ordinary to His Majesty William III of England."[4]

Nothing is known of Caius Gabriel's first wife, but on November 24, 1670, at St.-Giles-in-the-Fields, he married his second one, Jane, daughter of William and Jane Colley of Glaston, Rutlandshire. Her mother was the daughter of John Wirly of Dortford, Northamptonshire, and her grandfather was Sir Anthony Colley, a distinguished and staunch Royalist who had spent most of his fortune in support of Charles I. There was still enough in the family coffers, however, for Caius Gabriel to receive with his new wife a dowry of £6000. The Cibbers' first child was born in the fashionable new suburb of Southampton Street, Bloomsbury Square, on November 6, 1671, and christened on November 29 at St.-Giles'. He was named for his

maternal uncle, the last male heir of the Colleys. Later there
was a sister Veronica and a brother Lewis.[5]

As a very young child Colley saw Charles II sporting with
his spaniels and feeding the ducks in St. James's Park, and
once he saw both the King and the Duke of York at chapel in
Whitehall. He recalls these details in his autobiography,[6] but
others he omits. Apparently his was not a happy childhood.
Caius Gabriel took to gambling (later a favorite pastime of both
his son and his grandson), was jailed for debt, and for a time
"went backwards and forwards daily" to work from Marshalsea Prison.[7]

In 1680 Caius Gabriel sculpted perhaps his most famous
works, two huge statues in Portland stone for the gates of the
new madhouse, St. Mary's of Bethlehem ("Bedlam") in Moorfields. Probably influenced by Michelangelo's tomb of the
Medicis, they represented Melancholy and Raving Madness.[8]
When the asylum moved from Moorfields, these statues were
transferred to the South Kensington Museum. A visitor may
see them today in the Guildhall. However in their own day they
were not museum pieces but popular landmarks, and their
maker's name was known to everyone.

In 1682 Colley was sent to Grantham, Lincolnshire—his
mother's part of the country—to a free school, "where," he says,
"I staid till I got through it, from the lowest Form to the upper-
most." His school life was not pleasant, for his sarcastic wit
and incessant teasing of his companions made him unpopular
among both masters and boys, so that Colley early developed
a haughty air, an expectation of opposition, and a contempt
for criticism. Thus in later life he was able to withstand many
satirical sallies—but there was something about him that invited
them too. When he picked a fight with the school bully—and
was soundly trounced for his foolhardiness—even Colley's best
friend was shouting "Beat him, beat him soundly!" He, too,
had suffered from Colley's jibes.

Cibber almost deliberately made himself unpopular. When
Charles II died (February 6, 1685), the master set the boys of
Colley's class to write a funeral oration. All but one felt them-
selves unequal to the task. But, says Colley,

> I, Sir, who was ever giddily forward, and thoughtless of
> Consequences, set myself roundly to work, and got through
> it as well as I could. . . . This Oration, such as it was, I
> produc'd next Morning; All the other Boys pleaded
> their Inability, which the Master taking rather as a mark

of their Modesty than their Idleness, only seem'd to punish,
by setting me at the Head of the Form: A Preferment
dearly bought. Much happier had I been to have sunk my
Performance in the general Modesty of declining it. A
most uncomfortable Life I led among 'em, for many a
Day after! I was so jeer'd, laugh'd at, and hated as a
Pragmatical Bastard (School-boys language) who had be-
tray'd the whole Form, that scarce any of 'em would keep
me company. . . .⁹

Two months later Cibber made the same mistake again. (He
was to be "giddily forward" all his life and was forever being attacked by the envious and cantankerous.) When the schoolmaster
promised a holiday if anyone would produce a poem to mark
the coronation of James II (April 23), young Cibber's abundant
self-confidence once again manifested itself; he bent to his task
for a full half hour, infelicitously striving to engender an ode.
He earned the holiday for the boys, but his consequent vanity
so irked them that they shunned him for the rest of the day.
Cibber retained his pride: "But their Ingratitude serv'd only to
increase my Vanity; for I consider'd them as so many beaten
Tits, that had just had the Mortification of seeing my Hack of
a *Pegasus* come in before them."¹⁰
   Later, he continues, he realized the lesson to be learned:
"That when we are conscious of the least comparative Merit
in ourselves, we shou'd take as much care to conceal the Value
we set upon it, as if it were a real Defect: To be elated, or
vain upon it, is showing your Mony before People in want; ten
to one, but some who may think you have too much, may
borrow, or pick your Pocket before you get home."¹¹ If, in later
life, Cibber did not always follow his own good advice, and
suffered therefore from the envy of inferiors and the ire of
equals, he was at least willing to accept with good humor the
troubles and attacks he brought upon himself. He took criticism
with a smile of tolerance and amusement, a method which only
goads enemies to renewed assaults.
   At sixteen Cibber was ready for a public school, and his
father, who destined his son for the church, a comparatively
comfortable vocation which in those days demanded no particular piety, sent him to compete for election to Winchester
College and to claim descent from its founder, William of Wykeham, on his mother's side.¹² However this "pompous Pedigree"
was all he had and was insufficient to gain him acceptance.
He might as well have been sent, said Colley, "by the Carrier

to the Lord Mayor of the Town, to be chosen Member of
Parliament." Having failed to gain admission to Winchester,
Colley took the rest of his expense money and hastened to
London to spend it on entertainment—"to see a Play (then my
darling Delight) before my Mother might demand an account
of my travelling Charges. . . . 'Twas about this time I first
imbib'd an Inclination, which I durst not reveal, for the Stage;
for, besides that I knew it would disoblige my Father, I had
no Conception of any means, practicable, to make my way to
it."[13]

Colley had only a few months to pursue this interest, however, before he was summoned to appear at Chatsworth, the
Derbyshire seat of William Cavendish, Earl (and later first
Duke) of Devonshire. There Cibber's father was employed in
executing £1000 worth of sculpture,[14] and he decided that the
boy should stay with him until he could arrange to have Colley
accepted at Cambridge. The elder Cibber hoped to use his
connections to accomplish his son's admission: he had done
some decorations for the New Library at Trinity College and
the Master was a friend of his. Meanwhile, he thought it best
to have Colley at Chatsworth, away from the temptations (and
the expenses) of the capital. Reluctantly, Colley left London for
Derbyshire. He was loath to leave London for the rustication
of the Earl's remote country seat, but he lacked both the means
and the courage to disobey his father. As it turned out, however,
he never had to pine at Chatsworth. William of Orange's sixteen
thousand troops had already landed on the rocky coasts of
Devon: and, as he went North, Colley Cibber met the Glorious
Revolution.

Arrived at Nottingham, Colley took the place of his aging
father in the Earl's retinue and girded himself to battle for
Protestant William. His role in the revolution, however, was
to be an inglorious one. His only real duty that winter was to
ride out to meet the Princess Anne and to serve at the subsequent
banquet which the Earl tendered her and other dignitaries.[15]
With the new year William's convention Parliament assembled, declared the throne of James (who had fled to France,
throwing the Great Seal in the water *en route*) vacant, and
offered the crown to William and Mary jointly. The revolution
was over, and Colley Cibber was only one of the many young
men who were forced thereby to consider their prospects. Must
it be Cambridge and a benefice? Perhaps the Earl could find

him some other niche, some preferment. Colley Cibber stunned him with a tedious petition in Latin. His father, he explained, wished to avoid the expense of educating him at Cambridge. Could the Earl remember his father's service with any favor? The Earl gave him some vague promises of a post in London and sent Colley there to await further developments.

Whether Colley feared that the Earl's influence would find him some dreary office under Shrewsbury (then Secretary of State) or whether he independently determined to be beholden to no one and to indulge his own preference cannot be known. But the next we hear of Colley Cibber he was anything but waiting patiently for some uncongenial job in government. He was busily attempting to launch himself as an actor. When not frequenting the gaming house, he was to be seen in the company of the equally stagestruck young John Verbruggen, hanging about at Drury Lane. Each night Colley watched the glamorous performers and, perhaps, in the privacy of his dismal lodgings, mimicked them before a glass and dreamed his dreams of glory. At the same time, ever the "Pragmatical Bastard," he sought the influence of the powerful. But this time it was not an Earl: he was cultivating John Downes, the prompter at Drury Lane.

In time Cibber eased himself into the company as an unpaid probationer. He served the usual six-month apprenticeship and more, unpaid and unnoticed. He carried spears and swelled the scenes. He kept his eyes and his ears open and learned his trade, not hesitating to be critical of the established performers. He even felt competent by then to judge the great Mr. Dryden, who appeared to read the script of his *Amphytrion*—and read it, brash young Cibber observed, in a flat, dull, uninspiring way.

Finally Master Colley, as he was called, began his professional career—with a blunder, so the story goes. Intimidated by the audience, perhaps elbowed by one of the gallants seated on the stage or distracted by some remark from the pit, he blew up in his lines and threw even the redoubtable Thomas Betterton out of his stride. The old man ceased in mid-oration and was livid with rage. Betterton should have sympathized with the gawky young man's problem—he used to blow up occasionally himself—but perhaps his gout was particularly troublesome that day.[16] In any case the star demanded that nincompoop Colley, who came on as a servant and ruined a scene, be fined for incompetence. "Why, sir," replied Downes, the prompter;

"he has no salary." "No?," said Betterton, not to be cheated of his just revenge, "why then put him down [for] ten shillings a week and forfeit him five!"[17]

And so Master Colley was hired as an actor at The Theatre-Royal in Drury Lane.

CHAPTER 2

The Actor

TEENAGER Cibber's debut was not encouraging, nor were the other parts he played in 1691,[1] but a lucky opportunity rescued him from being immediately stamped as a bit player. His performance as the chaplain in Otway's *The Orphan,* though not a lead, brought him his first applause from an audience and heady praise from Cardell Goodman, a well-known though by then retired actor, who clapped him on the shoulder and predicted a successful career.[2] Cibber says in his *Apology* that he nearly cried.

In 1693 his only new role was that of Aminadab in *The Very Good Wife,* a very bad play. He was sinking back into obscurity. Then in 1694 he got another break, the sort that young actors dream about and that old actors fondly recall in their ghost-written autobiographies. Kynaston, cast as Lord Touchwood in Congreve's *The Double Dealer,* had to be replaced at the last minute. Cibber was given the part; and, to make it doubly exciting for him, it was to be a command performance before the Queen. Years later Cibber recalled the excitement of that January 13:

> Queen *Mary* having commanded the *Double Dealer* to be acted, *Kynaston* happened to be so ill, that he could not hope to be able next Day to perform his Part of the Lord *Touchwood.* In this Exigence, the author, Mr. *Congreve,* advis'd that it might be given to me, if at so short a Warning I would undertake it. The Flattery of being thus distinguish'd. . . made me blind to whatever Difficulties might attend it. I accepted the Part, and was ready in it before I slept; next Day the Queen was present at the Play, and was receiv'd with a new Prologue from the Author, spoken by Mrs. *Barry* . . . . Two lines of it, which though I have not since read, I still remember.
> > *But never were in* Rome, *nor* Athens *seen,*
> > *So fair a Circle, or so bright a Queen.*
> After the Play, Mr. *Congreve* made me the Compliment of saying, that I had not only answer'd, but had exceeded his Expectations, and that he would shew me he was sincere, by his saying more of me to the Masters—He was

as good as his Word, and the next Pay-day, I found my
Sallary, of fifteen, was then advanc'd to twenty Shillings
a Week.[3]

On this salary, and £20 a year from his uncle's estate, Cibber
married Katherine Shore, daughter of Matthias Shore, Sergeant
Trumpet to His Majesty. The whole Shore family was musical:
the two sons William and John also played the trumpet, and
Katherine studied voice and harpsichord with Henry Purcell.
Indeed, their daughter Charlotte said Colley and Katherine
met because Cibber heard her singing one day while he
was visiting John, then a musician at Drury Lane, and asked
to be introduced.

The marriage took place on May 6, 1693. Katherine's father
opposed the match; and, instead of giving Colley Katherine's
dowry straight off, he spent it on Shore's Folly, a showboat on
the Thames, a kind of floating Vauxhall. Though cranky old
Matthias did eventually leave Katherine her share of his property,
he apparently never warmed to his son-in-law.[4] The young
couple did not, therefore, have an easy time of it. Children
arrived with startling regularity. Cibber's salary from Drury
Lane was not only small but undependable; for Christopher
Rich, the tightfisted manager, paid as little and as infrequently
as he could; and what little money Cibber did have he was
inclined to fritter away on fripperies or to squander at the
gaming tables of Groom Porter's. In 1697 he was, very briefly,
jailed for debt, just as his father had been. Katherine was
obliged, for a time, to take small roles at the theater to augment their income and pay off their bills.[5]

Cibber's prospects seemed dim. He could scarcely hope to be
a leading man, for he was in a strong company and his assets
were few. He tells us that, when he joined the Drury Lane
troupe in 1690,

> the principal Actors then at the head of it were,

Of Men	Of Women
Mr. *Betterton,*	Mrs. *Betterton,*
Mr. *Monfort,*	Mrs. *Barry,*
Mr. *Kynaston,*	Mrs. *Leigh,*
Mr. *Sandford,*	Mrs. *Butler,*
Mr. *Nokes,*	Mrs. *Monfort,* and
Mr. *Underhill,* and	Mrs. *Bracegirdle.*[6]
Mr. *Leigh,*	

Betterton had been since the Restoration one of the great

tragic actors of the English stage, a man of electric personality with eyes that flashed command. Kynaston was so handsome
that in his youth he had played women's parts and was considered the most ravishing of the belles. Moreover, he had
"true and masterly touches of Nature" in his acting and the
happy knack of speaking lines so naturally that they sounded
as if they had just occurred to him. Monford (or Mountfort)
was renowned as a dashing lover in tragedy. Sandford was a
famous "heavy" with a face of striking villainy and an in-
exhaustible bag of tricks. Nokes was a popular comedian and,
like Cave Underhill, a darling of the pit. Nokes' feigned distress
when he aroused laughter was irresistible; and squat, awkward
Underhill delivered the most risible lines in a "churlish Voice"
that convulsed the spectators.

And Cibber? What had he to offer? A very unsympathetic,
anonymous writer described him in *The Laureat*: "He was in
stature of the middle size, his complexion fair, inclinable to
the sandy, his legs somewhat of the thickest, his shape a little
clumsy, not irregular, and his voice rather shrill than loud or
articulate, and crack'd extremely when he endeavour'd to raise
it. He was in his younger days so lean, as to be known by the
name of Hatchet Face."[7] If there was any grain of truth in this
description, we cannot wonder that Cibber abandoned all hope
of playing the lover opposite the stalwart Mrs. Bracegirdle.
He could never be one of those tragic heroes stalking (as
Belvedira says in *Venice Preserv'd*) "to eternal honour," following the glorious models of the oratorical Betterton and the
monumental Charles Hart. Cibber's piping treble would be
worse than useless in loud, rhetorical dramas—plays in which
elocution replaced emotion. It was a day in which the thunder
of the actors disguised the emptiness of the tragic speeches
they roared. In fact, for such as Betterton, the emptiness seemed
only to provide a sort of resonance. Cibber had a good ear
for lines, but he could never hope to deliver them like that.
How could he manage that low growl with which, Tony Aston
says, Betterton "enforced universal attention even from the
fops and the orange girls"? No, Cibber would never play tragedy
effectively: his voice quavered as he intoned his half-sung lines
of "high heroics."[8] Nor would he ever be an acceptable romantic
hero: his impudent pale face, his graceful but slender figure,
his *rétrousé* nose and vapidly smiling mouth—all these were
against him. Very well, he would turn them to his advantage.
He would be a comedian!

Meanwhile, he bought a fashionable, full-bottomed, flaxen periwig and swaggered about like a beau, gambling, dueling, running up debts, frequenting brothels and coffeehouses, rubbing shoulders with the highest and the lowest. The highest, preferably, for Cibber all his life was a snob and would rather be slightly acquainted with a parcel of peers than beloved by a few close friends of lower rank. At Will's Coffeehouse he knew Dryden, no longer Poet Laureate (since the Protestant succession) but still a literary lion. Cibber remembered him many years after as "a decent old man, arbiter of critical disputes."[9]

His acting career went on. When Queen Mary died on December 28, 1694, the theater was closed until the next March. When it reopened, Cibber not only wrote the Prologue the occasion demanded but was allowed to speak it. He was making progress. Then, when Betterton left Drury Lane in disgust at Rich's management and opened a new theater in Lincoln's Inn Fields (April, 1695), Cibber was among the actors Rich retained. Cibber found his salary raised to thirty shillings a week; and, in the absence of those actors who had joined the mutiny, he began to get better roles. George Powell undertook to do *The Old Bachelor* in imitation of the now-rival Betterton. Cibber was given the part of Alderman Fondlewife, a "cameo" in the fourth act. He mimicked curmudgeon Thomas Doggett so well, borrowing not only his costume but his voice, that for an instant the audience thought that Doggett must have quit Betterton's rebellion and returned to Drury Lane. The great applause that greeted Cibber's performance disappointed Powell, who had cast him in desperation, thought he might fail, and had said: "*If the Fool has a mind to blow himself up, at once, let us ev'n give him a clear Stage for it.*"[10] Cibber's triumph, though his applause was "more than proportional," was shortlived. It was clear to him that he was getting such chances only occasionally and then rather by accident.

He realized that if he wanted a really good part he would have to write it for himself. Most actors have this thought at one time or another, but Cibber was capable of translating his wish into fact. With the same application and confidence with which he had produced schoolboy odes, Cibber busied himself during the winter with his new task. He decided, of course, upon a comedy, and he carefully constructed one in which the star part called for all the special talents he himself had as an actor—and all the particular knowledge he himself had picked up as a man about town. He gave it the catchy title of *Love's Last Shift, or the Fool in Fashion.* Thomas Southerne, who "pandered to the vicious tastes of his audience" and who had made as much as £500 out of so slight a thing as *The Spartan Dame,*[11] gave Cibber the approving verdict of an eminently successful commercial dramatist: *"Young Man! I pronounce thy Play a good one! I will answer for its Success, if thou dost not spoil it by thy own Action."*[12] Cibber, who had written it to act in, was not going to be deterred. His wife could manage the role of Hillaria; he would coach her at home. He would star as Sir Novelty Fashion, "a good Portrait of the Foppery then in fashion," an egregious dandy, always *en cavalier,* gossiping and fluttering, the prototype of Lord Dundreary and dozens of others.

The managers accepted the play. After a slight skirmish, Powell got to speak the Prologue instead of Cibber, but afterwards that night was Cibber's. The audience cheered. Charles Sackville, Earl of Dorset and Lord Chamberlain, paid Cibber a compliment: *"viz. That it was the best, First Play, that any Author in his Memory, had produc'd; and that for a young Fellow to shew himself such an Actor, and such a Writer, in one Day, was something extraordinary."*[13] John Dennis and some other enemies paid the fledgling dramatist the supreme compliment of alleging that the play was far too good to have really been written by Cibber, then only in his twenties. Cibber was delighted. At last he had found his *métier;* playing the fop with solemn insignificancy, creating a series of eccentric coxcombs, drawling and snuff-pinching and mincing through comedy after comedy. The success of his first major characterization set his style of delivery for comedy: an affected accent in which all the "O" 's were "A" 's, all sung to what Roger North is said to have called the "court tune." Of Cibber's voice the comedian Samuel Foote said in his memoirs: "It is true his voice partook of the *old school,* and therefore differed in some respect from that familiarity in modern dialogue which Garrick introduced; but it was, upon the whole, a fine picture of the manners of the age in which the play was written, and had a very impressive effect."[14]

So well did Cibber play the dandy who believed "One had as good be out of the world, as out of the fashion," that the next year Sir John Vanbrugh produced as his first play a sequel to *Love's Last Shift,* pointing up *The Relapse* that must surely have followed the contrived *dénouement* of Cibber's last act. Vanbrugh raised Sir Novelty to the peerage as Baron Foppington, and Cibber played him in triumph. He went on to play Sir Courtly Nice and other men of mode such as Sir Fopling Flutter, Tattle, Tinsel, and a host of other social butter-flies whose fictive names (in the fashion of the time) indicated their frivolous nature. He also played similar characters in earlier plays—Osric in *Hamlet*, for instance. Perhaps in tragedy of the period "declamation roar'd while passion slept," but in comedy Cibber was introducing a new lightness, deftness, and charm. In enormous wig, outsized lapels, cocked coat-tails and per-fumed, lace-trimmed, orangerie gloves, he pranced and shril-led, sneered and fidgeted his way to success. Spectators said that Cibber onstage occasionally looked so vapid that it seemed he didn't know what he was doing. Cibber did know: he was building a character and a career for himself.

It was perhaps not surprising that there developed a certain sameness in his roles. Bishop Newton wrote to Garrick (whom he was praising for having more range than his predecessors) that "Cibber is something of a coxcomb in everything; and Wolsey, and Syphax, and Iago all smell strong of the essence of Lord Foppington." But Cibber did have some variety. For example, he was remarkably effective as Sir John Brute in *The Provok'd Wife*: "Two years Marriage has debaucht my five Senses. Every thing I see, every thing I hear, every thing I smell, and every thing I taste—methinks has Wife in't. . . . Wou'd my Courage come up but to a fourth part of my Ill Nature, I'd stand buff to her Relations, and thrust her out of Doors."[15] Garrick took over this role and eventually overshadow-ed Cibber, though Cibber once returned for a benefit perform-ance and proved he could still draw much bigger audiences.[16] Nor could "Natural David" rival the effectiveness of Cibber's somewhat extravagant performance as "Your most obsequious and most observant very servant, sir" Bayes in *The Rehearsal*: for, as snobbish Horace Walpole was quick to note, Garrick was a country boy at heart and ever rather weak on stage as a man of fashion.

Cibber, on the other hand, was a superb mimic and a snob. His first play may have been dedicated to plain Richard Norton, but later plays were addressed to the Marquis of Kent, to the Duke of Argyll, to the King himself. Cibber was always culti-vating the nabobs of the society of his time. Eventually Cibber— not merely a rich and influential theater manager (and "Gentle-man of the Great Chamber," with a scarlet livery) but Poet

Laureate as well—was able to dress himself in public as finely as he ever did for the stage, to move in the highest circles, and, to some extent, to play the part on the stage of the world that he played in the world of the stage. He knew more of the fads and foibles of the *haute monde* than did Garrick, who forever retained a slight if ingratiating touch of the boy who had come up from Litchfield with his schoolmaster to seek his fortune, with but five pence between them.

Garrick could never be, therefore, quite light enough to equal Cibber's Sir Courtly Nice, a performance favorably compared with Mountfort's for "insipid, soft civility" and "drawling delicacy." Perhaps Cibber did obtain laughter by caricaturing himself as an exquisite, but then his friend Steele testified to the fact that Colley excelled in roles that contained "anything that tends to the personal mortification of Mr. Cibber."[17] It may be that one of the reasons Cibber was able to survive all the satire that was directed at him in later life was that very early he had learned to laugh at himself, that for all his self-confidence and occasional overdone *eutrephilia* he had a sound appreciation of who and what he was.[18] He answered spite and spleen with humor, and nobody could caricature Colley Cibber better than he could.

Not all Cibber's roles were successful, of course. When he played Careless in Drake's play *The Sham Lawyer* (1697), he (or one of his colleagues) so botched it that the irate author had it published with this comment on the title-page: "As it was damnably acted at The Theatre-Royal in Drury Lane." In other comedies, however, he seems to have had a distinct flair for characterization and rode many dramatic Rosinantes to victory.

But he was not good in tragedy. His "honest Iago" was hissed as too patently a villain to make Wilks' deception as Othello creditable. His Wolsey lacked stature. His Scipio in *Sophonisba* was received on two successive nights with clamorous catcalls, and one critic averred that "Cibber was as much exploded as any bad actor could be." In any case, he was forced to resign this plum of a part to Charles Williams. When Williams made his entrance as Scipio on a subsequent evening, he was at first mistaken for Cibber and was nearly jeered off the stage. Then the audience discovered its mistake and gave Williams such a round of apologetic and encouraging applause that it threatened to stop the play cold. Cibber must indeed have felt that this demonstration was adding insult to injury, but he was

not often so condemned. Ordinarily he was "endured" in tragedy, Thomas Davies tells us, "on account of his general merit
in comedy."

He did succeed in tragedy as that determined villain Richard
III, stalking the stage and sometimes howling until his face was
as red as a pulpit cushion; but then he had the opportunity to
alter Shakespeare and to tailor the part to his own abilities.
Moreover, Richard (as portrayed by Shakespeare and even more
so by Cibber) is rather more sneaky than grand.[19] The newspapers of the period indicate that Cibber played up Richard's
slyness—some were unkind enough to say that he slunk around
like a pickpocket—and Aaron Hill characterized Cibber's Richard as "an unjointed caterpillar." But John Downes, whose career
as prompter connected him with the great and near great of the
stage from 1663 to 1706, points out that Cibber was not at all
bad in certain kinds of tragic roles, that he was "not much
inferior in Tragedy, had Nature given him Lungs Strenuous to
his finisht Judgment." Frankly, all the nineteenth-century
tragedian Charles Kean had that Cibber lacked was lung-power
(and limelight), for he shared Cibber's short stature and piercing
nasal voice, yet he was favorably compared with his famous
father Edmund Kean, and he filled the vastnesses of The Princess's Theatre. But Cibber drew spiteful notices such as these:
"I have seen the original Syphax [Cibber] in 'Cato' use as
many ridiculous distortions, crack in his voice, and wreathe
his muscles and limbs, which created not a smile of approbation,
but a loud laugh of contempt and ridicule of the actor." And,
as Richard III, "our comic-tragedian" Cibber "screamed thro'
four acts without dignity or decency. . . . [and] in the fifth
act, he degenerated all at once into Sir Novelty . . . . [so that]
when he was kill'd by Richmond, one might plainly perceive
that the good people were not better pleas'd that so *execrable
a tyrant* was destroy'd, than that so *execrable an actor* was
silent."[20]

In truth Cibber never was comfortable in tragedy, for
there the "comic shruggings," grimacing, and mugging of his
comic portrayals were out of place. If he did not understand
Iago, he *was* Sir Novelty Fashion. When he forgot his lines,
as he sometimes did because business or social life had kept
him from rehearsing adequately, he was all poise. He would
slowly take a pinch of snuff or drawl "Your humble servant,
Madame," bowing low. If the lines still eluded him, he would
only gain more applause by bending over the prompter's box

and calmly inquiring what came next. (This was even funnier when the audience knew that he had written the play or had played the role often.) As Justice Shallow he could play that solemn dodderer as slowly as he liked; the audience relished every word, every gesture, almost hoped (as in our day with the incomparable Bert Lahr) that he would *not* get on with it, that he would bumble and temporize hilariously. Cibber made the part his own.

De Witt Croissant is not overstating the case when, on the very first page of his study, he calls Cibber "the greatest actor of his day in comic roles."[21] Cibber surpassed even Doggett (a great clown, "very aspectabund, wearing a farce in his face"); played more often than almost anyone but the indefatigable Robert Wilks; and created a far greater number of roles in his long career. Steele himself credited Cibber with doing much to ensure the success of *The Conscious Lovers*, in which Colley was not the least distinguished member of an all-star cast; and Cibber did a great deal for lesser plays too. In a perfect part, say the superb dressing scene of *The Relapse*,[22] he was hilarious. He "stopped the show" with the description of his day, perhaps the best "counter-tenor aria" in all eighteenth-century literature:

> LORD FOPPINGTON. Far example, madame, my life; my life, madame, is a perpetual stream of pleasure, that glides through such a variety of entertainments, I believe the wisest of our ancestors never had the least conception of any of 'em. I rise, madame, about ten a-clack. I don't rise sooner, because 'tis the worst thing in the world for the complexion; nat that I pretend to be a beau; but a man must endeavour to look wholesome, lest he make so nauseous a figure in the side-bax, the ladies should be compelled to turn their eyes upon the play. So at ten a-clack, I say, I rise. Naw, if I find 'tis a good day, I resalve to take a turn in the Park, and see the fine women; so I huddle on my clothes, and get dressed by one. If it be nasty weather, I take a turn in the chocolate-house; where, as you walk, madame, you have the prettiest prospect in the world; you have looking-glasses all raund you.—But I'm afraid I tire the company.

> BERINTHIA. Not at all. Pray go on.

> LORD FOPPINGTON. Why then, ladies, from thence I go to dinner at Lackit's, where you are so nicely and deli-

cately served, that, stap my vitals! they shall compose you
a dish no bigger than a saucer, shall come to fifty shillings.
Between eating my dinner (and washing my mouth,
ladies) I spend my time, till I go to the play; where, till
nine a-clack, I entertain myself with looking upon the
company; and usually dispose of one hour more in leading
'em aut. So there's twelve of the four-and-twenty pretty
well over. The other twelve, madame, are disposed of in
two articles: in the first four I toast myself drunk, and in
t'other eight I sleep myself sober again. Thus, ladies, you
see my life is an eternal raund of delights.

The parts Cibber played from 1691 to 1745 have most of them
been mentioned in the Chronology as he created them year by
year. They cannot suggest any more than the wide variety of
his roles. Cibber began at Drury Lane and almost all these
roles were played there, for The Theatre-Royal in Drury Lane
was his home, as actor and manager.[23]

Of course, when Cibber came to be a director of that theater,
he had a profitable share in what was virtually a monopoly on
the drama, but even before that he was earning considerable
sums as an actor. In 1709 he got five pounds a week. For the 1708-
1709 season (135 playing days) he collected, with tips,
£162.10.10.[24] To give a modern equivalent of this sum would be
extremely difficult. Perhaps we can simply say that Cibber was
earning weekly about as much as the average Broadway actor
today, that he was (unlike the average actor today) working
regularly, and that he was paid only a trifle less than the great
stars of his company and others of the London stage. Cibber
acted seventy-one times "certain" that season. Of the major actors
only Wilks, with a hundred appearances, performed more than
Cibber.

After Cibber became one of the managers of Drury Lane,
his income rose considerably. His own hard work—he was usually
delegated to handle all legal and business affairs and got along
well with tradesmen, though his "tyranny" sometimes made him
unwelcome in the actors' Green Room—made the theater
ever more prosperous; and he shared in its success.[25] But 1709
is perhaps the last season for which we have details of his
income from acting alone. For a stagestruck fellow who began
by hanging around the stagedoor, who worked for longer than
usual as an unpaid apprentice, who finally got started at a
bare ten shillings a week, Cibber had already come a long way.
He no longer had to write plays to augment his income—he

had to act because he was "an actor by temperament"[26]—but he continued to do so. It was his philosophy rather than his poverty that led him always to make them commercial plays, vehicles for actors, commodities adapted from life (or Shakespeare, or anyone) to the public taste of the time. Of some of his plays it may now be asserted that they do not read well. Of none could it then be said that they could not run well.

Cibber retired from the stage in May, 1733, after a busy career in acting and managing as well as writing. By then Booth and Wilks and Nance Oldfield had all gone. Cibber was old but still vigorous, but in acting as in playwriting he always quit when he was ahead. Like many another theatrical personality, however, he was loath to leave. He haunted the scenes, loved to sit "out front," visited backstage with the performers, even came back for farewell appearances in his most popular roles. Aged and toothless at last, he might occasionally wish that he was home by his fireside and not waiting in the wings to go on as Cardinal Pandulph, but he could still "pack them in" to the point where the management was glad to pay him substantial amounts for single appearances and to erect temporary boxes on the stage to hold the overflow audiences these gala events drew. These audiences came to recall their youth or to see this legend about whom old theater hands still told so many stories: the great successes of glittering first nights and the less happy occasions when Cibber, as author, had to come on stage during a badly received performance and beg the audience not to be so violent and so noisy in its displeasure. As a playwright he never misjudged the taste of the town; as a personality, however, he once in a while was booed and his play suffered the fate of its author. As an actor he had generally been applauded. When as an old man he made a special appearance, this compliment was paid him: there was no other name on the bill. And everyone came to see *him*.[27]

His last appearance, fittingly enough, was in a play of his own devising and, strangely enough, in a serious role. He strode the boards with stilted grandeur in the flowing ecclesiastical robes of the papal legate in the tragedy of *Papal Tyranny in the Reign of King John,* adapted from Shakespeare. He had tried to stage this piece in 1736 but had failed.[28] By 1745 what Cibber would have regarded as the public's prejudice had changed. Bonnie Prince Charlie had created a climate that promised *Papal Tyranny* a better opportunity. Cibber knew that the play's politics were right and that its anti-Catholic bias was box-office material. Cibber gave it a try at Covent Garden,[29] opening on February 15 with Quin as King John, Mrs. Pritchard as Constance, Mrs. Bellamy as Blanch, Theophilus Cibber as the Dauphin, and Colley Cibber as Cardinal Pandulph. The reception was mixed.[30] Cibber, his voice quivering with age and his syllables indistinct without his teeth, wished that he had not cast himself in a part. He was as bad as his play. Davies, who attended one of the performances, reported: "He affected a stately magnificent tread, a supercilious aspect, with lofty and extravagant action, which he displayed by waving up and down a roll of parchment in his right hand; in short, his whole behaviour was so starchly studied that it appeared eminently insignificant, and more resembling his own Lord Foppington than a great and dignified churchman."[31] After the tenth performance (February 26, 1745), Cibber took his £400 profit— even his bad plays made money—and prudently purchased an annuity with it. After that he was seen no more on the public stage.

An actor's art is evanescent. Cibber's verse remains, though the circumstances which produced it have disappeared. Cibber's pamphlets to Pope are here, the echoes of an argument which has long since been stilled. Cibber's plays can be fully understood only when we can visualize their presentation and recreate the world of their reception, but at least we have the texts. Cibber as an actor is gone. He remains to us only in the paintings of Grisoni (who captured a striking pose of Cibber as Lord Foppington) and others and in the descriptions of his work penned by enemies and friends. The best of these word pictures speaks of Cibber at about the time of his official, though not actual, retirement from the stage around 1733. Aaron Hill wrote in *The Prompter* for November 19, 1734, without flattery but with great skill:

> As to his person, his shape was finely proportioned though not graceful, easy but not striking. Though it was reported by his enemies that he wanted a soul, yet it was visible enough that he had one, because he carried it in his countenance; for his features were narrowly earnest and attentively insignificant. There was a peeping pertness in his eye, which could have been spirit had his heart been warmed with humanity or his brain been stored with ideas. In his face was a contracted kind of passive yet protruded sharpness, like a pig half roasted; and a voice not unlike his own might have been borrowed from the

same suffering animal while in a condition a little less desperate. With all these comic accomplishments of person, he had an air and a mind which complete the risible talent, insomuch that, when he represented a ridiculous humour, he had a mouth in every nerve and became eloquent without speaking. His attitudes were pointed and exquisite, and his expression was stronger than painting; he was beautifully absorbed by the character, and demanded and monopolized attention; his very extravagances were coloured with propriety; and affectation sat so easy about him that it was in danger of appearing amiable.

CHAPTER 3

The Playwright

COLLEY CIBBER was writing plays before Vanbrugh and Farquhar, and he did not stage his last work until 1745. During his extraordinarily long career he wrote a dozen comedies, half a dozen tragedies, a "comical-tragedy," a handful of masques and libretti, and perhaps a dozen prologues and epilogues for other people's plays—not to mention various odes and lyrics, four public letters to Alexander Pope, several miscellaneous prose works, and one of the best autobiographies in English. In this chapter I propose to treat his more important dramatic works in some detail and to say something about most of the rest. I omit little but his last play, *Papal Tyranny in the Reign of King John,* for it is discussed in Chapter Ten in the context of his last years.

Cibber's comedies are his best theater pieces, but even these are not all first-rate. There is a modicum of truth in Alfred Bates' comment: "As a dramatist, he has neither the broad humor and strong comic vein of Vanbrugh, nor the fine diction and masterfulness of Congreve, nor the frolicsome gayety and airy fancy of Farquhar. His characters are flat; his plots are neither natural nor well conducted; his dialogue is often flippant."[1] Cibber's tragedies, generally poor, are effective only when melodrama creeps in.

But occasionally Cibber shows a master hand in both comedy and tragedy. He was capable of turning essentially dramatic ideas into fully realized plays, of integrating striking scenes into successful dramatic unities. He was a man of the theater who well understood the necessary, though secondary, non-verbal aspects of production and staging, matters with which we shall deal in subsequent chapters discussing his long and close association with practical theater management, and the selection and direction of plays for a repertory company. More often than luck can explain, Cibber built sturdy dramatic machines that could, artistically and financially, run. He had a shrewd sense of the commercial potential of a play script, a good ear for the playable line, a good eye for the scene *on the stage.* He knew his theater and his actors, and he wrote for them (and himself, as an actor) purposefully and success-fully, planning for the dramatic gesture, for the actor's stance and expression, for the right costume, the enhancing lighting, the property's positioning, the effective entrance and the elect-rifying exit. To appreciate how well Cibber's plays went on the stage it is necessary to read them so that the words come off the page, to put them in imagination on the boards of his theater so that the characters stalk before the mind's eye. We shall attempt—by describing not only his writings but his theater, his company, his audience, and the times—to enable the student to consider them in the light of how Cibber, and the people for whom he wrote them, saw them.

Perhaps Cibber has been cheated of just praise because he has been assessed by literary critics who do not take these matters into account, who read his scripts as literature rather than as dramatic literature, who examine his characters and ideas solely in their relationship to real life and not at all in connection with the stage's world of make-believe. Cibber was a professional man of the theater who wrote professionally for the theater, not for posterity. He addressed posterity only, perhaps, in his *Apology,* for which posterity remembers him best; the rest of the time he was an actor-manager and com-mercial playwright. It could be said that in some instances Cibber, writing so much for his time, has left us plays which mean little to ours. It could never be said of him what George Jean Nathan so aptly said of Luigi Pirandello's more wordy, intellectual debates—what we can say of much of modern drama—that these plays seem to have been written by a blind man.

Mrs. Inchbald had a good point when she observed: "Whilst many a judicious critic boasted of knowing what kind of drama the public ought to like, Cibber was the lucky dramatist generally to know what they would like, whether they ought or not."[2] It was more than luck. Dennis might dogmatize, but no one seems to have written a great play to his formula, which is suspicious. Jeremy Collier might rave—even try to reform the licentious stage—but he was of little fundamental use to the dramatists, for he basically did not like the theater. Cibber did not learn from them. He came by his knowledge by daily study and practice in the theater, not luck. He gave freely of his formulae too, but they were practical, not theoretical ones. He offered dramatists examples more useful than John Dennis' theories. He offered audiences and readers pleasures more moral than those derived from following Collier's well-meaning signposts to indecencies.[3] Not only did Cibber contribute to other dramatists by showing them how (or how not) to throw together a complex plot—or a viable play from discarded or forgotten old plays—but he established, for them to copy, a wholly new kind of play: the sentimental comedy. For this alone his position in histories of dramatic literature is secure.

Others had paved the way—Thomas Shadwell, for example—for few things happen suddenly in an art as conventional as that of the theater. But Cibber produced one smashing original success that created a significant demand for brilliant mixtures of the old comedy and the new morality. He put a new emphasis on *feeling*—especially on pity, repentance, duty, and sympathy. Thomas Otway, who rang these changes in tragedy, should logically have done this in comedy too, but theatrical history does not work that way. He did not. It was left to Cibber to blend the intrigues of a dissolute rake and the pathetic plight of a distressed wife, to combine tergiversation and tears to the popular taste.

Sir Richard Steele, a rake turned sentimental himself, encouraged the vogue. Eventually he wrote *The Conscious Lovers* (1722). Cibber advised him, perhaps helped him write it. Here was the height of the style, a play determined to "please by wit that scorns the aid of vice," a play that combined sentiment not with the comedy of manners (as Cibber had done at the beginning) but with farce, leaning heavily on pathos in the serious parts. Steele had only varied Cibber's recipe. And he lacked some of Cibber's restraint: the play is a trifle too saccharine for modern palates; unlike Cibber, Steele did not know when to stop adding sweeteners. As the century went on, the vogue of sentiment increased; and the sentimental comedy was debased by too much popularity. It degenerated into the formula-plays of Thomas Holcroft, Hugh Kelly, Richard Cumberland, and their ilk; and the stage which had been a "school of abuse" and a showcase of licentiousness gradually transformed itself into "a school of morality." The public tired of sentimental comedies, but not completely. Things change slowly in the drama. (After all, Steele had got part of *The Conscious Lovers* from Terence.) The sentimental drama is still with us: we still have on the stage, on television, and in the films, plays that teach "by precept and example," that sermonize, that lecture on the humanitarian belief in the essential goodness of man. "Let the common Practice of Mankind be what it will," declared Cibber, "it is not Unnatural to be Virtuous"[4]—nor to write dramas that preach that. This view ruled the drama absolutely until Goldsmith, and it is not dead yet. It was Cibber who introduced it to the stage, as surely as it was the Earl of Shaftesbury who introduced it into English philosophy.

If Cibber was lucky, it was in his timing. When he came along, a general reformation of the stage was imminent. The pendulum was swinging: the public had had enough of smutty, witty dialogue and of lack of feeling. The public that thought Charles II's fourteen illegitimate children a "merry" prank had become stricter, and the changing economy was bringing the rising middle class to the fore (and to the theaters, where they sat in "the middle row"). With that class came its sobersided mercantile ethic. Had this not been so, Cibber's success could never have been so immediate and so wholehearted. Tuke, Shadwell, Mrs. Behn, Ravenscroft, Crowne, and others had given copious hints of what was coming. It remained for Cibber to come along at the right time and, whether from moral duty or from sheer opportunism no one can say, to seize upon it and make it pay. There seems to be, no matter how imperfect his morality nor how commercial his successes, no reason to doubt that Cibber truly had "the Interest and Honour of Virtue always in view." He might have said with Addison, "I shall endeavour to enliven morality with wit, and to temper wit with morality."[5] In *Love's Last Shift* (1696) Cibber began to moralize the drama by capping a play of diverting dissipation with a contrived but morally acceptable conclusion, replete with tearful confessions and guarantees of mended ways (which, being less dramatic, are for offstage). His hero, whom Shadwell would have called "a Swearing, Drinking, Whoring Ruffian," grew regenerate before the very eyes of the audience in a Grand Transformation Scene of unparalleled effectiveness. The audience delighted in the spicy Restoration intrigue and then, just as the bourgeois "city gentlemen" were beginning to feel guilty at so enjoying it, came the edifying end which excused it. At this they could laugh *and* cry. Cynical Vanbrugh could not accept the end. He predicted a relapse. But Cibber, a man who could give a happy ending to *Le Cid*, was sincere in his last act, proud of the "moral Delight receiv'd from its Fable," and it showed. The audience which came to laugh remained to cry—and loved doing so.[6]

When the initial effect of *Love's Last Shift* began to wear
off, Cibber reinforced it with another moral and sentimental
triumph, *The Careless Husband* (1704). He (and Mrs. Oldfield,
whom he trusted to carry a large part of the play) firmly
established the vogue once more. Cibber had not only made a
momentous discovery, he had capitalized it, for which Thomas
Davies praised him fulsomely: "To a player we are indebted
for the reformation of the stage. The first Comedy, acted since
the Restoration, in which were proferred purity of manners
and decency of language, with a due respect for the marriage
bed was C. Cibber's *Love's Last Shift*."[7]

I Love's Last Shift

It has often been noted that there are conflicting theories
of comedy. Ben Jonson, for example, at his best removed the
gall and copperas from his ink ("only a little salt remaineth"
for bite) and ridiculed strays back onto the path of reason. In
plays that instructed delightfully, Jonson presented Comedy
> When she would show an image of the times,
> And sport with human follies, not with crimes.
Others burlesqued, satirized, kidded, or excoriated follies
and exhorted their audiences to avoid looking as silly or
acting as unwisely as the people they laughed at in the plays.
Cibber held to another theory and made popular a sentimental
comedy in which the stock characters of the Restoration comedy
of manners were purged of their vices (but retained, fortunately, some of their old spirit and dash) and presented to the
audience as models of virtue to be emulated rather than as
horrible examples of what to avoid. Instead of starting, like
Jonson, with "manners," creating caricatures to embody "humours" and a plot to exhibit and satirize them, Cibber—rather
like the writer of a nineteenth-century thesis play—starts with
a moral problem. His play is devoted to stating it and resolv-
ing it. He brings his essentially good people—even his wayward
protagonist is an *"honest"* rake—from distress to happiness.
As the curtain falls, however many tears have been shed, the
good have their reward and the bad are punished—or, better,
reformed by an appeal to their better natures, by sentiments
of pity or gratitude or (closely related to both) love. No one
is essentially evil or irremediably unsocial; and all men, at last
if not at first, are ashamed of folly and dedicated to virtue.
Virtue conquers all.

Cibber's sentimental comedy contained an admixture of other elements: manners, "humours," satire, burlesque, even the barest trace of the Shakespearian or "romantic-commercial" view, as Bernard Shaw calls it. Four of the five acts of *Love's Last Shift* are much in the vein of the Restoration intrigue comedy. But the last act of that play is thoroughly moral-sentimental, and throughout the whole play every character motivation and plot development is imbued with the sentimentalism that comes to the fore at the end. *Love's Last Shift* was the inheritor of Thomas Heywood's Elizabethan sentimentality and the forerunner, as we have said, of Steele and Vanbrugh, Farquhar, Mrs. Centlivre, Addison, Charles Johnson, Edward Moore, and many others. It ousted aristocratic cynicism; it introduced bourgeois moral preachment. Its effect was seen not only on the stage but in novels like *Pamela*, in poems like Gray's *Elegy*, in periodicals like *The Tatler*, in lives such as Dr. Johnson's and Goldsmith's. Could Cibber at twenty-four have fully realized that *Love's Last Shift*, written with a shrewd eye on the box-office and with the pragmatic purpose of creating an outstanding role for its author to act, was to be a milestone in the English drama, to be regarded as the first sentimental comedy?

The conception of comedy on which *Love's Last Shift* is constructed is one not far developed beyond the definition from Cicero:

> *Illud genus narrationis quod in personis positum est, debet habere sermonis festivitatem, animorum dissimilitudinem, gravitatem, leniatem, spem, metum, suspicionem, desiderium, dissimulationem, misericordiam, rerum varietates, fortunæ commutationem, insperatum incommodum, subitam letitiam, jucundum exitum rerum.*

> That kind of narrative which is represented by persons [that is, drama] ought to have liveliness of dialogue, diversity of characters, seriousness, tenderness, hope, fear, suspicion, desire, concealment, pity, variety of events, changes of fortune, unexpected disaster, sudden joy, a happy ending.[8]

This play of Cibber brought a new sensibility to the stage. Emotional relationships between characters, relegated to the subplots if they occurred at all in Restoration comedies, were stressed. Insensitive self-seeking, heartless intrigue, superficial love games—all these were unpalatable to the middle clas-

ses who were now thronging the pit and demanding once again
sensitive heroes and distressed heroines, hearts of gold rather
than flowers of eloquence. Perhaps Cibber's characters did not
have brains as quick as those in Congreve's plays, but they had
hearts.

Such ideals are not likely, however, to produce realistic or
even credible characters, and those in Cibber's epoch-making
comedy are less than vital personalities. None can be said
entirely to transcend specimen. Loveless, the debauched "hero,"
returns to London after eight years abroad, away from his wife.
Despite his advertised worthlessness, we sense from the start
that he will be redeemed from his life of depravity and (one
can almost hear the good burghers of the audience tut-tutting)
financial recklessness. His wife Amanda, "a woman of strict
virtue" and intolerable patience, whom he abandoned, still loves
him. With the aid of Young Worthy, whose name tells all, she
devises a bed-trick to win back Loveless. We are supposed to
consider neither Shakespeare nor ethical protest as Amanda
rhapsodizes:

> I can't help a little concern in a business of such moment.
> For tho' my reason tells me my design must prosper, yet
> my fears say 'twere happiness too great.—Oh! to reclaim
> the man I'm bound by heaven to love, to expose the folly
> of a roving mind, in pleasing him with what he seem'd
> to loath, were such a sweet revenge for slighted love,
> so vast a triumph of rewarded constancy, as might per-
> suade the looser part of womankind ev'n to forsake them-
> selves, and fall in love with virtue.

Amanda sets the trap; she appears "*loosely dress'd*" to
Loveless; and, after his protestations—"I like and I love you,"
"my own excess of burning passion," and so on—she "*Runs into
his arms.*" "Can all this heat be real?" she asks. They go off
to "be lavish to our unbounded wishes," presumably with more
effectiveness than they had ever done before, since Loveless
was "within two women of my maiden-head" when he knew
Amanda previously; but since then he has had eight years
of incontinence on the Continent.

The next day she gives him a sermon and a surprise. Upon
learning her identity, he dissolves into a rant of repentance: "Oh! thou hast rouz'd me from my deep lethargy of
vice: for hitherto my soul has been enslav'd to loose desires,
to vain deluding follies, and shadows of substantial bliss;
but now I wake with joy, to find my rapture real.—Thus let

me kneel and pay my thanks to her, whose conquering virtue
has at last subdu'd me. Here will I fix, thus prostrate, sigh my
shame, and wash my crimes in never-ceasing tears of penitence."
Amanda raises him with forgiveness (and the information that
her late uncle, Sir William Wealthy, has left her £2000 a year).
A few other loose ends are tied up, and the play termi-
nates gaily with a masque featuring Love and Honour, "the
subject perhaps not improper to this occasion," and giving the
audience time to dry its tears.

The subplot, owing most to the comedy of manners, features
a couple of *soubrettes,* Hillaria and Narcissa; and it stars the
fool in fashion, Sir Novelty, who gets some of his laughs with
his lines,[9] some with his costume (his buttons are "not above
three inches in diameter"), and some with his farcical falls.
Cibber romped in this role, and it was his first real hit as an
actor. The public approved him quite as much as "the mere
moral Delight receiv'd from the Fable."

Sir Novelty Fashion rings true, for all the exaggeration. Loveless does not. His excuse (" *'Twas heedless fancy first that made
me stray*") seems unacceptable; his repentance ("Pray give me
leave to think" at the disclosure of his wife's identity and "I
have wrong'd you" a moment later) is incredible. It is clear
that his heart was never in his licentiousness (which has
diverted us for four acts), and his virtue seems sham. His "love"
is really nothing more than the Restoration sex game again.

Henry Fielding was one of the few who were annoyed at
the hypocritical morality in the play. Vanbrugh, after a life in
the army and a term in the Bastille, was more cynical. He
could not credit Loveless' conversion. In six weeks he penned
what he considered to be a fairer, less sugary picture of human
nature, a sequel which showed *The Relapse; or, Virtue in
Danger.* Loveless and Amanda are seen again, and this time
the libertine is once more on the loose and the wife herself
is sorely tempted. The fop was brought back by popular
demand—as Lord Foppington, ennobled by purchase but not
ennobled in spirit—and once again Cibber was the ostentatiously
vapid popinjay, "industrious to pass for an ass." *The Relapse,*
testified Cibber in the *Apology,* "by the mere Force of its agreeable Wit, ran away with the Hearts of its Hearers." Though it
had been dashed off, Captain Vanbrugh (of Lord Berkeley's
Marine Regiment of Foot) traveled in a brilliant set; he
had only to commit his ordinary conversation to paper to have
brilliant dialogue.

Vanbrugh's dialogue is easily more sparkling than Cibber's. Cibber always relied more upon plot than on dialogue and many times his characters speak no living language. Vanbrugh's structure is better too: it is more of a piece. Cibber brought the action of *Love's Last Shift* to a moral end only by a wrench which strains the plot as well as our credulity, and it remains a question whether four acts of frivolous (or immoral) bandinage can be excused or atoned for by an ending drenched in sentiment. Are we asked to feel so deeply that we stop thinking? The conclusion of Cibber's play seems to me to have as little necessary relationship to the rest, despite the sentimental motivations throughout, as the endings Sir Robert Howard wrote for *The Vestal Virgin* (1664); he provided two fifth acts, to be played on alternate nights. True, Cibber asserts (as Shadwell had done) that he is introducing immorality only for the purposes of correction, but there is the distinct impression that he has his fingers squarely on the public pulse. Here is some of what Miss Cross (still dressed as Love from the masque) delivered as an Epilogue:

> *NOW, gallants, for the author. First to you,*
> *Kind city gentlemen o' th' middle row;*
> *He hopes you nothing to his charge can lay,*
> *There's not a cuckold made in all his play.*

And to the beaux:

> *He fears he's made a fault you'll ne'er forgive,*
> *A crime beyond the hopes of a reprieve:*
> *An honest rake forgo the joys of life,*
> *His whores and wine, t' embrace a dull chaste wife!*
> *Such out-of-fashion stuff! But then again*
> *He's lewd for above four acts, gentlemen.*[10]
> *For faith he knew, when once he'd chang'd his fortune,*
> *And reform'd his vice, 'twas time—to drop the curtain.*

And we turn from the beaux to the ladies, now tucking away their handkerchiefs:

> *Four acts for your coarse palates were design'd.* ⎫
> *But then the ladies taste is more refin'd.* ⎬
> *They, for Amanda's sake, will sure be kind.* ⎭

Cibber, tyro though he was, had hit upon "the understanding of the Galleries" and "the applause of the Boxes." So cleverly was it done that his enemies paid him the compliment of saying "That, to their certain Knowledge *it was not my own.*" Some

years later John Dennis continued to refuse Cibber credit for
Love's Last Shift: "When The Fool in Fashion was first acted,
Cibber was hardly Twenty Years of Age. Now could he at
the Age of Twenty write a Comedy with a just Design, distinguished Characters, and a proper Dialogue, who now at
forty treats us with Hibernian Sense and Hibernian English?
Could he, when he was an arrant Boy, draw a good Comedy,
from his own raw uncultivated Head. . .?"[11]
 The answer was that Cibber could, and his "own raw uncultivated Head" swelled to think that a work of his should be
attributed to Dryden or to any other such skillful hands. Loud
applause told Cibber that he had found his character as an
actor. Jealous opposition told him better than any of the flat-
teries he cherished that he was on to something important as
a dramatist. With *Love's Last Shift* he had arrived. It was
even presented in France, they said, as *La dernière Chemise
de l'Amour*!

II Womans Wit *and* The School Boy

 Cibber's second play was *Womans Wit* (1697), "intended,"
as he said, "to have made the town some amends in this play
for their extraordinary favours to my first." To stress the relationship to his first play, Cibber changed the original subtitle
of *The Devil to Deal With* to *The Lady in Fashion*. He and
his young wife both appeared in *Womans Wit* and did their
best to ingratiate themselves with their audience. So did the
author, but there were "considerable hindrances": "My first
hindrance was want of time; for rather than lose a winter (the
profits from my other being so considerable) I forc'd myself
to invent a fable: now my first was spontaneous, and conse-
quently more easy: the one was the kindly product of my
fancy, this of my judgment (I mean of that little judgment I
have); that was a cherry gathered in *July*, this was merely
ripen'd by artifice in *April* . . . ."[12]
 Not only was Cibber working too fast; he was guilty also
of "too nice observation of regularity." Perhaps the influence
of French classical models and theories had produced in England
chiefly outward changes only, but the production of versions
of French pseudo-Classical plays—mostly Corneille and Racine[13]—had had its effect, even though the native English tradition
predominated in Otway, Southerne, Rowe, and the rest. Somehow Cibber felt obliged to crowd all the improbable incidents

of *Womans Wit* into five hours and to set them all in St. James's (including the first scene of the last act, set in the real-life fashionable "Indian House" run by a Mrs. Siam, a notorious place of assignation in London). The attempt to abide by Classical rules, as his age understood them, put an added burden on our fledgling author and caused him to be pedestrian and dull more often than "regular" and "diverting."[14] Moreover, while he was writing the first two acts, Cibber was "entertained at the New Theatre," and so he tailored the play for the Haymarket's actors. By the time he came to work on the third act, he was back at Drury Lane, had to toss in a low-life character (Mass Johnny) to be played by Doggett, and thus concluded the play with a different stock company in mind than that for which he had begun it.

"Every one did their best, and I thank them," said Cibber, but the Drury Lane company was "uncertain" in the roles, the performance was bad, and the play failed. In his *Apology* Cibber asked that *Womans Wit* be peaceably forgotten, but he himself went back to it late in 1702. From the farcical scenes that constitute a large proportion of the last three acts, he confected an afterpiece, *The School-Boy, or The Comical Rival.* He himself played Mass Johnny, the impish trickster, and the farce became very popular. Whether *Womans Wit* be said to have a plot and a subplot (which came into English drama with Henry Medwall) or "more serious" and "less serious" plots interleaved (a practice common with Dryden and other playwrights), the farcical elements were clearly the more vital and in *The School-Boy* they survived.

III   Xerxes

Womans Wit had been put together too quickly and too carelessly. Cibber's first tragedy, *Xerxes* (1699), took two years to write. It transpired that he could no more write tragedy, however, than play it successfully. An enemy claimed that Cibber could not get his tragedy presented at Drury Lane and was compelled to underwrite its performance at Lincoln's Inn Fields, where it closed, unlamented, on opening night.[15] Addison's mock inventory of Christopher Rich's theatrical paraphernalia seems to bear out this charge, listing "the imperial robes of Xerxes, worn but once."[16] Constructed on the frigid model of the late heroic play that crutched its feeble sense on verse, *Xerxes* lamely tells the story of Tamira, a lady in distress, and it makes plentiful recourse to bombast, the supernatural, and French claptrap.

Perhaps in those days, when audiences had been trained by Dryden and his followers to pay no more heed to tragic declamation than to the libretti of opera, Betterton's stentorian Artabanus and Verbruggen's sonorous Xerxes may possibly have been endured for a performance, especially when there was plenty of gore in evidence, rich costumes, and a plethora of melodramatic moments—as for example this one in the last act when Tamira, clutching her baby to her bosom, is being dragged off, by the hair, screaming "O cruel! cruel men!" at the top of her lungs. Enter Mardonius and Aranthes, two Persian generals, attended. Mardonius speaks, asking the pretty obvious question:

> *Mar.* What means this strange disorder, friends?
> Why is this woman rudely dragg'd along?
> > *[They loose her, as half afraid.*
> *Tam.* Relieve me, heav'n!
> *Mar.* Now, by my soul! the fair *Tamira.* Help ho!
> *Tam.* Protect me, brave *Mardonius.*
> > *[They raise her.*
> *Mar.* Protect! yes, and revenge thee too—Villains!
> *Tam.* Hold! I conjure you, hold Good Sir, be mild,
> And speak 'em fair, or that revenge
> May cost me dearer than my life—my child!
> *Mar.* Ha! forego the infant, slaves!
> Or by the lifted fury of this arm—
> *Tam.* Oh! do not fright 'em, Sir! see! they're merciful
> And kind! they will not hurt the babe!
> > *[They set down the child, which runs into her arms.*

This may have all the coldness and pomposity of the painter David's *Battle of the Romans and Sabines*—without his perfection of finish—but, when Cibber forsook original scripts and turned to the adaptation of Shakespeare's *Richard III* in the next year, his apprenticeship in melodrama with *Xerxes* stood him in good stead.

IV   Richard III

Margaret Webster has remarked that *Richard III*, "which cannot be placed anywhere near the top of Shakespeare's greatest plays . . . was the most constant Shakespearian vehicle for all the greatest actors who dominated the English-speaking theatre for a period of a hundred and fifty years."[17] For most of

this time this "Shakespearian vehicle" was in fact the brilliantly
stageworthy adaptation by Colley Cibber. Cibber took the character of Richard III, more familiar from Restoration plays than
from Shakespeare,[18] and he produced on July 9, 1700, at Drury
Lane a play which some critics have called a tragedy and which
Odell is rash enough to say is better than Shakespeare's.[19]

Cibber played Richard himself, as much in the manner of
the villainous Sanford as he could manage; and Vanbrugh com-
plimented him on the acting, though others reviled it. David
Garrick made his memorable debut as Cibber's Richard and
played it often.[20] He also chose it for his farewell to the stage
in 1776. He and Quin played Richard in 1746 on alternate
nights, using it to debate the merits of Quin's old-school his-
trionics against Garrick's more modern style. Apparently Cibber's
character could be played successfully either way, for it was
a great play for actors. John Philip Kemble and Mrs. Siddons
appeared in it. George Frederick Cooke brought it to America
in 1810 and so did Edmund Kean.[21] Junius Brutus Booth
essayed the part in an attempt to rival Kean. Charles Macready
attempted to restore Shakespeare's text (in 1821) as a novelty,
but after a couple of performances he was compelled to return
to the Cibber version. Samuel Phelps had more success with
Shakespeare's *Richard III* at Sadler's Wells in 1845, but once
again the Cibber version returned. When Edmund Kean's son
Charles produced his magnificent *Richard III* at his Princess's
Theatre in 1850, it was Cibber's durable play he used, and it
was Cibber's version in which he toured America and Australia.
It was not really until Sir Henry Irving and the 1870's that
Shakespeare's text recaptured popular favor, and even in the
twentieth century Walter Hampden, Robert Mantell, and others
played Cibber's version in preference to the original. *Richard
III*—"as dramatized by Colley Cibber," one critic said—became
the play that, even more than *Hamlet*, every aspiring Roscius
had to attempt.

It was Cibber's Richard Crouchback, not Shakespeare's slightly more complex but (to use a favorite word of Cibber's) less
theatrical villain, that fired the popular imagination. William
Hazlitt deplored Cibber's "patch-work" and cited the "idle and
misplaced extracts from other plays" used "to make the character
of Richard as odious and disgusting as possible."[22] But it was
futile. In the fashionable drawing rooms of London and in the
raw opera houses and Gold Rush settlements of America, in
the Victorian nurseries where children acted out the play in

their "tuppenny-coloured" paper theaters, it was Cibber that was preferred.[23]

So far as the actors were concerned, Cibber definitely improved upon Shakespeare's *Richard III*, that peculiar amalgam of chronicle history and morality play. Cibber concentrated the spotlight on Richard, omitting scenes in which he does not appear and heightening the "bottled spider" villainy of those in which he does. To do this, Cibber had to handle his material freely.[24] He added speeches and self-explanatory asides to Richard's part to make him deeper-dyed, more obviously guilty of the death of King Edward's sons, more ruthlessly conscienceless, more intolerant of virtue, more deliberately diabolical, more ranting. Cibber's Richard is even more the "cruel monster, deformed in body, mind and soul" than the Tudor historians and Shakespeare manufactured out of the handsome historical Richard. Modern historians have shown that the real Richard was far from the fiend that Shakespeare's portrait makes him out: but Cibber makes him worse. Cibber's Richard, for example, pauses on an otherwise empty stage to fling exit lines like these: "Conscience, lie still, more lives must yet be drain'd;/ Crowns got with blood, must be by blood maintain'd." Who would not thrill to this variation on the theme:

> Conscience avaunt, *Richard's* himself again;
> Hark! the shrill trumpet sounds, to horse, away,
> My soul's in arms, and eager for the fray.

Cibber's debt to Shakespeare was enormous, of course, but he managed to make the play his own. He introduced some *coups de théâtre* and some ringing lines that, like "The aspiring youth that fired the Ephesian dome," gained him fame, at whatever cost.

Cibber's *Richard III* is written in pure "Cibberian" style. Note the use of villainous asides; the decision to show, rather than to describe as Shakespeare does, the murder of the princes in the Tower; Richard's heartlessness: "How are the Brats dispos'd?"; the playing down of Richard's pangs of conscience after his dream, when Shakespeare has him confess:

> My conscience hath a thousand several tongues,
> And every tongue brings in a several tale,
> And every tale condemns me for a villain.
> . . . .
> I shall despair. There is no creature loves me;

> And if I die, no soul shall pity me:
> Nay, wherefore should they,—since that I myself
> Find in myself no pity to myself.

The whole emphasis is concentrated on Richard's evil, though, of course, the compulsory eighteenth-century love interest is tossed in near the end and handled better than the affair between Edgar and Cordelia that Nahum Tate introduced into *King Lear*. In Cibber's play Richard becomes the utterly conscienceless but clever malefactor; his antagonists, sincere but simple men. The melodramatic struggle is more direct and more dramatically striking than in Shakespeare's more diffuse and complex drama. Cibber's Richard stands out more forcefully, with all the villainous grandeur of Kean in those "penny plain" engravings our great-grandfathers used to color. The sympathy which in Shakespeare's play is "wasted" on the unfortunate Clarence, on Rivers, on Grey, on Hastings, Buckingham, Edward, and the wailing women—all this is conserved. Mad Margaret is cut: her big scene would challenge the star's preeminence. Richard stands alone; or he appears, as did the great actors, "with a supporting cast."

When Richard has the stage to himself Cibber allows him to revel in his soliloquies, but the rest of the play is speeded up. In a sense it is the same technique William Gillette later used as Sherlock Holmes: while the rest of the cast plays at a hectic pace, with comparatively staccato speeches and quick, nervous gestures, the leading actor delivers his lines with all deliberation, slow, calm, assured, commanding.[25] Shakespeare's Act III, Scene 1, exchange is leisurely:

> *Prince.* My lord of York will still be cross in talk.
> Uncle, your Grace knows how to bear with him.
> *York.* You mean, to bear me, not to bear with me:
> Uncle, my brother mocks both you and me.
> Because that I am little, like an ape,
> He thinks that you should bear me on your shoulders.
> *Buckingham.* With what a sharp provided wit he reasons!
> To mitigate the scorn he gives his uncle,
> He prettily and aptly taunts himself:
> So cunning and so young is wonderful.

Cibber was cunning too. Though he was apt to pad his comedies with polite persiflage that was wholly inconsequential, and (when he aimed at wit) took such careful aim that he missed being witty, he achieves a fine economical effect in his *Richard*

III by a different distribution of speeches and an accelerated delivery:

> *Prince Edward.* I hope your Grace knows how to bear
> with him—
> *Duke of York.* You mean to bear me—not to bear with
> me—
> Uncle, my brother mocks both you and me;
> Because that I am little like an ape,
> He thinks you should bear me on your shoulders.
> *Prince Edward.* Fye, brother, I have no such meaning.
> *Stanley.* With what a sharp, provided wit he reasons!
> To mitigate the scorn he gives his uncle,
> He prettily and aptly taunts himself.
> *Tressel.* So cunning and so young is wonderful!

In little tricks like these, perhaps even more than in the elaborate shifting around of scenes, we see Cibber's theater sense and his tinkering at its best.[26]

At its worst his tinkering tends to eliminate the "quaint" images that color Shakespeare. He flattens the poetry and interjects a rather uninspired product of his own devising, though Cibber does seem to have been aware of the deficiency of his verse and anxious to keep his additions to a minimum. He is also aware, however, that in *Richard III* the Bard himself was far from his poetic best, so Cibber does not balk at enlivening *Richard III* with bits of *Richard II, Henry IV (Part I), Henry V,* and (to clarify certain details of the political situation) some gems of purest ray serene from the dark, unfathomed caves of the *Henry VI* plays. After all, Cibber was only stealing jewels to deck the rightful owner. Once in a while he adds a flashing Cibberian ornament. Surely any producer of *Richard III* owes his audience the thrill of experiencing Richard's wide-flung gesture, his imperious sneer, and the dramatic delivery of Colley Cibber's most famous line: "Off with his head—so much for *Buckingham.*"

I have gone into some detail here because Cibber's *Richard III* was for generations one of the theater's warhorses and also because I want to dispel the false notion that Cibber butchered Shakespeare. Actually Cibber's success derived from the fact that he knew precisely how to serve up Shakespeare to the public of his time. He did not hack Shakespeare—but he himself was axed. At the time of the first performance, the Master of the Revels (acting as censor under the authority of the Lord Chamberlain) lopped off the first act of Cibber's *Richard III*. The death of Henry VI—which Cibber borrowed from Shakespeare's *Henry VI, Part III*—would, the censor thought, put the audience too much in mind of James II, then languishing in exile in France.[27] The censor had, Cibber remarked bitterly, "not Leisure to consider what might be separately offensive," so he expunged not just the scene which referred to the pitiful end of a king but the whole act.

There is, in fact, no convincing proof that Cibber ever presented the entire five acts of his *Richard III* at any time during his life.[28] Certainly the censor's action got the play off to a bad start: without the first act, the original production of 1700 was tepidly received and fairly unprofitable.[29] In modern times, strangely enough, it is usually the first act material as arranged and augmented by Cibber that is, along with Edmund Kean's now standard stage business and John Barrymore's as-well-as-possible-disguised limp, incorporated into productions of *Richard III* when Shakespeare is altered.

V Love Makes a Man

The hero of one of Cibber's plays asserts that "a single intrigue in love is as dull as a single plot in a play," a remark that tells us as much about the survival of Restoration dramaturgy as it does about the persistence of Restoration morality, even in Cibber's more "decent" age. In an attempt to keep *Love Makes a Man, or The Fop's Fortune* (1700) from being dull, Cibber went back to two late Elizabethan plays and combined them in the late Restoration style. From John Fletcher's two plays *The Elder Brother* and *The Custom of the Country*, he took two series of tragi-comic adventures, hair-raising dangers, and romantic reversals. He tells his complicated new story in rather artificial but passable prose, as was characteristic of the time, and purges it of indecency, as was characteristic of Cibber, who was always more restrained than his predecessors or even his contemporaries in an age when sometimes "Ev'n Bullies blush'd, and Beaux astonish'd stood" at what they heard from the stage.

For himself Cibber wrote the part of Clodio, The Elder Brother's younger brother, a Frenchified fop with a peruke like a frozen mop. Cibber had plenty of opportunity to play the role, for *Love Makes a Man* became a standard light comedy, although in its first run it eked out five nights only with the help of added, entr' acte French acrobats, an intrusion then becoming very popular. The play ends, like other comedies of the time, with a dance. It had nothing to do with the plot: it was merely a conventional, flashy closing for the rapidly moving succession of sprightly scenes. One might compare the end of the Pyramus and Thisbe play in A *Midsummer Night's Dream* (Act V, Scene 1) where Theseus is asked by Bottom the Weaver: "Will it please you to see the epilogue, or to hear a Bergomask dance between two of our company?" Theseus, dispensing with the apologetic epilogue, calls for "your Bergomask" and the stage direction reads "*Here a dance of clowns.*"

Love Makes a Man is one of those dated but attractive trifles that lead critics who write surveys, such as E. J. Burton, to say of Cibber: "His plays are not 'literary'—indeed, why should a play script be so?—but they are skillful and appealing. He can catch the character and affectations of the period. . . . His is the scripting of the professional."[30]

VI She Wou'd and She Wou'd Not

The Victorian Mrs. Inchbald found that *She Wou'd and She Wou'd Not* has "neither wit nor sentiment, but instead it has swearing, lying, and imposture." Generations of less sanctimonious theatergoers, however, have applauded this romantic comedy of 1702 that, while its initial run was a meager six nights, soon earned a place in the repertoire which it did not lose until the end of the nineteenth century. Maybe the charm of what Dryden would have called "The Songish Part" helped. The songs were particularly catchy, and a critic of Cibber's time complained: "Of late we have been disturbed by a shoal of seamstresses, whores, and shoplifts, with a gang of highwaymen, pickpockets and footboys a-humming your *Caelia my Heart.*"[31]

It has been said that Cibber got his plot from Leanerd's *The Counterfeits* (1678), but both probably derive from a common Spanish source. There was a little borrowing from Spanish sources in the eighteenth century: by Steele and Mrs. Susanna Centlivre, for instance. But, wherever the story came from, Cibber made it his own. Getting the exposition out of the way in a somewhat crowded first act, "Our humble Author" proudly sticks to the Neoclassical unities: Act I takes place at an inn in Madrid and the rest of the play is one continous action at the house of Don Manuel, for throughout Acts II, III, IV and V "*The SCENE continues.*"

Here, from the Prologue, is Cibber's design for the play:

View then in short the method that he takes: ⎫
His plot and persons he from nature makes,   ⎬
Who for no bribe of jest he willingly forsakes. ⎭
His wit, if any, mingles with his plot,
Which should on no temptation be forgot:
His action's in the time of acting done,
No more than from the curtain, up and down.
While the first music plays, he moves his scene
A little space, but never shifts again.
      From his design no person can be spar'd,
Or speeches lopt, unless the whole be marr'd:
No scene[s] of talk for talking's sake are shewn,
Where most abruptly, when their chat is done,
Actors go off, because the poet—can't go on.
His first act offers something to be done,
And all the rest but lead that action on;
Which when pursuing scenes i' th' end discover,
The game's run down, of course the play is over.

These certainly are ideals that a dramatist could do worse than follow. Fully realized, they would have solved every one of Cibber's playwriting problems with the possible exception of his tendency to write lines that (as Congreve said) *looked* like wit but were *not* wit.

Cibber's comedy does not, however, seem crippled by theories of dramaturgy. It tells a breezy tale of "The Kind Imposter" Hypolita (a fetching, feminine version of Cibber's daughter, Charlotte Charke) who turns down her suitor Don Philip and then, when he goes to Madrid to marry another girl, follows him in disguise. Don Philip proposes to marry Rosara, but Octavio is in love with Rosara and so, to prevent her marriage to Don Philip, Octavio goes into disguise as a friar. Intrigues develop rapidly, assisted by the clever servant Trappanti, a device as old as the Roman comedy and as hilarious as Pinkethman can make it on stage. Hypolita appears in a "breeches part" as a young gallant, claims to be Don Philip, duels with the real Don Philip, and marries Rosara! Then she promises to have the marriage annulled—if Rosara will marry Octavio. Rosara's father, Don Manuel, with an "Odzook," agrees. Hypolita reveals her identity. The lovers *"advance slowly, and at last rush into one another's arms,"* a stage direction that was still being used (and kidded) when Sandy Wilson wrote *The Boy Friend.* Don Philip embraces Hypolita (after nine or ten lines of the "O ecstasy! distracting joy" variety). The "some-

thing" of the first act is "done," and a little dance is thrown in
for a festive finale.

The curtain falls on perhaps the best constructed play Cibber
ever wrote, one so fine that even George Farquhar learned from
it. What matter if the elements be conventional, if the ghosts of
Shakespeare and Fletcher stalk, if the disguises get so involved
as to recall Ben Jonson in his dotage? The play moves so
quickly and so amusingly that criticism is stilled, disarmed.
All we can remember is the captivating Hypolita, a creature of
many madcap moods, and the enjoyment of a rattling good
yarn told with economy and *élan*. We are almost persuaded to
accept the moral: *"O! never let a virtuous Mind despair,/
For constant hearts are Love's peculiar Care."*

VII The Careless Husband

First presented at Drury Lane on Thursday, December 7,
1704, the comedy *The Careless Husband* was one of Cibber's
major works and long a favorite, for it combined the best of
two dramatic worlds: the witty, aristocratic intrigues of the
Restoration comedy and the new sentimentalism recently popular
in the plays of Richard Estcourt (*The Fair Example: or The
Modish Couple*) and of Sir Richard Steele (*The Funeral* and
The Lying Lover). *The Careless Husband* clinched the success
of the sentiment that characterized *Love's Last Shift* but which
had suffered a temporary setback with the arrival of the masterpiece of the Restoration comedy of manners, William Congreve's
The Way of the World (1700). *The Careless Husband* appeared
in two editions in 1705 and was thereafter frequently reprinted
as well as revived on the stage. Pope praised it. Wilkes' *General
View of the Stage* extravagantly said that, except for one scene,
it was "not only the best comedy in English, but in any other
language." Dibdin discussed it as "a school for elegant manners,
and an example of honourable actions," and Barker claims that
"it helped to fix standards of gentility and politeness which were
profoundly to influence comic writing throughout most of the
eighteenth century."[32]

Cibber began the play while the Drury Lane company was
playing at Bath during the summer of 1703, but the death of
Mrs. Susanna Verbruggen "in child-bed" caused him to lay
aside the script until a suitable Lady Betty Modish could be
found.[33] The sudden success of Mrs. Anne Oldfield encouraged
him to complete the part for her. She well repaid his confidence:

Whatever favourable Reception, this Comedy has met with from the Publick; it would be unjust in me, not to place a large Share of it to the Account of Mrs. *Oldfield;* not only from the uncommon Excellence of her Action; but even from her personal manner of Conversing. There are many Sentiments in the Character of Lady *Betty Modish,* that I may almost say, were originally her own, or only dress'd with a little more Care, than when they negligently fell, from her lively Humour: Had her Birth plac'd her in a higher Rank of Life, she had certainly appear'd, in reality, what in this Play she only, excellently, acted, an agreeably gay Woman of Quality, a little too conscious of her natural Attractions.[34]

Cibber not only made the part fit Mrs. Oldfield but gave quickening highlights to the portrait of Lady Betty by drawing from life, for he limned the wife of his old friend Henry Brett. Cibber had assisted that handsome gallant to win the lady, and now Mrs. Brett helped Cibber clothe his character.[35] Cibber always kept an eye on fashionable circles and from Mrs. Brett he learned the accent of a modish lady of quality. Some of his dialogue, he claimed in his Dedication, was inspired by an equally prominent personage: any "easy turn of thought or spirit" came from the Duke of Argyll's "manner of conversing." We begin to understand why Cibber's plays are so significant as social history, such an important key to fathoming the society of his age.

Cibber, never of these high circles, strove to be in them; and the folly and affectation of such people as these (whom he always snobbishly admired) gave him the subject of *The Careless Husband*—his bourgeois view of the *beau monde.* Scorning "the incorrigible Fool" and the inmates of Bedlam and Newgate, he presents a picture not of vice and depravity but of frailty and foolishness among "the better sort." His Prologue is Jonsonian in explicitness but not in content:

> *We rather think the persons fit for Plays,*
> *Are those whose birth and education says*
> *They've every help that shou'd improve mankind,*
> *Yet still live slaves to a vile tainted mind;*
> *Such as in wit are often seen t' abound,*
> *And yet have some weak part, where Folly's found:*
> *For follies sprout like weeds, highest in fruitful ground.*

The main plot of *The Careless Husband* deals with Sir

Charles Easy who, like a typical Restoration rake, has long engaged in affairs. He has now fallen out with his mistress, Lady
Graveairs. ("What a charming quality is a woman's pride, that's
strong enough to refuse a man her favours, when he's weary
of 'em.") He has even grown tired of his wife's saucy maid,
Edging. But he is more refined than the standard dramatic
cavalier, and much more sentimental in his sensuality. The most
famous scene of the play is that in the last act in which the
long-suffering Lady Easy, finding her husband and Edging
asleep in armchairs and fearing that he might take cold without
his wig, *"Takes a Steinkirk off her neck, and lays it gently on
his head,"* moved by "my heart-breaking patience, duty, and
my fond affection." Sir Charles wakes—and to his wife's love as
well:

Sir *Char.* She certainly has seen me here sleeping with her
woman:—If so, how low an hypocrite to her that sight
must have proved me?—The thought has made me des-
picable even to myself—How mean a vice is lying? and
how often have these empty pleasures lull'd my honour
and my conscience to a lethergy,—while I grossly have
abus'd her? poorly skulking behind a thousand falsehoods?
Now I reflect, this has not been the first of her discoveries
—How contemptible a figure must I have made to her?
—A crowd of recollected circumstances confirms me now,
she has been long acquainted with my follies, and yet with
what amazing prudence has she borne the secret pangs of
injur'd love, and wore an everlasting smile to me? This asks
a little thinking—something should be done. . . .

He begs his wife's pardon, stirred "with so severe a proof of
thy exalted virtue, it gives me wonder equal to my love"; and
he is converted. Too suddenly? So think some critics. A Farquhar
or a Fielding would have said *yes*; a Steele or a Cibber, *no*.

The superbly carpentered subplot concerns the coquetry of
Lady Betty Modish, who is loved by Lord Morelove but is
flirting audaciously with the shallow Lord Foppington (played
with verve by Cibber). After a great deal of highly artificial
dialogue that Cibber counted upon to be rescued by Mrs.
Oldfield's charm, Lady Modish at long last abandons Lord
Foppington and is happily received by her true love.

We may compare the elements of *The Careless Husband* to
those of the Restoration comedy of intrigue as exemplified by
Dryden, D'Urfey, Ravenscroft, and Mrs. Aphra Behn, and as
succinctly summarized by John Harold Wilson:

This consisted of a plot involving one or more cynical gallants who sought to seduce (or marry) a like number of brisk young ladies, and who had to overcome or circumvent a heavy father, an old husband, or a set of rivals. Fortified with a variety of fools, country bumpkins, braggarts, fops, and half-wits (all of whom provided broad physical comedy by their appearance and behavior in farcical situations), and spiced with erotic bedroom scenes, pretty actresses in breeches, and passages of *double entendre*, a merry intrigue comedy was sure to please the taste of the town. Sometimes a setting in France, Spain, or Italy added a touch of variety.[36]

The scene of Cibber's play is Windsor. There is no profanity. The very few lines that might bring a blush to the sensitive are confined to the subplot. The play ends with a wayward husband won back to virtue and with a coquette about to marry a tried and true lover. The dialogue is anything but coarse. Croissant claims that it "approaches the finest of the period," but Barker is closer to the truth: "One feels stifled in this atmosphere of well-bred chitchat, one longs for a little coarse and unrefined humanity." The structure of the play is admirable, but its equally consistent moral tone is offensive. Cibber, objecting to "the coarseness of most characters in our late Comedies" as "unfit entertainments for People of Quality, especially the Ladies," has clearly striven to produce a popular piece in which virtue is rewarded and vice—folly, rather—punished.

His hero, Sir Charles, is conceived too simply. Quite apart from the facile reformation is the question of his rationale for wrongdoing in the first place. He is accused of being untrue to his "Human Nature," of not being informed by what Steele would call his "good natural impulses," of not "thinking." A moment's reflection is then supposed to produce a permanent reformation: his "want of Thinking" is cured abruptly by a single act of his wife's thoughtfulness. This action reawakens his reason, rouses his dormant conscience, and effects his regeneration, causing him without further ado to abandon the delusive pleasures of vice for virtue, now recognized as the sole source of all true and lasting bliss. What a generous and feeling rake! What transformation can be effected in the most evil man by an appeal to his *better nature!* But suppose he was evil, suppose he had no better nature, suppose he had been a shameless or a heartless rake, suppose he had more than "want of Thinking" to atone for. Has the new sentimental drama, of which *The Careless Husband* was one of the best and most loved examples, no place for villainy or even insensitivity? Must no vice go unrepented and no virtue unrewarded? Apparently. "There the dread Phalanx of Reformers come," cried one playwright who spotted the new Men of Feeling on the horizon. With their "Pensive Homilies" all rakes turn reformers; all punks, proselytes. In *The Careless Husband* we have "stuffy morality and snobbish manners" with a vengeance. Sir Alphonsus Ward is grossly understating the case when he concedes that this play "fails to treat vice from the loftiest of stand-points."[37]

Ward is on firmer ground when he discusses characterization and dialogue. The skirmishes of Lady Betty and Lord Morelove (and of Lord Foppington and Lady Graveairs) are indeed "in the best style of later English comedy." Lady Betty is truly "a most delightful coquette—*with a heart*," and Lord Foppington "one of the best easygoing fools ever invented." Foppington completely fits Etherege's definition of the exquisite gentleman, one who "ought to dress well, dance well, fence well, have a genius for love letters, an agreeable voice for a chamber, be very amorous, something discreet, but not over-constant."[38] Lady Easy is another fine portrait and in her the Patient Griselda is not soppy.

With such excellent acting parts it is not surprising that *The Careless Husband* was a milestone in genteel comedy, both in its original form and in its adaptations.[39]

VIII   Perolla and Izadora

Perolla and Izadora, a tragedy acted at the end of 1705, was designed to satisfy the needs of the time. John Dennis only a few years before had written in the Epistle Dedicatory to *The Advancement and Reformation of Modern Poetry: a Critical Discourse* (1701) of what he and his contemporaries expected of tragic drama: "Every tragedy ought to be a very solemn lecture, inculcating a particular Providence, and showing it plainly protecting the good, and chastizing the bad, or at least the violent." Anything else, said Dennis with his accustomed dogmatism, was "empty amusement, or a scandalous and pernicious libel upon the government of the world." All that can be said for *Perolla and Izadora* is that in it the author of *The Careless Husband* and other such plays probably conscientiously designed "a very solemn lecture." I find no "empty amusement" in it—nor any other kind. The view of human nature

presented is precisely what one might have expected from the
man who established the sentimental comedy; but, from one
who confessed that he wrote more to be fed than be famous,
it is surprising to have a work so altruistically devoted to giving
people what they said they wanted rather than what they really
wanted and would pay to enjoy.

Of course the play pleased no one, not even Dennis. The
diction recalls the worst of Nathaniel Lee. Pope called it *"thick
Fustian* and thin *Prosaic*," and Dennis hopped on it immediately. He spoke of it feelingly and forcefully, alleging that
Cibber's "Masterpieces in Tragedies, *Perolla,* and *[Ximena]
the Heroic Daughter* . . . are . . . full of Nonsense and False
English . . . and are full of stiff, awkward, affected Stuff, and
Lines that make as hideous a Noise, as if they were compos'd
in an Itinerant Wheel-Barrow."[40] Richard Savage spoke true
when he said that John Dennis was often "Too dull for laughter,
for reply too mad," but in this case Dennis hit the nail squarely
on the head. Like so many others whom we have been told
to despise because Pope attacked them, Dennis was not the
hopeless fool he was made out to be. Though he was immoderate
in his damnation of Cibber, whom he both envied and de-
tested, calling him a *caput mortuum* for putting down some
plays of real merit—Dennis'—Dennis was right about *Perolla and
Izadora.* Fortunately, an occasional play such as this unfortunate
tragedy does not compel us to identify dramatists and managers
such as Cibber with what Dennis called them: *The Causes of
the Decay and Defects of Dramatic Poetry, and of the Degen-
eracy of Public Taste.*[41]

IX   The Double Gallant

Pierre Corneille's younger brother Thomas wrote about forty
plays including *Le Galant double,* and Cibber's comedy *The
Double Gallant* (first acted at the Haymarket, November of
1707) sounds as if it might be a translation. But, Cibber tells
us, his *Double Gallant* is "made up of what is tolerable in
two or three" other plays: Mrs. Susanna Centlivre's *Love at a
Venture* (which is from Corneille) and bits of *The Ladies'
Visiting Day* and *The Reformed Wife* (both by Charles Burna-
by), all considerably cleaned up.[42] Taking what he could
use from these old failures, Cibber constructed an extremely
complicated plot, far too intricate to recount here, which moves
so fast as virtually to exclude sentiment. The piece is remarkable
chiefly because it shows that Cibber was more moral than the

Restoration (as befitted a man of his time) and capable of cooking up a palatable hash out of unpromising leftovers without using too much spice (as befitted a commercial playwright of his era).

The single final scene—"worthy of Wycherley or Vanbrugh," says Thorndike—[43] is that in which Lady Sadlife's letter from Atall, her secret lover, is intercepted by Sir Solomon, her husband. She quakes as her lord reads the missive, but Atall has taken the precaution to address it to Wishwell, her maid, so Sir Solomon is thrown off the track:

> Sir *Sol.* I have made a discovery here—your Wishwell I'm afraid is a slut—she has as intrigue.
> Lady *Sad.* An intrigue! heavens, in our family.

Surely any competent performers could make that a great moment in the theater. Wishwell thinks quickly and accepts the letter as her own—and then asks Lady Sadlife to draft a reply for her. So Sir Solomon stands by, all unsuspecting, while we watch his wife writing to arrange an assignation with her lover.

No amount of opposition to Cibber as a person could keep a scene this effective from gaining favor at last. The *Biographia Dramatica* tells us Barton Booth wrote to Aaron Hill that "we learn that the play, at its first appearance was, as he expressed, hounded in a most outrageous manner. Two years after, it was revived, with most extravagant success, and has continued a stock play ever since."[44]

X   The Comical Lovers

The title of *The Comical Lovers, or Marriage à la mode,* a comedy first presented at the Haymarket in 1707, points up its derivation from John Dryden's play of 1673. To this was added a generous portion of the comic elements of *Secret Love,* and the result was happy in the extreme in that it provided opportunities for Mrs. Bracegirdle (Melantha) and Mrs. Oldfield (Florimel) to rival each other as charming impertinents. But even after Mrs. Bracegirdle "retir'd from the Stage in the Height of her Favour from the Publick" after playing the "breeches part" of Florimel, the play continued to draw audiences.[45] It was one of the features of the gala Coronation program in 1714. When the revivals of Restoration plays were few indeed, Dryden survived in this adaptation, a sparkling play from which, even after more than two centuries, the bubbles have not all escaped.[46]

XI   The Lady's Last Stake

In the Preface to *The Lady's Last Stake*, a very didactic
comedy from Cibber's most prolific year of 1707, the author,
addressing the Lord Chamberlain, writes: "If I would have been
less instructive, I might easily have had a louder, tho' not a
more valuable Applause. But I shall always prefer a fixt and
general Attention before the noisy Roars of the Gallery. A Play,
without a just Moral, is a poor and trivial Undertaking; and
'tis from the Success of such Pieces, that Mr. *Collier* was furnish'd with an advantageous Pretence of laying his unmerciful
Axe to the Root of the Stage."

This serious comedy was acted with some success at the
Haymarket on December 13, 1707; sold a considerable number
of copies at 18d. (the standard price for a printed play in
those days); and was still on the boards as late as 1786. It was
intended, says Thorndike, as a "pendant" to *The Careless Husband*. To the critics who found Lady Easy in that play "a
poor-spirited creature," Cibber replied:

> *He gives you now a Wife, he's sure in Fashion,*
> *Whose Wrongs use modern Means for Reparation.*
> *No Fool, that will her Life in Sufferings waste,*
> *But furious, proud, and insolently chaste;*
> *Who more in Honour jealous, than in Love,*
> *Resolves Resentment shall her Wrongs remove:*
> *Not to be cheated with his civil Face,*
> *But scorns his Falsehood, and to prove him base,*
> *Mobb'd up in Hack triumphant dogs him to the Place.*

So Lady Wronglove, the jealous wife, is persuaded to try
sweetness and tenderness to win back her erring husband.
"Husbands," advises Lady Gentle, "must be smil'd upon." Of
course "soft affection" works wondrously, and Lord Wronglove
succumbs, confessing, "I cannot bear that melting eloquence of
eyes." Sir Friendly Moral, who introduces ethics into the comedy and exhorts to virtue on every possible occasion, is partly
to be credited with the victory. A sentimental guide, philo-
sopher, and friend, Sir Friendly was to have many imitators
during the century, to become a stock character. Cibber's was
"the first full-length portrait of the type."[47] Certainly Sir Friendly is very useful: he sees to it that Lord and Lady Wronglove
are reconciled, that the profligate Lord George Brilliant (Cibber
as the fop again) is taken in hand by Mrs. Conquest, that

everything comes out right in the end, even for the minor
characters:

> Ld. *Geo.* Confess me victor, or expect no mercy: Not all
> the adamantine rocks of virgin coyness, not all your trem-
> bling, sighs, prayers, threats, promises or tears shall save
> you. Oh transport of devouring joy!
> *Closely embracing her.*
> Mrs. *Con.* Oh!–Quarter! Quarter! Oh spare my perriwig!

The authentic voice of the most dismal melodramas of the
nineteenth century, saved in the nick of time by a light touch!
Miss Notable, summed up by Thorndike as "an amorous
tell-tale who plays tricks on every one and does all she can to
thwart the moral stratagems,"[48] rounds out the cast. These
seven carry a subplot as well as the main action, and the play
not only gives us the prescription for a happy marriage—sincerity,
fidelity, good humor, and a double bed—but also cautions
against gambling: "Some other Follies too, our Scenes present;/
Some warn the fair from Gaming, when extravagant." This was
a popular occupation in the eighteenth century and a common
topic in plays,[49] but no one else approached it with the earnest-
ness of Cibber. Witness his Preface: "Gaming is a Vice that has
undone more innocent Principles than any one Folly that's in
Fashion; therefore I chose to expose it to the Fair Sex in its
most hideous Form, by reducing a Woman of Honour [Lady
Gentle] to stand the presumptuous addresses of a Man [Lord
George], whom neither her Virtue nor Inclination would let her
have the least taste to."

Cibber, who put an allusion to gambling into the mouth of
Lord Stanley in his *Richard III*, was well equipped to preach
on gambling: he knew it from experience. Himself, his father,
and his son were all addicted to betting. It was not merely that
he risked as much as £1500 in a speculation like the South Sea
Company—everyone was doing that, albeit with smaller
amounts—but in his youth he haunted Groom Porter's and in his
later life he was frequently to be seen gambling at White's in
London and at the fashionable spas. Sir Richard Steele once
indignantly had to insist that the rumor that Cibber had lost
£6000 in one year was unfounded. Victor, a friend of Cibber's
old age, joked that Cibber was frequently seen at prayers—and
that that was only right, since the vicar always accompanied
him to the gaming house. But, though Cibber was an inveterate

gambler himself, he would not praise it from the stage: the theater had "to entertain the Town, without giving Offence, either to Virtue, Decency, or Good Manners;"[50] the theater had to be more moral than the dramatists. When Mrs. Porter objected that he personally did not live up to the virtuous models he created for the stage, Cibber replied sincerely: "Madame, the one is absolutely necessary, the other is not." He was not being hypocritical when he insisted that the moral be writ large after the fable. In 1707 he was right: sentiment and morality ruled supreme—on the stage.

XII   The Rival Fools

First acted January 11, 1709, *The Rival Fools*, a slight far-rago, was an inconsequential attempt to put *Wit at Several Weapons*, by John Fletcher, into Queen Anne dress. As Cibber often did, he belittled in the Prologue what he had received from his source; a bold undertaking, considering that Henry Vaughan had written "Upon Mr. Fletcher's Plays" (1647): "This age or that may write, but never see/A wit that dares run parallel with thee." Undaunted, Cibber confessed frankly:

> From sprighly Fletcher's loose Confed'rate Muse,
> The unfinish'd Hints of these light Scenes we chuse;
> For with such careless Haste this Play was writ,
> So unperus'd each Thought of started Wit;
> Each Weapon of his Wit so lamely fought,
> That 'twould as scanty on our Stage be thought,
> As for a modern Belle my Grannam's Petticoat.
> So that from th' Old we may with Justice say,
> We scarce cou'd cull the Trimming of a Play.

The Elizabethans and Jacobeans lived in a far more boisterous but more barbarous era and were satisfied with a good deal less than Cibber's sophisticated audience demanded! (We recall the statement of seventeenth-century diarist John Evelyn who commented that crude and barbarous works such as Shake-speare's *Hamlet* "begin to disgust this refined age.") Cibber did, in fact, make a few improvements on Fletcher: the exposition in Cibber is a good deal clearer, the conclusion is more effective, and *The Rival Fools* is in prose. It is true that Fletcher wrote the most conversational of all blank verse and it can scarcely be said to obtrude; but verse of any sort was really unnecessary both in his play and in Cibber's. Still Cibber's entertainment cannot be rated as wholly acceptable. We fail to appreciate the "keen Satire's Jerk" of which Cibber boasted. We cannot say that we are conscious of the advertised "Profit and Delight" now that we have turned its tedious pages. Cibber truly was, as William Hazlitt said, "one of the best comic writers of his age," but this particular effort does nothing to support that statement. There must be easier ways for us to learn of the fatuities and futilities of polite society in the reign of Good Queen Anne.

XIII   The Non-Juror

Molière indirectly gave English literature a number of its most notable plays, and the most famous of all Cibber's *rifacimenti* was from Molière: *The Non-Juror* was based on *Tartuffe* (1667).[51] The Author's purpose in reworking this material was eminently serious and patriotic, as he explained to the King in the Dedication:

> Your Comedians, SIR, are an Unhappy Society, whom some Severe Heads think wholly Useless, and others Dangerous to the Young and Innocent: This Comedy is therefore an Attempt to remove that Prejudice, and to shew, what Honest and Laudable Uses may be made of the *Theatre*, when its Performances keep close to the true Purposes of its Institution: That it may be necessary to divert the Sullen and Disaffected from busying their Brains to disturb the Happiness of a Government, which (for want of proper Amusements) they often enter into Wild and Seditious Schemes to reform: And that it may likewise make those very Follies the Ridicule and Diversion even of those that committed them.[52]

Cibber's opponents, professional and political, did not for a moment accept this righteous stance. He was, they said, just trying to write a pennycatching play, and plagiarizing at that:

> Yet to write plays is easy, faith, enough,
> As you have seen by—Cibber—in Tartuffe.
> With how much wit he did your hearts engage!
> He only stole the play;—he writ the title-page.[53]

But Cibber had done very much more to make this a popular, partisan play than to translate Molière. He went back, to some extent, to the early drama of the Restoration, which put a distinct emphasis on contemporary political affairs, but he gave everything his own particular touch. If his *Apology* is to be trusted, he was once again consciously introducing that didactic tone with which (along with greater refinement in both language and structure) he modified the Restoration comedy of intrigue:

> About this Time *Jacobitism* had lately exerted itself, by the most unprovoked Rebellion, that our Histories have handed down to us, since the *Norman* Conquest: I therefore thought that to set the Authors, and Principles of that desperate Folly in a fair Light, by allowing the mistaken Consciences of some their best Excuse, and by making the artful Pretenders to a Conscience, as ridiculous, as they were ungratefully wicked, was a Subject fit for the honest Satire of a Comedy, and what might, if it succeeded, do Honour to the Stage, by shewing the valuable Use of it. And considering what Numbers, at that time, might come to it, as prejudic'd Spectators, it may be allow'd that the Undertaking was not less hazardous, than laudable.
> To give Life, therefore, to this Design, I borrow'd the *Tartuffe* of *Moliere*, and turn'd him, into a modern *Non-Juror*: Upon the Hypocrisy of the *French* Character, I ingrafted a stronger Wickedness, that of an *English* Popish Priest, lurking under the Doctrine of our own Church, to raise his Fortune, upon the Ruin of a worthy Gentleman, whom his dissembled Sanctity had seduc'd into the treasonable Cause of a *Roman Catholick* Out-law.[54]

The Tartuffe character becomes Dr. Wolf, a Jesuit priest posing as a nonjuring (Anglican) clergyman.[55] Nonjurors were not ordinarily traitors, for they did not advocate violent opposition to established authority, but Dr. Wolf is no dissenting Protestant: he is a papist spy. Nonetheless, he contrives to convince the gullible Sir John Woodvil that he is a member of the Church of England, not the Church of Rome, and gains refuge in his household. An unmitigated villain, Wolf proposes to repay this kindness by seducing his benefactor's wife, seizing the estate, and disinheriting young Woodvil. His hypocrisy threatens to make impossible the discovery of his nefarious plans, but love finds a way: he is betrayed by his assistant Charles who, though a former pupil and a Preston rebel, is touched by a deep, Cibberian, and sentimental attachment for Maria, the Woodvils' daughter. Sir John is directed to hide under a table and he hears the hypocrite Wolf make advances to Lady Woodvil. The plot becomes so clear that even the naïve Sir John cannot doubt; the jig is up. After this service neither the audience nor the author can be ungrateful to the repentant

Charles. Cibber grants him a royal pardon[56] and, for good measure, restores him to his long-lost father. Dr. Wolf, exposed, is punished as befits his crime. The Woodvils are happy once more.

The subplot features Maria as a coquette. She dallies with Charles and (especially) a certain, patient Mr. Heartly, a gentleman prodigiously equipped with moral pronouncements for all occasions. The saucy Mrs. Oldfield, however, managed to enliven this part of the play by putting a good deal of sparkle into Maria. She assisted Cibber in making this role of the impudent flirt a much more entertaining one than that of Marianne in Molière.

Though Cibber in effect added Charles to the play,[57] he generally economized and cut out Molière's Dorine, Cléante, and Madame Pernelle. His Lady Woodvil (Molière's Elmire) is less lively than her original, probably because Cibber had decided to adopt the usual moral main plot and witty subplot arrangement; he therefore gave all of the glitter to Maria. His Sir John (Orgon) is closer to the French model. The greatest changes are in the major figure: Molière's romping rogue becomes a slinking villain, less hypocritical but even more dishonest. Tartuffe is a fat, florid, gormandizing mountebank, teetering on the brink of farce; Dr. Wolf has a lean and hungry look, is more dangerous, less outwardly demanding, more insidious, verging on melodrama. He appears in the first act—much earlier than Molière's main character—and his treasonous machinations are soon patent: he will not pray for the Royal Family by name, he visits the Continent, he is clearly trying to put the Old Pretender back on the throne. When we hear of his connection with the Rebellion of 1715, we are not surprised; when we see his downfall, we are not unhappy.

Miles is the authority for stating that about three-quarters of *The Non-Juror* is new material. His thesis laid stress on the originality of the love interest in Cibber's plot, and he concluded that "Cibber does not owe much to Molière. He has a good many scattered reminiscences embodied in free paraphrase, three copied scenes in which many phrases are borrowed, and two passages translated quite closely from the French. Still the language of the adaptation as a whole is distinctly Cibber's."[58] Not only are the language and the significant plot devices largely Cibber's but the very tone of it all is Cibberian—Barker calls it "his own spurious conception of gentility"—even to the touches of sentimentalism designed to "coerce" the passions.

So soon after the Old Pretender and the Earl of Mar, such a play, as Cibber well knew, necessarily offended some. Because it was Cibber's play, it was especially opposed. Though *The Non-Juror* ran for eighteen successive nights in December, 1717, and through five editions in the next year, it called forth a flood of protest. Some of this was, of course, attributable to Jacobite sentiment, which did not die easily; but most was less in support of the divine right of kings than in rebellion against the divine right of theater managers. There was a flurry of vituperative pamphlets and several "keys" to the drama (including Joseph Gay's *Compleat Key to the Non-Juror* and an ironic one by Pope).[59] Christopher Bullock rushed *The Per-Juror* onto the stage at Lincoln's Inn Fields in an attempt to cash in on the publicity and one "W. B." (advertised as "late of St. John's Colledge, Camb.") penned a farce called *The Juror*.

The newspapers were full of jokes, criticism, and counter-criticism; for Cibber had boldly discussed from the stage one of the most debated issues of the day. *Mist's Weekly Journal* was but one of the many periodicals that took up the question on the personal as well as the political level. It printed a diatribe against Cibber purportedly by the author of *The Wife's Relief* and signed "Charles Johnson," which showed scant gratitude to Cibber for the kind reception Johnson had received at Drury Lane. Barker quotes it in full, and it is studded with phrases like "more malice, nonsense, and obscenity"; "a stolen, malicious, insulting performance"; and *"would-be wit."*[60] It alleges that Cibber made £1000 out of *The Non-Juror* (and promptly lost it all gambling).

As late as February 3, 1731, the *Grub-Street Journal* recalled the fuss that *The Non-Juror* had raised. The anonymous author is insulting Cibber (recently appointed Poet Laureate) by comparing him with a rhyming shoemaker named Carpenter ("Deputy Bellman of the City of Hereford"):

> CIBBER is also a *Translator* and Cobler, but in no degree equal to his rival. He has *translated,* as I am told, two pair of CORNEILLE's and MOLIERE's old shoes, in such a manner as to fit no mortal. The *Pompey,* the *Cid,* &c. were despised by many in our Society, who wear none but second-hand shoes: and even the *Nonjurors* themselves have chosen to go almost barefoot, rather than to appear in a pair of patch'd shoes of *Tartuffe,* or to tread one step like him.

The point is that years later it could be assumed that the public would still recognize allusions to Cibber's play of 1717. *The Non-Juror* had been a huge success. Like many another thing with which Cibber had been associated, it had been widely discussed, and it left its mark. It made for Colley Cibber some extremely vocal political enemies (who turned out regularly to damn his plays for years thereafter, regardless of their merit). It also made him some extremely valuable political friends; and, regardless of Cibber's merit, he was eventually to become the chartered bard of Whig sentiments, the Poet Laureate of England. He owed that honor, he himself said, to *The Non-Juror.* If he thereby incurred a debt to Molière's memory, perhaps it was canceled when someone "borrowed" the play from Cibber: in 1769 Isaac Bickerstaffe reworked *The Non-Juror* into *The Hypocrite.*[61] Once again it was a hit. A good thing has a long life in the theater.

XIV   Ximena, or The Heroick Daughter

Aimez donc la raison; que toujours vos écrits
Empruntent d'elle seule et leur lustre et leur prix.

—BOILEAU

We have above quoted a reference to Cibber's version of *Le Cid.* It was *Ximena* (failed, 1712; printed, 1719), and in the Preface Cibber explained that his purpose in tinkering with Corneille's masterpiece of 1637 was to make it more reasonable, to improve it. Though the impeccable taste of George Saintsbury caused him to hail *Le Cid* as "perhaps the most epoch-making play in all literature,"[62] Cibber, who was no more afraid of classics than he was of controversy, felt that he could regularize it along Neoclassical lines, make it less romantic, render it more credible. He always thought that French plays were too unrealistic. As late as November 21, 1749, he wrote to his friend Benjamin Victor that "the French Plays I never had any great opinion of; their Comedies want Humour and their Tragedies credible Nature; that is, they are too heavily romantic."

Sometimes Cibber follows Corneille's text closely—clearly there were some things in the play which he much admired—but he does not hesitate to alter. He gives the tragedy a new first act, for he complains that Corneille has been lax in opening with "a cold conversation between Chimène, and her Suivante" (at the end of which Chimène "quaintly walks off, to as little purpose as she came on"). He is obviously treating Corneille's masterpiece in precisely the same way he would a new script submitted to him at Drury Lane—and the author is not there to defend his work against Cibber's practical, slashing quill. Chimène, he feels, is not built up enough to serve as a fit heroine. Cibber's first scene is a chatty but highly purposeful exchange between Don Alvarez (Don Diegue in the original) and his son Don Carlos (Corneille's Don Rodrigue, the Cid) which establishes Don Carlos' love for Ximena (Chimène) and gives the audience cause to concern itself over them.

Occasionally Cibber makes an improvement only to cancel it out again: he wisely cuts the Infanta from Act I and then adds Belzara and complications which only hinder the necessary business of the play. Some of his changes are interesting: he makes the Count (Ximena's father) "more civilized and rational," more dignified than Corneille's character, and the King likewise is more reasonable and less tyrannical. Some of the changes are indefensible: he gives the original's somber end a happy (but infelicitous) twist. Dorothy Canfield Fisher explains that "he thought the French ending too sad a one, and adopted the most childlike method of making it cheerful—that is, the resurrection of a character supposed to be dead."[63]

The whole adaptation is free and cannot in any major respect be said to be either very faithful or superior to the original. Much as it might help Cibber's reputation could we divide the blame, there seems to have been no truth in the rumors that Pope had a hand in the play.[64] Parker in 1717 in his Complete Key to the farce *Three Hours after Marriage* announced that Cibber had "Naturaliz'd the *Cid* of *Corneille* into an *English Heroick Daughter*, Which will see the Light, as soon as Mr. *Pope* has touch'd it up, who has it now for that Purpose, the Diction being somewhat *obnubilated*." The diction remained obnubilated, and the play and the blame are all Cibber's.

XV The Refusal

In *The Author's Farce* Henry Fielding deals in Aristophanic directness and personal allusion. He has Marplay Senior (Colley Cibber) explain to Marplay Junior (Theophilus Cibber): "The Art of Writing, Boy, is the Art of stealing Old Plays, by changing the Name of the Play, and new ones by changing the Name of the Author." In *The Refusal, or The Ladies Philosophy*, however, Cibber was no simple plagiarist; he changed quite a bit more than the title of Molière's satire *Les Femmes savantes* (1672).[65] He altered plot, characterization, and dialogue. He raised

Molière's bourgeois main characters to the minor nobility and thoroughly Anglicized them. He switched the satire from philosophy (typically French) to business (typically English): Chrysale becomes a typical promoter: Sir Gilbert Wrangle, a director of the South Sea Company.[66] A little of the satire deals with idealized love (in Plato and Milton),[67] none with the clumsy grammar lampooned in Molière. (Style was a touchy point with Cibber, whose own was constantly under attack.) For the most part, Cibber cashed in on the South Sea craze, much as he had exploited the anti-Catholicism and the Bangorian controversy of the time in *The Non-Juror*. Molière's satire of typical individuals becomes in Cibber's hands satire of individual types, and the very character names in *The Refusal* underline this: Wrangle, Frankly, Witling. In Cibber, each character has "some distinguishing quality"[68] but the satire is broader, more like Shadwell's. The plot, as is usual with Cibber, thickens. Here is the Plotwell of *Three Hours after Marriage* hard at work. Croissant says that the *dénouement* is accomplished by Cibber by "more characteristically English means" and that, because of its increased complexity, it is less amusing than Molière's.[69]

This lively comedy of manners did not deserve the cold reception it met in 1721, one due to opposition to Cibber as a person, not as a playwright. It was widely read, reaching four editions by 1737 and being reprinted in 1753 and 1764. It still repays reading, not only for its intrinsic merit but because of the picture it presents of the era.[70] It must be confessed, however, that the diction of such characters as Sophronia sounds more like that of a Sir Walter Scott heroine than the speech of human beings. Since the wit is not particularly clever, many of the lines have gone flat over the years, while an unintentional humor of artificiality strikes the modern reader, as sometimes happens as he peruses Samuel Richardson's *Pamela* or John Cleland's *Fanny Hill*.

XVI   Caesar in Aegypt

First acted December 8, 1724, and published a week later, *Caesar in Aegypt* is carpentry. Most of the materials come from *The False One* (a collaboration by John Fletcher and Philip Massinger),[71] a tragedy of 1674 which reminds one of Shaw's *Caesar and Cleopatra* and treats of the treacherous murder of Pompey by Septimus ("The False One"); the intrigues of Photinus against Ptolemy and Cleopatra (joint rulers of Egypt); the

Alexandrian revolt and Caesar's suppression of it; the death of Ptolemy; and Caesar's affair with Ptolemy's celebrated sister, Cleopatra. To this material is added some ormolu from Corneille's *Pompée* (1642 or 1643) and a little scrollwork of Cibber's own. Cibber gave no indication that the whole work was not his own.

In its day *Caesar in Aegypt* competed successfully with the splendiferous operas and extravagant entertainments at rival theaters, for it offered sumptuous and exotic settings and good bravura roles for Booth (Caesar) and Wilks (Antony), Mrs. Oldfield (Cleopatra) and Mrs. Porter (Cornelia, "The relict of *Pompey*"), Cibber (Achoreus, counselor to the King of Egypt) and Theophilus Cibber (Ptolemy). Downes' *Roscius Anglicanus* defined an "opera" as a play with "machines"; though *Caesar in Aegypt* had incidental music at most, it had plenty of machinery in both its production and its plot and was Drury Lane's sort of answer to the musical extravaganzas at the Haymarket and elsewhere. Mrs. Oldfield in the Epilogue asks: *"Was it not bold, from stated rules to rove,/And make the Tragic Muse commode to love?"* Bold, yes; but without the spectacle that accompanied it the play is "scarcely worth mentioning."[72]

XVII   The Provok'd Husband

In the period of Garrick's contribution to what Samuel Johnson called "the gaiety of nations" and "the public stock of harmless pleasure" Cibber was second only to Shakespeare in popularity as a writer of comedies, and *The Provok'd Husband*, with eighty-two performances in twenty-six seasons, was the most acclaimed of all Cibber's works. [73]

The Provok'd Husband was a sentimental comedy of manners combining feeling and wit, imbued with the bourgeois morality—perhaps we should say *respectability*, or desire for it—which had come to dominate England, the nation of shopkeepers. Bellmour in William Congreve's first play had succinctly stated Restoration irresponsibility: "Come, come, leave business to idlers, and wisdom to fools: they have need of 'em: wit, be my faculty, and pleasure my occupation; and let father Time shake his glass." But how different Cibber's age had become, and Cibber wrote "to expose, and reform the licentious Irregularities that too often break in upon the Peace and Happiness of the married State." With this serious purpose Cibber took up the "occasional papers" of *A Journey to London*, a play left unfinished by Sir John Vanbrugh at his death in 1726. Out of them Cibber fashioned *The Provok'd Husband*.

Cibber claims that he attempted to preserve as much of "Sir John" as possible, and even the new title recalls Vanbrugh's masterpiece *The Provok'd Wife* (1697); but he softened the characters and the story line by numerous changes and "he unconsciously stamped his individuality upon almost every scene."[74] The play became more moral, more sentimental, more regular, more probable. Two plots are neatly stitched together, and all that Vanbrugh left "irregular" or "undigested" is carefully ordered, as befits the serious intent of the author's *utile dulce*. As George Farquhar, close friend of Cibber's partner Wilks and the author of several comedies in which Cibber was featured, wrote about the intent of comedy of the day:

> Comedy is no more at present than *a well-framed tale handsomely told as an agreeable vehicle for counsel or reproof*. This is all we can say for the credit of its institution, and is the stress of its charter for liberty and toleration. Then where should we seek for a foundation but in Aesop's symbolical way of moralizing upon tales and fables? with this difference: that his stories were shorter than ours. He had his tyrant Lyon, his statesman Fox, his beau Magpie, his coward Hare, his bravo Ass, and his buffoon Ape, with all the characters that crowd our stages every day; with this distinction, nevertheless, that Aesop made his beasts speak good Greek, and our heroes sometimes can't talk English.[75]

Cibber's "fable" is in two parts, as we have said. Plot number one concerns serious Lord Townly (Lord Loverule in Vanbrugh) and his sister Lady Grace, who are annoyed by the gay irresponsibility of Lady Townly (Lady Arabella). Manly, Lady Grace's *fiancé*, advises Lord Townly to threaten his pleasure-mad wife with divorce. (In Vanbrugh there was some talk of throwing her out of the house.) She is thereby brought to her senses, and Peace and Happiness are restored with a maximum of wit and surprisingly little sententiousness, considering Cibber's didactic intent. Plot number two concerns the country-cousin family of Sir Francis Wronghead (Headpiece in Vanbrugh). Though Cibber played Sir Francis, this more breezy, somewhat farcical subplot is basically Vanbrugh's; Cibber should therefore, receive credit for the major plot's handling. Of course Cibber, alert to the opposition accorded him as a personality,

announced it *vice versa,* confounding his critics. On opening
night he was treated to the spectacle of his enemies applauding
the Cibber scenes and nearly stopping the play with hisses
for Vanbrugh's. It was devious of Cibber thus to ascribe the
sentimental parts which he himself had added to the play to
an aged Vanbrugh, converted from cynicism, but it was both
clever and justified. Personal antipathies were so strong that
any work announced as Cibber's seldom got a fair hearing.
Even after Cibber retired from the stage, the works of other
authors—Theophilus Cibber and Charles Boadens, for example—were hissed when they were falsely suspected of containing parts by the old man.

Opening night was a triumph for the stately and sparkling
Nance Oldfield. The reviews damned Cibber, however. *Mist's
Weekly Journal* announced on January 13, 1728: "On Wednesday
last a most horrid, barbarous, and cruel murder was committed
at The Theatre-Royal in Drury Lane upon a posthumous
child of the late Sir John Vanbrugh by one who for some time
past has gone by the name of Keyber. It was a fine child born
and would certainly have lived long had it not fallen into such
cruel hands."

Actually the foundling would never have lived at all had
Cibber not adopted it. Mist was wrong and as usually vicious,
and his outbursts looked pretty silly when the shares of Cibber
and Vanbrugh were identified on January 31. Others attacked
the Wronghead scenes, thinking that what Cibber had played
he had written; but, despite carping critics, the play was a
success. It was not only well written and well acted, the audience
liked its message or moral:

> For in the Marriage-state the World must own,
> Divided Happiness was never known.
> To make it mutual Nature points the Way:
> Let Husbands govern: Gentle wives obey.

If the solution of the play's problem is more than a little contrived, well, Mozart managed to get away with a Da Ponte
Marriage of Figaro libretto that ends like this:

COUNT: *Contessa perdono!*	Forgive me, Countess!
COUNTESS: *Più docile io sono,*	I am more gentle
e dico di sí	And answer you "yes."
ALL: *Ah tutti contenti*	We all are delighted
saremo cosí	To have it end thus.

The public welcomed *The Provok'd Husband.* In 1728 good
comedies in London had long been too rare. The play ran for

a month and, though its success was then eclipsed by the prodigious reception of *The Beggar's Opera* at the rival house, it meant a new prosperity for Cibber and his theater. *The Provok'd Husband* brought in more than any other single play done at Drury Lane in fifty years.[76]

XVIII The Rival Queans

The year 1703 is a probable date for the première of Cibber's "Comical-Tragedy" *The Rival Queans. With the Humours of Alexander the Great*, actually a mock-heroic parody of the false fire and fustian of Nathaniel Lee's famous, fatuous heroic tragedy *The Rival Queens* (1677). Lee's "furious Fustian and turgid Rants" tell the tale of the first and second wives, Roxana and Statira, of Alexander the Great. The rival queens bombast and recriminate, Alexander goes spectacularly mad, and Lysimachus emulates Samson (tearing a lion to pieces with his bare hands) while the actors do everything but subject the scenery to the same fate. Cibber bravely essays the task of making these materials even more ridiculous. He reduces the queens to *queans* (that is, sluts) and strains even harder than Lee to produce prodigious similes but fails amusingly. It all sounds a good deal like the business in the last act of Farquhar's *The Constant Couple* (1699), not only in the bustle of the action but in the burlesque of Lee's rhetoric. (In Farquhar's play Sir Harry Wildair listens to Angelica's overblown speechifying and comments wryly: "This is the first Whore in *Heroicks* that I have met with.")

Cibber may have lacked originality in *The Rival Queans*, but the work pleased. At the beginning of the eighteenth century the English were developing a new and immensely popular offshoot of the *commedia dell'arte*. Taking Harlequin and some of the other vivid characters from the Italians, the English produced elaborate spectacles in which dialogue and music were added to the mime of the harlequinade. The public flocked to see these frothily fabulous entertainments and thrilled to the great "transformations" and the increasingly fancy and pictorial scenery (which greatly influenced the drama of the next century). Cibber and his colleagues inveighed against these "non-rational" entertainments but were compelled to compete with the other theaters, so they presented them. *The Rival Queans* lay somewhere between these spectacles and farce and was probably presented with verve and with plenty of mime

and mugging, appealing to those elements of the audience that
would concur in the opinion that "the pantomime is a kind of
stage entertainment which will always give more delight to a
mixed company than the best speaking farce than can be composed."[77]

Pantomime and farce, slapstick and rowdy burlesque, had
drawing power and were not to be gainsaid. Cibber deplored
their excessive popularity and fundamental foolishness, but he
was too acute as a manager to banish them from his theater
and too enterprising as an author to omit them from his works.

XIX   Love in a Riddle

The vogue of Italian opera in England, dating probably from
Arsinoe (1705), "was demolished by a single stroke" of John
Gay's pen, said Pope, when *The Beggar's Opera* appeared in
1728. Gay's sprightly mixture of simple comedy and simple melody, tunes "commonly sung up and down the Streets," created
a rage for ballad opera—*The Quaker's Opera* (1728), *The Village Opera* (1729), and so on—that persisted nearly unabated
until mid-century.[78]

As manager of Drury Lane, Cibber had read Gay's manuscript and declined it. Then he had to watch, with what discomfort we can imagine, as John Rich's production of it proceeded to smash all records. Rich netted some £4000 from his
production, plus the satisfaction of lording is over his rival as
Cibber sat down to imitate the very piece he had rejected. In
1729 Cibber came up with *Love in a Riddle,* exploiting the
ballad-opera vogue but claiming to have written the piece "upon
a quite different Foundation that of recommending Virtue, and
Innocence." In addition to the sentimental didacticism, however,
it had an elaborate plot, a comic subplot, fifty-five rousing songs
of high moral tone, Cibber himself as Philautus (a Corinthian
fop), and Catherine Raftor (later famous as Mrs. Kitty Clive)
in her debut as the heroine.

The ravishing Mrs. Raftor nearly saved *Love in a Riddle*
despite all, but it was damned. Cibber's enemies, of course,
all knew that he had rejected *The Beggar's Opera,* and they
were ready to adduce that fact as proof that he had no taste.
His imitation signified to them that he had no principles. The
rumor that he was responsible for the suppression of Gay's own
sequel *Polly* they took as evidence that Cibber had no scruples.[79]

On the opening night of *Love in a Riddle* the audience was

restless. On the second night (January 8, 1729) Cibber's enemies destroyed the work entirely. Cibber had expected trouble and had taken the precaution of installing Frederick, Prince of Wales in the royal box, hoping that the presence of royalty would discourage rowdiness. The stratagem didn't work. The catcalls were so frequent and the boos so vociferous that Cibber was forced to step out of character to beg the audience's indulgence while the actors finished the play, promising that they would never again be insulted by it. In an age when duels between members of the audience on the stage were not unknown and bloodshed in the pit was not uncommon, it was dangerous to provoke the audience.

With a "prodigious Concourse of Gentry and Nobility" flocking to see Gay's "Newgate pastoral" at another theater,[80] one might think that the musical pastoral Cibber was offering at Drury Lane would gain acceptance. But the power of Cibber's enemies was great enough to ruin anything of his if they exerted themselves. Nathaniel Mist had been preparing for six months scathing articles in *Fog's Weekly Journal* to axe this entertainment. Even before he saw it, he hated it. When it was hooted down, he was delighted. An enemy of Cibber both personally and politically, Mist gloated as he reported:

> On Tuesday night last a ridiculous piece was acted at the theatre in Drury Lane which was neither comedy, tragedy, opera, pastoral, or farce; however, no thief or robber of any rank was satirized in it and it could be said to give offense to none but persons of sense and good taste: yet it met with the reception it well deserved and was hissed off the stage. However, it may serve to bind up with the rest of Keyber's works.

XX Damon and Phillida

Love in a Riddle had, nonetheless, some sturdy theatrical lumber in it, and this Cibber was able to salvage. In the same way that he made a popular farce (*The School-Boy*, 1703) out of the subplot of *Womans Wit* (which failed in 1697), Cibber now created a famous afterpiece out of the comic underplot of *Love in a Riddle*. It too dealt with comic rivals—the booby brothers Crimon and Mopsus who woo the fair Phillida—and it was called *Damon and Phillida*. Cibber took care to present it anonymously in 1729, lest it meet with the fate of its parent. It became immensely popular—as *Love in a Riddle* ought to have done—and Baker's compendium *Companion to the Play-*

house praised it for "a Simplicity of Manners and a Uniformity of Conduct that render it most perfectly and truly pastoral." Today the piece seems rowdy, noisy and dull, but fifteen sparkling songs and plenty of slapstick kept it in the repertory for years.

XXI   Polypheme

Another musical venture by Cibber was *Polypheme,* an opera by Paul Rolli with music by Nicola Antonio Porpora.[81] Cibber translated the Italian libretto of *Polypheme,* one of five presented in London for the Opera of the Nobility, a group set up to rival Händel. It was presented at the Haymarket at the beginning of February, 1735. Cibber seems to have known Italian, therefore, as well as French.

XXII   Venus and Adonis *and* Myrtillo

Cibber was the author of the libretto of *Venus and Adonis. A Masque,* first performed March 12, 1715, with music by Dr. John Christopher Pepusch, director of music for Lincoln's Inn Fields.[82] For that theater Dr. Pepusch wrote not only *Venus and Adonis* but also *Apollo and Daphne* (1716), *The Death of Dido* (1716, with text by Barton Booth), and *The Union of the Three Sister-Arts* (1732).

Cibber and Pepusch also collaborated on *Myrtillo. A Pastoral Interlude,* first performed November 5, 1715. Like *Venus and Adonis* it recalls Dryden's ode *Alexander's Feast.* Neither of Cibber's libretti for masques is of interest today except as "representative of a vogue which was popular but which left no permanent impress on the English drama."[83]

XXIII   Works Attributed to Cibber

A number of works have been attributed on more or less evidence to Cibber. The earliest of these is *Cinna's Conspiracy,* a tragedy first performed at Drury Lane on February 19, 1713. Lintot, the publisher, paid Cibber thirteen pounds for the manuscript of this play.[84] "In a pamphlet by Daniel Defoe, written about 1713, this play is," says Baker in the *Biographia Dramatica,* "and we think not without probability, ascribed to Colley Cibber, who spoke the prologue." But Barker does not think this version of Corneille's *Cinna* "Cibberian," and neither do I.

The Secret History of Arlus and Odolphus is probably not by Cibber. The only "evidence" is the fact that this work, published anonymously in 1714, was advertised by a publisher as "By Mr. Cibber."[85] More of a case has been made for Cibber's authorship of *Hob, or the Country Wake. A Farce*, first presented at Drury Lane on October 6, 1715, and published that year with *By Mr. Doggett* on the title page. The source was a longer play, *The Country Wake* (1696), more certainly by Thomas Doggett. *Hob* was first assigned to Cibber by the theater historian William Rufus Chetwood in the eighteenth century, and this bold ascription was picked up by D. E. Baker in *The Companion to the Playhouse* (1764). John Genest argued against Cibber's authorship, but Richard Hindry Barker accepts it, saying that Chetwood is "too good an authority to be set aside on *a priori* grounds." Nevertheless I do not think the farce to be Cibber's.[86]

I have not been able to find *The Tell-Tale, or The Invisible Mistress. By Mr. Cibber*, so listed by Lintot in the publisher's advertisement following Barton Booth's *Death of Dido* (1716). As for *Chuck*, an opera attributed to Cibber in the *Biographia Dramatica* and by the editors of the fourth edition of the *Apology*, I accept Croissant's statement that it is "entirely without value" and probably not by Cibber. I do think, however, that the epitaph on Pope in *The Gentleman's Magazine*, XIV (June, 1744), 330, which I reproduce in the chapter on Cibber and "The Literary Quarrel with Pope," might be added to the canon. Barker says all that can be said: "It is Cibberian in thought and style and may possibly be genuine."[87]

Despite the arguments of G. W. Whiting,[88] I do not think Cibber to be the author of *The Temple of Dullness*, a comic opera published in 1745 without Cibber's name on the title page but with credit to the composer, *The Music by Mr. Arne*. In 1759 or later an undated edition was published of *Capochio and Dorinna. An Interlude for Music of Two Acts. Translated from an Italian Intermezzo of That Title, by the Late Colley Cibber, Esq., Poet Laureat. The Music Composed by Dr. Arne*.[89] In this latter case I can agree with Whiting, for he pretty much establishes that Cibber had nothing to do with this piece, which is more closely related to Lewis Theobald, author of *The Happy Captive*.

In 1752 the Epilogue to *Eugenia*, a tragedy by Philip Francis, was attributed to our author. The Earl of Chesterfield wrote to his son (February 20, 1752) that the epilogue was "old Cibber's,

but corrected, though not enough, by Francis." Cibber did, however, write eleven other prologues and epilogues, and these
are listed, with details, in the Selected Bibliography.

Colley Cibber and the Earl of Rochester are each said to
have contributed a song to *The Devil to Pay*. The earliest
edition I can find is undated but was printed in London about
1838. The title page reads: *The Devil to Pay; or, The Wives
Metamorphosed: A Comic Opera in Two Acts, by Charles
Coffey. Revised by Colley Cibber.* Coffey and John Mottley
had in turn reworked Thomas Jevon's *The Devil of a Wife.*
This version, whose title page I quote, was in reality revised
by Theophilus Cibber, the error being that of the printer,
J. Cumberland.[90]

CHAPTER 4

Drury Lane

A bare outline of the history of the London stage from the end of the Commonwealth to the time of Cibber is essential if we are to put in perspective the changes wrought by Cibber and his colleagues in the business of theatrical management and to understand the plays which Cibber wrote for the theater he ran. At the Restoration (1660) a number of acting companies sprang up, but soon two men dominated the scene: Sir William D'Avenant (who claimed to be the bastard son of Shakespeare) and Thomas Killigrew (unofficial court jester to Charles II). Each was furnished with a royal patent and founded theaters whose history was tremendously vicissitudinous, even more complex than our brief recapitulation can suggest.[1]

During the Puritan interregnum (1642-1660), when the public theaters were officially closed, the old traditions of the Elizabethan and Jacobean open-air theaters perished. With the Restoration, the indoor theaters, descendants of the private playhouses of Shakespeare's time, were firmly established; and it was in roofed buildings that D'Avenant and Killigrew set up their acting companies. By 1663 Killigrew's company had a new Theatre-Royal in Drury Lane at Bridges Street, the first to be erected cn that still-famous site.[2] Half a dozen years after it was built, an Italian visitor to London described it as nearly circular; and Pepys' diary tells us it had three balconies: a tier of boxes for the carriage trade, a balcony of boxes and benches for the beaux and belles, and a shilling gallery for the gods. Its stage jutted out into the auditorium in the Elizabethan fashion, though its front was rounded, and there were three proscenium doors on either side of the stage. This theater stood about eight years before it was destroyed by fire, always a danger in that candle-lit age; but it helped to establish some of the conventions of Cibber's stage.

D'Avenant's company, The Duke of York's Men, had its own new establishment by 1671: the Duke of York's Theater in Dorset Gardens, a handsome structure in Fleet Street (near the river) and purportedly designed by Sir Christopher Wren more for spectacle than for drama.[3] By this time the company had passed to D'Avenant's heirs, and it came under the control of the actors Betterton and Harris. The actor-manager tradition which so affected Cibber was being strengthened.

When Killigrew's company was driven out of Drury Lane by fire, it moved to the Lincoln's Inn Fields building that D'Avenant's company had vacated, but this was only a temporary expedient. The rivalry which Cibber was to feel so keenly later on was already strong. Killigrew's company wanted its own new theater too. Sir Christopher Wren built for it a playhouse in Drury Lane which cost £4000. It was less ornate than that of the rival company (which had cost £5000), but it too had the three balconies and a seventeen-foot stage jutting into the pit. This time there were only two proscenium doors on either side of the stage. The auditorium was raked for better sight lines and provided with benches which curved with the stage front. There were ample boxes for the people of quality and plenty of room backstage for the actors and the machinery which created the popular stage effects. These, common by Cibber's time, were already being greeted warmly.

With all this outlay it might seem that theatrical business was booming. It was not.[4] For a while it looked as if these brave new buildings might have to be deserted, that where plagues and Puritans had failed to quench the drama financial distress might succeed. The two companies were forced to consolidate to survive. In 1682 they joined forces at the Theatre-Royal in Drury Lane, using the Lincoln's Inn Fields building only occasionally. The theater with which Cibber was to be chiefly associated was already establishing itself as the more important.

Things went from bad to worse but, as always, businessmen were found who would take a flyer on The Fabulous Invalid. Chief among these was Christopher Rich, a lawyer turned impressario.[5] Even Cibber, who became Rich's personal friend and benefited under his management, admitted that Rich was a wily customer, "a close subtle Man," a grasping tyrant who snatched his two shillings profit out of every pound and often left the actors to wait for their salaries.[6] If Philip Henslowe, the theatrical entrepreneur of Shakespeare's time, was shrewd, Christopher Rich represented even rougher management. He came in time to control both patents, and he strove mightily to make money out of his monopoly despite rising costs, declining interest in the theater, and a prevailing public taste for increasingly vapid and dazzling entertainments. He adopted the most businesslike (if not artistic) methods. Cibber must have learned efficiency from him, but Cibber could never have welcomed Rich's policy of skimping on necessities in order to be able to afford showy extravagances. That was rather like debasing the product so that more cash would be available for advertising. It led to more and more superficial theater. Rich put on splashy spectacles when he could and cut four feet off the stage apron to install £10 worth of extra seats—in case his hodgepodges drew larger audiences. A crafty manipulator, he did away with the time-honored system of sharing profits with the actors; he instituted regular salaries, which he paid as irregularly as possible. He deprived actors of their pay, lent them money in their extremity, and then kept them in line by threatening to jail them for debt. Later, when we read of Cibber's being criticized for his managerial manners, let us remember his predecessor.

In 1695 the actors rebelled. The great Thomas Betterton, who had been a star since the Restoration and who had had some experience of his own in managing, led the revolt, broke away from Drury Lane, finagled a license, and opened his own theatre in Portugal Street (Lincoln's Inn Fields). He took with him such stalwarts as Cave Underhill, Mrs. Bracegirdle, and Mrs. Barry. He lined up a dramatist· for a share in the profits, William Congreve contracted to write one new play a year specifically for this company. To open the theater he prepared a fine new comedy of manners, *Love for Love.*

Despite these advantages, Betterton's group almost immediately ran into trouble. The theater (another former tennis court) was small and out of the way; once the novelty wore off, the public lost interest in it. The new company lacked both the space and the means to mount the extravaganzas that would draw new customers, or perhaps Betterton's integrity would not allow him to present "squeaking Italians and capering Monsieurs." Meanwhile Drury Lane was not above doing so, and it offered increasing competition. The ceaseless battle between good plays and cheap spectacles—one with which Cibber and his colleagues were to become all too familiar—raged until the aged Betterton was only too happy to sign over his license to two more hardy adventurers: William Congreve, the dramatist, and a stagestruck soldier, Captain (later Sir John) Vanbrugh. These two launched enterprisingly, even recklessly, on what was announced as an idealistic venture designed to uplift the stage and to improve the drama. They built a brand new theater in the Haymarket.[7]

Vanbrugh was also an architect—among English architects only he and Hawksmoor seriously attempted the Baroque—and he designed the new Haymarket theater in his most exuberant Baroque style, adapting (as he did with most of his plays) from the French. Its most striking feature comprised three tiers of boxes arranged in a horseshoe around the pit, rather like some opera houses with which we are familiar today. He opened with an opera, sumptuously mounted, which immediately made the impracticality of the building apparent. It ran only three performances. Soon the owners were searching for foreign novelties to fill the boxes. Business declined. Congreve pulled out, leaving Vanbrugh with his elaborately decked white elephant. Within three months it was obvious that the Haymarket had failed to check or to rival Rich's Drury Lane. Vanbrugh petitioned the Lord Chamberlain to unite his company with Rich's.

The Haymarket Theatre today is Her Majesty's, a few blocks from the bustle of Piccadilly; but in those days it was off the beaten track and patrons were liable to be ambushed by highwaymen. (Years later things were still bad. George II, who made Cibber his Poet Laureate, was attacked by highwaymen while he was strolling alone in Kensington Park and lost even his royal shoe buckles.) Moreover, as might be expected from the Vanbrugh who built Blenheim Palace, the theater was too vast. The architect had sacrificed acoustics to magnificence; Vanbrugh had constructed a grandiose monument, not an auditorium. Today electricity can throw light on the stage from the back of the galleries and can magnify voices from the stage. At that time this was impossible. Cibber complained that actors could be neither seen nor heard in this Baroque barn. And what the audiences could hear of caterwauling Italian singers, they did not like.[8]

Cibber was then firmly established in Rich's company at Drury Lane and could contemplate Vanbrugh's predicament with equanimity. Despite a raise in salary (to thirty shillings a week) designed to keep him at Drury Lane at the time of Betterton's desertion, Cibber had been tempted to join the new company and he had left Rich for Betterton in 1696. He soon returned to Drury Lane, however. It was, of course, illegal under the royal patents for actors to desert their companies.[9] Compelled to remain with Rich, Cibber determined to make the best of it. He could not hope always to play leads in a company that included Powell, Sandford, Swiney, Mills, Pinkethman, Bullock, and (after 1698) Wilks; but he could work his way into Rich's confidence and a position of power. Rich was ignorant of the drama and needed help. He had to hire a Captain Griffith, the actor George Powell, and Cibber himself in various assistant capacities. Professor Barker has found evidence that as early as 1704 Cibber had such power in the management of the theater that he was coming in for criticism in print.[10] This little dialogue involves "Colley C - - - - r, plagiary" and the famous Nathaniel Lee, popular author of the rhodomontade of *The Rival Queens* and of rather verbose tragedies on other polysyllabic personages such as Sophonisba, Mithridates, Theodosius, and Constantine:

CIBBER. The town has a [good] opinion of my parts, and my plays have raised me to a sort of viceroy in the theatres; for I try, acquit, or condemn; and there's nought to be represented but what is stamped by my approbation and tried by the touchstone of my own sense.

NAT LEE. Why the truth on't is, you are a very pretty deputy under Apollo, and the poets must need have a fine time on't, to be governed by such a quack of Parnassus, a stage tartar, that graze for your dialogues from the poets of the last age (for thank Heaven the ancients are far enough out of reach of your plagiarism). In short, your plays and your judgment are monstrous and defective.

CIBBER. Mr. R[ic]h and Mr. S[kipwi]t[h] think otherwise, and I value no one's opinion beside.

NAT LEE. I think it's almost upon the same footing of policy to make a militia captain a general, or give the Britannia to the care of a monkey, as to set you up as a theatric director. To be silent of how many better plays you have refused than you ever writ, and how many promising young authors your ignorance or malice have nipped in the bud; your absolute denial of *The Ambitious Stepmother* is an admirable test of your foresight and penetration, and shows how proper a person you are for that employ. Mr R[ic]h, no question, has given you thanks for it; and the town is satisfied just how much your judgment is good for. . . . Jonson, Shakespeare, Dryden, and some others of us not long since were discoursing of the poor estate of your theatre, and after several causes assigned, they all agreed the chief was owing to your mismanagement.

Clearly Cibber had achieved the position which enabled him
to act for the manager: to refuse plays he didn't like (such as
the bombast of Lee) and to accept others that met his standards
of charm and "prose and sense" (the new comedies of Steele
and Farquhar, for example). He forgot the difficulties he had
experienced in gaining a foothold in the theater and was ruthless
(and tactless) in rejecting plays that did not please him, that
did not offer him or one of the other principal actors a meaty
part, or that were not "theatrical." (This was Cibber's favorite word for plays that met the taste of the town, as he assessed
it.) He did not hesitate to fling back a play he thought uncom-
mercial—"Sir, this will not do!"—nor to tamper with one he knew
had literary value.[11]

It was inevitable that his treatment of authors ("choaking of
Singing-Birds," as he wryly called it) would render him unpopular. Hack writers objected that he set standards too high and
was unmindful that the theater was a commercial venture.
Talented dramatists objected that he had too businesslike an
approach, too little discrimination and appreciation of fine literature. It was always a battle between *belles lettres* and box office,
and Rich had been his mentor. Cibber infuriated disappointed
playwrights and their partisans, angered even the accepted
dramatists (whose work was being tampered with), and pro-
voked both professional enemies and such men as John Dennis,
an enemy by profession.

Impervious to criticism, aware of his limitations as a critic
of literature but proud of his undoubted success as a servant of
the public taste, Cibber blithely continued to suit himself.
He sat complacently with the other managers, smoked his long
pipe and tipped his head to one side as he listened and judged
the quaking dramatists who came to the theater office
to read their plays before a triumvirate who held the power
of life and death over the drama. Cibber usually delivered the
verdict, perhaps not always with as much consideration for the
playwright as for the commercial success of the theater. Cibber's power lead to bitter envy and detraction; his compla-
cency and invulvernability served but to goad his attackers
into ever more violent assault.

Cibber also annoyed his detractors by being clever. English-
men have always used "clever" in a derogatory way and looked
with ill-concealed distaste on those who deserved this adjective.
Cibber was more than clever: he was successful, drawing down
upon himself the envy of the lazy. He was not the "covetous,

sordid fellow" that Rich had been, but he was a businessman possessed of some of that ability for dissimulation which the Earl of Chesterfield said was a *sine qua non* for commerce. He added to this a positive gift for dealing in such a way that considerable sums of money found their way into his pockets and those of his fellow managers. He was pragmatic. He insisted on "theatrical" qualities in plays until the word became a joke around London. Surely he was aware that his job was to foster dramatic literature—not just literature—and to fill the auditorium not only on Saturday nights (when most people liked to go to the theater and the actors presented their best programs) but every night, if possible. He took to heart the lines Charles Hart spoke: "But we, the actors, humbly will submit,/Now, and at any time, to a full pit."[12]

"I go with the great stream of life," said Sir Joshua Reynolds: Cibber went along with the public taste, urging it now and then. He encouraged authors. He sought out good plays. But he knew that the actors, then as now, could often carry a bad play as well as ruin a good one. Mrs. Barry was dumpy and had a crooked nose; but she was able, Betterton testified, to give "Success to such Plays, as to read would turn a Man's Stomach." Cibber always thought, as he read a manuscript, how it would play, what his actors and his theater could do with it, how his audience would receive it.

His affection was chiefly for the actors, even for those who succeeded where his piping voice and slight build caused him to fail (in the historical oratorios that passed for tragedies and in the plays that demanded romantic ardor and pathos); but he had as well sympathy with playwrights. After all, unlike most managers, he was a playwright himself. However, he always insisted (and he was most often justified) that dramatists would have to defer to his superior knowledge of the commercial theater. If they would not admit that, like architects, they had to cope with the functional necessities as well as strive for the artisitic ideal, Cibber was likely to give them trouble. Indeed, playwrights ought to have been inured to trouble; they got it from so many quarters. In one of Fielding's pasquinades, a little "Dramatick Satire on the Times," his poetaster Fustian complains of the playwright's woes "before he comes to his third night" (that is, gets his money from his benefit performance).[13] Fustian speaks in *Pasquin* of what the dramatist undergoes

first with the muses, who are humourous ladies, and must

be attended; for if they take it into their head at any time
to go abroad and leave you, you will pump your brain in
vain: then, sir, with the master of a play-house to get it
acted, whom you generally follow a quarter of a year before you know whether he will receive it or no; and then,
perhaps he tells you it won't do, and returns it you again,
reserving the subject, and perhaps the name, which he
brings out in his next pantomime; but if he should receive
the play, then you must attend again to get it writ out into
parts, and rehearsed. Well, sir, at last, the rehearsals
begin; then, sir, begins another scene of trouble with the
actors, some of whom don't like their parts, and all are
continually plaguing you with alterations; at length, after
having waded through all these difficulties, his play appears
upon the stage, where one man hisses out of resentment
to the author; a second out of dislike to the house; a third
out of dislike to the actor; a fourth out of dislike to the
play; a fifth for the joke [sic] sake; a sixth to keep all the
rest company. Enemies abuse him, friends give him up, the
play is damned, and the author goes to the devil; so ends
the farce.[14]

Small wonder the playwrights complained. But, in an age
when the audience was frequently rowdy, dilettante, and drunk-
en, in both the footmen's gallery and the best seats, everyone,
managers included, was taking a chance when, instead of reviv-
ing an old warhorse of proved acceptance, he risked a riot with
an untried piece. We have seen that Cibber had good cause to
be cautious and fearful of the ire and orange peel of the
audience. *The Non-Juror* was hissed: *The Refusal* and *The
Provok'd Husband* were hooted—the actors pelted as if they
were in the pillory. Kitty Clive, vivacious darling of the stage
in ballad opera, made her debut to hisses and catcalls in *Love
in a Riddle*, an entertainment which had to be withdrawn, quite
apart from its merits, because of the opposition to Cibber.

Sometimes opening nights were in fact intolerable, for
not until Garrick that there was "predetermination of the
business of the scene" and the actors had perhaps only a fort-
night (playing other things every night) to learn their lines.
And even well-done plays might be damned for sport, as Grinly
tells us in Act IV of *The Modish Couple*, in which he says: "I
will wager you now five hundred Pounds that half a Score
of us shall quite demolish the best Piece that can come on any
Stage."[15] The play might begin quietly; but when the third
act arrived the obstreperous audience of 1732 took over—and

the first piece of Wit that is utter'd *Hiss* cry two or three
of us—In a little time after, a stroke of Humour comes
out, *hoh, hoh, hoh,* cry others. Then perhaps a serious
Scene comes in the Play, *Yaw* say the rest, and so on, till
the Play is pretty well over. And for the last two or three
Scenes, where the silly Rogue thinks he has shown his
Judgment the most, and on which the whole Business of the
Piece depends, we strike up such a Chorus of *Cat-calls,
Whistles, Hisses, Hoops,* and *Horse-laughs,* that not one of
the Audience can hear a Syllable, and therefore chari-
tably conclude it to be very sad Stuff.—The Epilogue's
spoke, the Curtain falls, and so the poor Rascal is sent to
the Devil.[16]

In those days a play might be hissed because its sentiments
were Whig or Tory, because it was a bad play by a friend, or
because it was a good play by an enemy. Party politics and
personal prejudice were as likely as its merit to affect its success.
All that could be done was to have a shrewd manager like Cibber
to make decisions; to rehearse the play as well as possible in
the time granted; to mount it as lavishly as money permitted;
to cast it with as many popular stars as were available; and,
for the author's sake, to pack the theater on opening night with
as many of his friends as could be assembled. Even so distinguished a writer as Addison had his opening night audience
handpicked by his friend Steele in order to avoid disaster. The
play was *Cato,* one of the smash hits of the century (largely
for political reasons, it is true); but at the first performance
Addison paced backstage, quivering like an expectant father.
Cibber had more gall.

Nicoll's *History of the Early Eighteenth Century Drama,* to
which we are all indebted, has a fine introductory chapter on
the nature of the audience in the theater of Cibber's time. He
concludes: "From whatever angle we look at it we find the drama
of the early eighteenth century, as the drama of all centuries,
more fully explained by a reference to the audience than by a
reference to any other thing."[17] That is one reason why we attempted to sketch in here how and why Cibber knew and
understood his audience. However tactlessly he gave his advice,
playwrights were wise to accept it. He not only helped dramatists
who heeded his suggestions but he was able to advance the
career of actors he thought deserving. One of these was of
particular importance to Cibber: he was Robert Wilks, a future
partner, one of the mainstays of Drury Lane (with brief

interludes at the Haymarket from 1706-1708 and from 1709-1710) from about 1699 to 1732.[18]

Wilks, who inherited some of George Powell's star parts and created many of his own, excelled in the role of the beseeching lover. He won his greatest applause in the genial and artificial comedies of the easy-going George Farquhar, becoming practically identified with the dashing Sir Harry Wildair in the play of that name.[19] The bluff and attractive character of Wilks fitted him for triumphs as Macduff in *Macbeth* and as Prince Hal in *Henry IV, Part I.* He also played many cavalier roles in the plays of his period, including Cibber's plays. Cibber, his friend and adviser for many years, attended Wilks' funeral at St. Paul's, Covent Garden, on September 27, 1732; and he perhaps was instrumental the next year in getting the infamous bookseller Edmund Curll to publish a best-selling *Life of that Eminent Comedian, Robert Wilks.*[20]

Cibber arranged good parts for Wilks, and this was a time when that mattered more than discovering new dramatists, for the fashion was to capitalize on good actors and to produce chiefly "acting plays," defined by Fielding as "entirely supported by the Merit of the Actor; in which case it signifies very little whether there be any Sense in it or no." Cibber made use of his drinking friendship with Christopher Rich to contrive the substitution of Robert Wilks for George Powell as *répétiteur* and stage manager at Drury Lane. Cibber's objections to Powell are detailed in the *Apology*: he was often drunk, perpetually overbearing, and sometimes ill-prepared in his parts, for he was not a "quick study" (unlike Wilks and Cibber) and was inclined like a schoolboy to postpone his study until the last minute. Moreover, Powell was unreliable in other matters: he fled to the rival company for a season and indeed would have remained there had not the competition of the other actors at the Haymarket deprived him of the best roles. And he was egotistical. Cibber didn't like people like that!

Cibber was later to find that Wilks was equally vain, jealous of preeminence, and not above self-serving at the expense of others. But a man of Cibber's character could understand such faults. Cibber made Wilks "first Minister, or Bustle-master-general of the Company" and watched him, less naturally endowed than Powell but immensely more industrious, go on to make himself admired by actors and audiences alike. Though sometimes lamenting Wilks' rashness and often suffering from his bad temper, Cibber chose him as a partner and was able to work rather harmoniously with him for the major part of his theatrical career.

Wilks, upon securing Powell's place, was given a contract paying him four pounds a week for acting and managing rehearsals. A month later Cibber negotiated for himself a five-year contract at £3/10/0 a week. This was ten shillings less than Wilks' salary, but by an oral agreement Cibber was awarded another thirty shillings for reading plays, casting parts, and generally helping out in production. At £5 a week all told, Cibber was the highest-paid member of the company. Moreover, he had installed his choice as stage manager.

Though it was only a century or so since English law had declared actors rogues and vagabonds, it looked at last as if Cibber were well launched on a respectable and even profitable career in the theater; and the theater gave fair promise of continuing to weather the storms. William Prynne's *Histriomastix* (1634) had reiterated the age-old attacks on the stage as the sink of sin. In the best traditions of the Church Fathers he had damned plays as the work of the devil, "sinful, heathenish, lewd, ungodly spectacles and most pernicious corruptions."[21] But Prynne had lost his ears and his case (albeit he was punished for political rather than theatrical libel), and he had been forgotten. The gallants and fine ladies of the stage grew increasingly smutty, profane, and licentious; but the theaters remained open. Even the more justified if not more temperate diatribes of the nonjuring clergyman Jeremy Collier could not eradicate these plays, though he took some effective swipes at Dryden, Congreve, Wycherley, Vanbrugh, D'Urfey, Otway, and a host of lesser fry.[22] Dryden was repentant, Congreve unregenerate; but the theater went on. And, adapting himself to the times, so did Colley Cibber.

CHAPTER 5

The Management

THROUGH a series of complicated managerial arrangements, which it is not essential to detail here, Cibber's employer Christopher Rich initiated a plan to corner the drama, to control both Drury Lane and the Haymarket. In 1706 Rich persuaded Owen Swiney, a clever and ambitious man, to leave the army and to take over the direction of the theater in the Haymarket, leasing it for seven years from Vanbrugh. Swiney was to be Rich's vassal.[1]

Once Swiney began working for Rich, however, Rich's cooperation was less than was promised: certain monies were not forthcoming, he haggled over details, he refused to allow Cibber and other actors to work for Swiney at the Haymarket,[2] and he lured away audiences from Swiney's theater by lavishly mounting operas at Drury Lane. Swiney battled bravely, but even well-cast productions of fine new plays (among them Cibber's *The Double Gallant* and *The Lady's Last Stake* and Farquhar's *The Beaux' Stratagem*) failed to keep the Haymarket in the black. It looked for a while as if Rich might force out even his satrap and rule like the Turk, no brother near the throne.

Rich's hope to be emperor of the London theater was stillborn. Just as it seemed that he was going to be able to seize for himself a lucrative monopoly on the drama, he was undercut by his hitherto silent partner, Sir Thomas Skipwith.[3] Suddenly Skipwith realized that he was getting nothing substantial from his investment and in the summer of 1707 he mentioned in a casual conversation with his friend Lt. Col. Henry Brett that the patent for the Theatre-Royal in Drury Lane was really more trouble than it was worth. It had not yielded him a profit in ten years. He offered it to Brett as a gift if he could make anything out of it. Brett at first demurred, then allowed his friend to persuade him. To make it all legal, Brett bought the patent for the nominal sum of ten shillings.

Then Brett came to London—he had been at the country seat of Sandywell Park in Gloucestershire—and immediately consulted Cibber as to how to make the most of the deed to Drury

Lane, now "sign'd, seal'd and deliver'd." Cibber was an old friend, having met Brett a decade earlier when Brett began to hang about the theater in the fashion of the beaux who crowded backstage to enjoy "the liberty of the scenes." They had often drunk together, and Cibber had hung on Brett's sparkling conversation, "as he had Wit enough for any two People, and I had Attention enough for any four, there could not well be wanting any sociable Delight, on either side."[4] Brett was not the "fine whoring, swearing, smutty, aetheistical man" that Jeremy Collier asserted the "fine gentleman" of the period had become, but he had sufficient wit and dash that Cibber's "Attention" might well have been prompted by more than friendship. Brett was a useful model for an actor who played men of fashion.

If Brett in this way had been able to help Cibber's career, Cibber was able to discharge the obligation and to assist Brett in his. Sir Thomas Skipwith had introduced Brett to "a Lady who had enough, in her Power, to disencumber him of the World, and make him every way, easy for Life." On that occasion Cibber, who happened to be stylishly decked out for the part of Young Reveller in *Greenwich Park*, lent him his clean shirt (for Brett had "been out all the Morning, upon Business, and . . . his Linnen was too much soiled, to be seen in Company") so that he could court her. In about ten days Brett married the lady.

It was to Cibber, then, who had literally given him the shirt off his back to help him gain his fortune, that Brett came for advice about what could be done to turn Sir Thomas' generous gift to advantage. Cibber, then engaged at the Haymarket, was not without ideas as to how Rich's grip on Drury Lane might be broken: "My first Advice, therefore, was, That he should produce his Deed to the other Menaging Patentee of *Drury Lane* [Rich], and demand immediate Entrance to a joint Possession of all Effects, and Powers, to which that Deed had given him an equal Title."[5] He counseled Brett to be firm with Rich and to proceed, as if he expected no opposition whatever, to unite the two companies of Drury Lane and the Haymarket. This was accomplished, and in January, 1708, Brett gathered all the actors together at Drury Lane (under Rich). He left Owen Swiney at the Haymarket in charge of opera, and he extracted a ruling from the Lord Chamberlain (who, as the head of the Royal Household, was technically in charge of all "Her Majesty's Servants") that this separation of interests was to be strictly enforced. As Cibber wrote, "The Scheme was, to have but one Theatre for Plays, and another for Operas, under separate Interests."

Swiney imported a Signor Nicolini to star in Händel's *Rinaldo* and for a while rejoiced in the new vogue for Italian opera. Things seemed to be going well at the Haymarket, but not at Drury Lane. Though Brett assigned his share in the patent (March 31, 1708) to the leading actors (Cibber, Wilks, and Richard Estcourt), the war between Rich and his performers continued, for he always had some skulduggery afoot to make extra money for himself. This time it was a demand that he receive a third of the money raised by the actors' benefit performances.[6] They strongly objected and immediately appealed to the Lord Chamberlain. They succeeded in silencing Rich. On June 6, 1709, Queen Anne closed the Theatre-Royal in Drury Lane.

"The Scheme" for "separate Interests" broke down. Since Drury Lane was "dark," Swiney was able to obtain permission to bring some of the actors into partnership with him at the Haymarket. The tradition of actor-managers, under which Cibber was to benefit so much, was being strengthened. Mrs. Oldfield eventually settled for £200 a year and the proceeds of a benefit performance—for Thomas Doggett objected to a woman in the management—but the other principal actors became sharers with Swiney and helped to run the theater.[7] Partnership articles were secretly signed in March, for it was clear that the downfall of Rich was imminent. In June the actors' most sanguine hopes were realized. Cibber watched Rich's discomfort as the Lord Chamberlain's silencing order was handed to "Our Politician" Rich and, gloating, flung at him a speech from Shakespeare:

> Read o'er this;
> And after, this: and then to breakfast with
> What appetite you have.[8]

Rich had lost Drury Lane by trying to seize too much power. He began to build another theater, but died before it was completed. His son John went on to be a famous impressario, producer of *The Beggar's Opera;* but the reign of Christopher Rich was over.

Soon, however, another owner-manager came along to tyrannize the actors. With Rich silenced, the way was clear for William Collier—another lawyer with a yen to make money out of Drury Lane—to obtain a license. He reopened Drury Lane on November 23, 1709, having broken into the theater, ejected Rich's staff, and scraped together a company of such actors as had not gone over to the Haymarket. Almost immediately he was in trouble. He quarreled with the actors. Business was slow and his sole consolation was that attendance was down at the Haymarket too.[9]

At the end of the season Swiney went to Ireland for the summer. Cibber and the others stayed on to keep the Haymarket open, running a series of special benefits for themselves. After a season that had ended with a loss of £206, they needed the money. Not only did they keep the proceeds for themselves —and Swiney was to be angry at that, since they were profiting and he had lost money that year—but they even took £350 from the Haymarket till to meet current expenses. Unwittingly, Swiney was underwriting their benefits. Confronted with this fact on his return, he wrote to the Lord Chamberlain that Cibber, Wilks, and Doggett were not abiding by their agreement. He was livid and prepared to go to any lengths to get his rights: "If that order is not observ'd I must Endeavour to preserve my Self from Ruin & have recourse to Such Methods as Shall be advised by the ablest Lawyers in England for my Security." And again: ". . . if there is any Prospect left me of getting any thing by the Play-house I will go on if there is not I hope it will be justification of me if I refuse."[10]

But Swiney lost. After many petitions, arguments, and agreements, Cibber, Wilks, and Doggett got control not only over Swiney but over the Theatre-Royal in Drury Lane. Collier wound up with the Haymarket, for opera only. Swiney dunned by creditors, fled to the Continent.[11] By 1711 Cibber, Doggett, and Wilks had formed a triumvirate at Drury Lane. They had a license, but it put them on a perilous footing for it was revocable at will. The three managers were on their best behavior. They remedied some of the evils of the stage, bettered the lot of the actors, were scrupulous in their weekly accounts, and introduced to the Theatre-Royal in Drury Lane a new era of prosperity such as had not been seen in thirty years. In all of this Cibber, combining firmness with practicality, was a leader.

The death of Queen Anne on the first of August in 1714 made a new patent mandatory. Cibber, Booth, and Wilks—knowing that they would have to pay £700 a year to some silent partner, and not wanting another Owen Swiney or a William Collier— elected to assign it to Sir Richard Steele. Accordingly Steele used his influence with the Duke of Marlborough to have his name inserted in the new document which was to regulate the theater. On October 18, 1714, he became a partner at Drury Lane with Cibber and the other actor-managers.[12] Later Steele was to cause trouble, but at first he was very congenial to work with.[13] He even contrived to get the theater a better deal by applying for it, with the managers' consent, under his own name. On January 19, 1715, Steele was personally granted the patent to Drury Lane, and then he immediately assigned equal shares to Colley Cibber, Robert Wilks, and Barton Booth.[14]

Booth's position in the mangement requires some explanation: the reader will wonder what happened to Thomas Doggett. Actually it was the question of Booth, on top of other arguments between the parsimonious Doggett and the extravagant Wilks, that drove Doggett out of the partnership. Booth used his influence at court to insinuate himself into the management.[15] By the time Steele first appeared on the scene, Booth was one of the three actor-managers of Drury Lane. Cibber, of course, had weathered all the storms. He had eased Wilks into the management. He had helped Swiney silence Rich and had then led the actor-managers against Swiney. He had refereed the battles between his partners Wilks and Doggett. And, insofar as it was he who cast Barton Booth as Cato, Cibber contributed to Booth's replacement of Doggett.

Booth became the talk of the town for his triumph in the title role of Addison's *Cato*. The play ran for an unprecedented month while Booth was cheered by both the Whigs and the Tories as he stalked "A brave man struggling in the storms of fate/And greatly falling with a falling state!" Cibber tells us that he had read *Cato* "privately with Sir *Richard Steele*" as early as 1703, "nine Years before it was acted." At that time only four acts existed, and Addison, protesting "that it had only been the Amusement of his leisure Hours in *Italy*," refused to have it produced, though he was assured that Betterton would undoubtedly make it a great success. By 1712 the political situation seemed to demand *Cato's* performance. Addison was prevailed upon to permit it, and Booth was handed one of the choicest roles of the century. It was the season of the year when actors' benefits were ususally given,

> But a Work of that critical Importance, was to make its
> way . . . it was therefore (*Mondays* excepted) acted every
> Day for a Month, to constantly crowded Houses. As the
> Author had made us a Present of whatever Profits he

might have claim'd from it, we thought ourselves oblig'd, to spare no Cost, in the proper Decorations of it. Its coming so late in the Season, to the Stage, prov'd of particular Advantage, to the sharing Actors; because the Harvest of our annual Gains was generally over, before the middle of *March;* many select Audiences being then, usually reserv'd, in favour to the Benefits of private Actors; which fixt Engagements naturally abated the Receipts of the Days, before and after them: But this unexpected After-crop of *Cato,* largely supplied to us, those Deficiencies; and, was almost equal to two fruitful Seasons, in the same Year; at the Close of which, the three menaging Actors found themselves, each a Gainer of thirteen hundred, and fifty Pounds. . . .[16]

After Booth had done so much for the management, it was inevitable that he would expect something of them. He used his fame and connections to become a shareholder as well as a star, despite Doggett's opposition to adding him to the directors of Drury Lane. Very soon the Lord Chamberlain decreed that Booth was to be allowed to buy an equal share in the partnership for £600. If the managers did not acquiese, they would lose their authority to operate.

It did not make sense to offer opposition to the Lord Chamberlain or to his underlings. The livelihoods of "His Majesty's Servants" depended upon the Lord Chamberlain's sufferance, and he was known to exercise his power. On December 19, 1719, for example, he suspended Cibber, charging that he had "insolently and traitorously" abused the Crown and its ministers in the Preface to *Ximena, or the Heroick Daughter.*[17] The remarks in the Preface, however, appear unexceptionable, or at least unworthy of this retaliation, short though Cibber's suspension proved to be. His real crime, it seems, was impertinence.

Cibber, used to ruling his company with an iron hand and "pert" by nature, was apt to be insolent on occasion. How one who did such yeoman service in keeping peace among the managers, however, could have been so foolishly tactless as Cibber was in this instance is hard to fathom. The Duke of Newcastle, who had taken an interest in the Irish actor Thomas Elrington, had asked Cibber to give Elrington the part of Torismond in a revival of *The Spanish Friar.*[18] Cibber refused, probably being impudent and imprudent enough to add that he knew his business and would run his theater without interference. Despite Newcastle's desire to advance Elrington, Cibber might well have rejected him with impunity had he only been more circumspect and more tactful. He appears to have learned from this incident: in later life, notably in the quarrel with Pope, he lost his patience and abandoned his tact only after much provocation.

On January 23, 1720, the Lord Chamberlain closed Drury Lane and revoked the license. He was going to make his authority clear for once and for all. Four days later Cibber, Booth, and Wilks received a new patent, having been compelled to swear obedience to the Lord Chamberlain and his officers. The Lord Chamberlain also took the opportunity to exclude Steele.[19] Steele despatched an angry note to Newcastle as soon as he learned that he was not included in the new patent. Newcastle's only reply was a curt directive, through his secretary, that Steele was never to address him again.

Steele started a new periodical, *The Theatre*, and argued his case under the pseudonym of Sir John Edgar.[20] The Lord Chamberlain was undaunted. The new license, issued January 27, 1720, empowered Cibber, Booth, and Wilks to reopen Drury Lane, but it did not mention Steele. The next day Steele wrote to the managers as if he were still the governor, peremptorily forbidding them to play "until you receive further orders." They ignored his communication, taking no further notice of him until May 2, 1721, when Steele contrived to get back the governorship of Drury Lane.[21] He immediately claimed from the managers his share of the profits withheld during the year and a half of his absence.

The three managers cannot have relished much having to pay, in a lump sum, all this money they had hoped to keep for themselves. By September 19, 1721, they had come to terms with Steele: he was to share equally with the three managers in the patent, the property, the profits, and the losses. But by December they were arguing again, this time about Sir Richard's creditors receiving the Drury Lane profits he should have been paid directly. A letter from Steele to Cibber (December 7, 1721) states in part:

> You have been the chief ingine in ensnaring me into a concession which I should have been ashamed to own, before you had the resolution to deny so equitable a demand as I made to you. But as it now is besides the folly of giving to men richer than myself, I have done it to those that have no regard for me, but as a tool and a screen against others, who want to treat you ill, and forbear only because of my relation to you; which shall not be very long, for it is in my power to get rid of my enemies much more easily than

> I can have common justice of my friends. This is evident
> in the monstrous hardiness of denying the Governor of
> your House, as you shall find I am, the superfluity of his
> income, which is liable to no demand or pretence. . . .[22]

No wonder Steele became estranged.[23] He worked ever less
closely with the actor-managers, though in 1722 he did sign two
documents with them.[24] That same year Steele's sentimental
comedy *The Conscious Lovers*, the play that Fielding's Parson
Adams declared one of but two "fit for a Christian to read,"
was produced at Drury Lane. Relations improved. Cibber
and Steele worked together on it.

In the Preface to the play Steele thanked Cibber for his assistance: "Mr. Cibber's zeal for the work, his care and application
in instructing the actors and altering the disposition of the scenes,
when I was, through sickness, unable to cultivate such things
myself, has been a very obliging favour and friendship to me."[25]
Cibber's son later claimed that Cibber had partly rewritten
the play, but Steele asserted that he had only meant to express
thanks for Cibber's staging it.

In any case, their truce was short. In 1724 they were at law
again, this time because Steele had assigned his Drury Lane
profits to a trustee to pay off some of his debts, and the managers
contended that this was tantamount to an illegal sale of his
share. In 1726 they were in court again, in countersuits about
Sir Richard's "natural Negligence of his Affairs," says Cibber,
explaining that

> upon Sir *Richard's* totally absenting himself, from all Care,
> and Menagement of the Stage . . . we were reduc'd to
> let him know, that we could not go on, at that Rate; but
> if he expected to make the Business a *sine Cure*, we had as
> much Reason to expect a Consideration for our extraordin-
> ary Care of it; and that during his Absence, we therefore
> intended to charge our selves at a Sallary of I 1. 13 s. 4 d.
> every acting Day (unless he could shew us Cause, to the
> contrary) for our Menagement. . . .[26]

The managers got away with this practice for several years.
Finally Steele, pressed by his creditors, advised by his lawyers,
or irritated by the managers' sudden decision to desist from their
practice of advancing him loans against profits, took them to
the Court of Chancery. We have heard Steele accusing Cibber
of being the "chief ingine" in an earlier instance, and indeed
Cibber does seem to have led the managers as *primus inter pares*.

On this occasion he certainly was the spokesman. Representing the managers, Cibber proved that Steele was not doing his share of the theater's work; and he convinced Sir Joseph Jekyll, Master of the Rolls, that the managers were entitled to the deduction they made. Both parties paid their own costs and shook hands amicably.

From then on Cibber's only real problem with his partners was with Barton Booth. Having married a woman of some wealth, Booth easily raised the money and bought his way into the partnership at the £600 price set by the Lord Chamberlain. Cibber and Wilks, realizing that they operated at the Lord Chamberlain's pleasure, readily accepted Booth, but Doggett was adamant. He took his case to the Court of Chancery.[27] Eventually Doggett obtained a judgment and by then he was ready to accept it. He took £600 and severed all connection with Drury Lane. He came out of the business, perhaps, less well than he might have done; but he was content. He apparently got along with Cibber—most people did, most of the time— but he had always fought with Robert Wilks. Cibber says Wilks had "a captious, overbearing, valiant Pride" and Doggett "a stiff, sullen Purse-Pride," so they inevitably clashed. The argument over the admission of Booth to the partnership gave Doggett a convenient excuse to quit it.

The company lost a fine actor in Doggett. He was especially good at portraying low-class comedy characters and Sailor Ben in Congreve's *Love for Love*. But the company also lost a contentious Jonsonian "humour" character, a man terribly difficult to please or to oppose. Doggett was a staunch Whig who loved to argue politics, and there was enough to bicker about in a large company of actors without that. He was also a reckless manipulator on the stock market but, when it came to laying out cash at the theater, tight-fisted in the extreme. He never really got along with his partners, despite Cibber's pouring oil on the troubled waters; and things went more smoothly at Drury Lane after his retirement.

For a time after the lawsuit, Doggett would not speak to Cibber or to Wilks, though he saw them every day at the coffeehouse which Button, a former servant of Addison, operated. Addison, Steele, Pope, and others were constantly to be seen there and so was Doggett, though he was sure to run into one or both of his former partners or maybe even Booth. Cibber bore Doggett no ill will and Doggett knew it, for he had heard tell that tricksters had informed Cibber that Doggett was dead in an attempt to provoke Cibber to unkind remarks, and Cibber would not utter a nasty word. Though he had been most active in the lawsuit, Cibber remained amiable toward Doggett and was able, by dint of much patience and charm, to regain his friendship.

Barton Booth, though he became lazier in later years, was never so much trouble as Doggett in the partnership and as an actor he was even more valuable.[28] He published a slight play of his own devising, *The Death of Dido. A Masque* (1716), and he remained a leading light of the stage until his retirement in 1727, half a dozen years before his death. Many years later he was still well enough remembered for Cibber's son Theophilus to find many readers for his *Life of Barton Booth* (1753).

With Doggett gone, Cibber's life was to be a trifle more peaceful, and he found more time for playwriting and interests outside the management of the theater. It is indeed amazing that he was able to find time for playwriting, caught up as he was in this series of skirmishes and internecine wars. Cibber, Booth, and Wilks reigned together for the next twenty years. As Cibber wrote in the *Apology*: "We had our clouded Hours, as well as our sunshine, and we were not always in the same Good-Humour with one another: Fire, Air, and Water, could not be more vexatiously opposite, than the different Tempers of the Three Menagers, though they might equally have their useful, as well as their destructive Qualities."[29]

CHAPTER 6

The Theater and the Company

WHEN he wrote his plays, Cibber had to take into account not only literary traditions and theatrical conventions but the capacities and limitations of the repertory company of actors for which he wrote, the theater in which they appeared, and the audiences that would attend the performances. He and his fellow actor-managers were at the head of an organization of impressive size.[1] Every week they had to meet a "constant charge" (payroll) and realize a profit in the face of competition.[2] In 1714 that competition increased, for Christopher Rich's son John opened a new theater in Lincoln's Inn Fields, lured away seven or eight of Drury Lane's younger actors, and began to produce popular entertainments, especially operas and imported novelties. Drury Lane's preeminence was threatened, and Cibber's theater went into a decline that lasted until about 1716.

But Drury Lane's prospects were good. The introduction of Sir Richard Steele into the partnership had put Cibber and his fellows on a firmer footing and offered them the security propaedeutical to long-range planning. With the Great Seal of England on a guarantee, their patent, the managers could set about refurbishing their Theatre-Royal. Drury Lane was closed for alterations in 1715 (which started a silly rumor that the building was unsafe) and reopened in new splendor.[3] Knowing what this theater was like is essential, for to read Cibber's plays intelligently we have to be able to visualize performances on the stage.

The most remarkable difference from the average theater of today—the first thing that would strike us if we were able to go back in time and walk into an eighteenth-century theater—was the apron that projected into the pit, the vestige of the platform stage of the Elizabethan playhouse and the ancestor of the "thrust stage" of the more *avant-garde* theaters of today. This apron, which was (as we have mentioned previously) a feature of the original Drury Lane theater, was retained when the theater was remodeled in 1715. So was the depth of the proscenium, which was sufficient to permit doors on either side. What resulted was precisely what these "new" thrust stages of the "modern" theater hope to produce—a style of acting wholly different from that possible or sensible on the typical, modern proscenium stage. To understand why Cibber's plays are as they are, we have to consider what that platform meant to actors and audience.

The actors moved chiefly on that apron, performing in front of the "picture" framed by the proscenium arch, not within the modern box set. When they were "discovered," by the opening of a pair of sliding flats, the stage directions very often required them to "come forward" immediately. They were always close to the audience, and this proximity made an intimate and subtle style of acting feasible, even in that era of flickering candles and lamps. Though the even and declamatory style of delivery popular at the end of the seventeenth century when Cibber first came to the stage still largely persisted, great stress soon came to be laid upon "the minutest Motion of a Feature" and natural-ness of facial expression. In the period after Cibber, David Garrick coupled this development with more restrained gestures and a more varied, a less stilted elocution, even in tragedy. Garrick was famous for being "natural."[4]

In Cibber's time the acting was still not "natural." It was in a more artificial art that Cibber and his colleagues trained the young actors, many of whom (as Irishmen without polish or girls with nothing but pretty faces to begin with) required a good deal of education. But generally Cibber could train them the way he wanted them—and then write plays to exploit their talents. Every manager was limited to some extent with regard to the plays he could accept, for he could only take what the resident company could perform. Cibber was a little luckier; to some degree he could train his company to perform the sort of plays he wanted, or he could train himself to write plays that suited them. He did both: he molded Mrs. Oldfield, and he coped with Barton Booth. He rose to the challenge of Mrs. Barry's "elevated dignity," all the more surprising in that Mrs. Barry got into the theater because she was a sprightly young flirt who caught the eye of the rakehell Earl of Rochester. Cibber provided parts for the dignified Booth, who was pom-pous; slow, even in the role of Hotspur; and almost as restrained as Betterton, of whom Tony Aston reported that he "kept his passion under, and shewed it most (as Fume smoaks most) when stifled." He used Mary Porter's coarse, rough voice in a cadenced, chantlike delivery. He made his comic heroines less flighty than those of the Restoration, for Mrs. Oldfield, one of the leading exponents of the "easy" school of comedy so popular in Cibber's time, was sparkling and coquettish but a lot more dignified than Nell Gwynn had been in good King Charles' golden days.

Mrs. Oldfield's career is a good example of Cibber at work, for she was one of the triumphs of his coaching. At first he thought little of her talent, and she did little for three or four years at Drury Lane until, in 1703, another actress fell ill and forced Cibber to share the bill with Nance Oldfield in a leading role. He found she had potential, a good "understanding," and was teachable. He not only helped her in her parts but wrote for her specifically the roles of Lady Dainty in *The Double Gallant* and the sprightly but substantial Maria in *The Non-Juror*. The part of Lady Modish in *The Careless Husband* he especially tailored to her measurement, but he also instructed her to essay tragic black as Mary, Queen of Scots, and in other parts—even as Cleopatra and as Semandra in *Mithridates*. Mrs. Oldfield developed into an astoundingly versatile and capable actress, considering that she was a simple sixteen-year-old when playwright George Farquhar discovered her (reading *The Scornful Lady* behind the bar at the Mitre Tavern), took her for his mistress, and foisted her off on the managers of Drury Lane as an ingenue.

Compared to her, Robert Wilks acted in a somewhat stilted way. He tended to strike poses or "moods" and to recite somewhat unevenly.[5] But he was grand and impressive. He might have been an even greater star in the Victorian theater in the days of such as Sir Henry Irving, an electrifying actor who had resonance where his brains ought to have been. In Cibber's theater it was not so necessary as it later became to "project"— which is why Cibber could make such a success with his small voice—but at the end of her career Mrs. Siddons, "The Tragic Muse" herself, warned a young actress that she would have to shout into a "wilderness," and even that was before the truly cavernous theaters of Victorian times.

The actor-managers of Cibber's time trained the company to intone tragedy, though it was not necessary to howl it as in Victorian times, and to play comedy in the "genteel" tradition. Farce, which depended largely on swiftness, asides, and ad-libs, was more "natural." Cibber mastered all these styles as director and as writer. As an actor he succeeded in comedy and farce, but his voice and bearing were not grand enough for tragedy, a question then more of elocution than of impersonation. He was at his best in the facile comedy of manners, as were the tall and striking Mrs. Oldfield and the dashing Robert Wilks; and for them and himself he saw to it that proper vehicles were selected or written. A good actor could do as much for a play as a play could do for him. Even feeble farces drew audiences when cut to the measure of Bullock and Pinkethman or enlivened by the skill of their delivery and ad-libbing.[6]

Although the student is advised to consult one of the several important histories of the eighteenth-century stage which have dealt with the physical theater in detail, it will not be out of place here to mention some of the facts of Cibber's theater which have been gleaned from study of the papers of the Drury Lane management—details which have not appeared in print.

The auditorium of Cibber's Drury Lane consisted of the boxes (at four shillings), the pit (at half a crown), the gallery (at 1/6), and the upper gallery (at a shilling). It held fewer than two thousand people. The boxes were lit by sconces or lanterns. Double boxes were kept for the Prince and Princess of Wales and their attendants, and a manuscript says these "wil hold Twenty People." These boxes were probably upholstered, like the stage boxes, with green baize and brass nails. The seats in the stage boxes were upholstered in green baize and padded with tow, as were the seats in the pit and the gallery. The boxes seem to have been level with the stage. We must see in our mind's eye, then, a theater in white, green, and gold—rather than the red plush and gilt theater of a later age, though one hardly less elaborate.

The green upholstery matched the carpet which covered the stage for tragedy.[7] Mrs. Barry once humorously complained in an epilogue:

> If this green cloth could speak, would it not tell,
> Upon its well-worn nap how oft I fell?
> To death in various forms delivered up
> Steel kills me one night, and the next the Cup.[8]

Dryden remarked in the Preface to *The Spanish Friar* that "The Dagger and Cup of Poison" were "alwaies in a readiness," and in Cibber's time the Restoration green carpet was still laid to protect the fancy costumes from the dust of the stage floor.[9]

The accounts of the Theatre-Royal indicate that Cibber, Booth, and Wilks mounted their productions lavishly. The women's styles of the period were elaborate. They stressed stiff gowns, be-ruffled, heavily embroidered, flowing with ribbons, and rich with lace. They were often of velvet, damask, or silk, and were frequently equipped with long trains.[10] The men strutted in flaring coats ("shapes"), closely fitted outfits of expensive materials, and fancy boots, often decked with ornamental chain. If the women had to worry about their trains, the male encumbrance was the "toor," a gigantic feathered headdress. This was the mark of the tragic hero, whether he was Oedipus or the Earl of Essex, Tamburlaine or Coriolanus, Caesar or Othello. At the end of Cibber's time, Quin was still declaiming the lines of Caius Marius looking like an Indian chief or some sumptuous stray from a chariot of Inigo Jones. It was not until the time of Garrick that the hero's headdress and traditional balletlike skirt were banished.[11]

If the actor did not move under a headdress of feathers he was almost certain to appear in a full-bottomed wig, a fashion introduced in imitation of the profuse locks of Charles II and which lasted until about 1720. At the height of his career Cibber in full dress sported a Chedreux periwig and so did his actors. His fashionable wig as Sir Fopling Flutter caused the beau Brett to come backstage to ask where he could get one like it. Hamlet, in the closet scene in Rowe's illustrated edition, wore a peruke and an eighteenth-century suit of black.[12] Wigs were also worn by pages and by women disguised as boys. This was a favorite device of Cibber and other playwrights, for it not only added intrigue and suspense to the plot but also permitted the audience to stare at the actresses' legs, otherwise hidden in oceans of furbelows. The managers had to pay actresses extra for appearing in men's clothes and wigs, but Dryden's *Marriage à-la-Mode*, Wycherley's *Plain Dealer*, and Cibber's *She Wou'd and She Wou'd Not* are but three of the many plays that required such disguise.

The use of rich materials and fancy ornament supplied in the costumes much of whatever spectacle was lost by the absence of elaborate modern lighting. English actors had long been famous (or notorious) for their sumptuous apparel. Edward Alleyn stalked the Elizabethan stage as Tamburlaine in gorgeous red velvet breeches laced with copper. The tailor probably earned more than the dramatist.[13] As early as 1579 the colorful and costly costume worn by the lowliest of strutting players came in for Puritan attack in Stephen Gosson's *Schoole of Abuse*. Before Cibber ever came to the stage, pageantry had won out over Puritanism. Sir William D'Avenant in *The Cruelty of the Spaniards in Peru* (1658) used not only semi-historical material but also

to some degree pioneered historical accuracy in costumes and
scenery.[14] Through the "First Entry" of his play moved a Chief
Priest, resplendent in feathers and sun-worshiper's regalia,
red-coated English soldiers, and other strikingly theatrical figures. Typically, these magnificent and unusual trappings did
double duty: the next year they reappeared in D'Avenant's
The History of Sir Francis Drake. D'Avenant knew with Mr.
Puff that a clock striking four in the morning "saves a description
of the rising sun and a great deal about gilding the eastern
hemisphere." He tended to gild his sets rather than his poetry.
This tradition remained strong throughout Cibber's career. Fortunately Cibber, woefully deficient in lyric poetry, had plenty
of theatricality.

Ben Jonson and Suckling, both famous for their exquisitely
mounted entertainments, had set standards before 1642 which
the commercial theaters strove to meet as well as they were
able. Thomas Betterton acted in *Love and Honour* in King
Charles II's own coronation suit; Mrs. Bracegirdle wore in *The
Indian Queen* the feather-decked costume that Mrs. Aphra Behn
had brought back from Surinam. Cibber himself tells us of the
expense of insuring that age would not wither nor custom stale
the appeal of Dryden's Cleopatra when *All for Love* was revived
at Drury Lane on December 3, 1718: "Upon the Revival of
Dryden's All for Love, the Habits of that Tragedy amounted
to an Expence of near Six Hundred Pounds; a Sum unheard of,
for many Years before, on the like Occasions."[15]

With the competition of the Haymarket and of Lincoln's Inn
Fields; the drawing power of harlequins, puppets, and other
novelties; French players doing *commedia dell'arte* and Italian singers presenting operas; pantomimes and extravaganzas—
it was not enough for Drury Lane to present good plays. Cibber
had to find or create plays that could compete in spectacle
as well as in wit. Hence *Xerxes* and *Ximena, Richard III* and
Caesar in Aegypt, Venus and Adonis and *Myrtillo,* gave scope to
the designers of expensive costumes and elaborate settings.

Because the main curtain was not used from the Prologue to
the Epilogue and the end of an act was signified simply by the
old-fashioned convention of emptying the stage, this scenery
had, therefore, to be changed in full view of the audience. The
spectators were not disturbed by this—they were used to the
incongruous but sometimes necessary ministrations of the candle
man who attended to the "rings" (chandeliers) and "floats"
(footlights)—but it did tempt the producers to stage occasional

"transformation scenes" and other spectacular effects. Scenery changes were patently easier in the eighteenth century, when flats slid in grooves in the stage, than in the modern theater of the "box set," where flats are lashed together and fixed to the floor with stage screws (that is, when overpriced union labor charges permit the use of much scenery). It is no longer feasible to have a scene such as Scene 4 of Act V of *The Careless Husband*, in which Cibber requires a setting for barely seven lines. Today Broadway producers are all looking for one-set plays.

The chief articles of scenery in the early eighteenth century were flats, "relieves," ground-rows, and curtains. The flat (or "flat scene") was a wooden frame, covered with calico or muslin, sized, and painted with a scene or part of one. These flats slid in grooves (top and bottom) on the stage, closing in the center to present a background for the action. Though actually shutters, rather than a curtain, they were in appearance and in function much like the modern "drop." Other flats extended from the wings only part way toward the center of the stage, much like the modern wings used to create depth and perspective (and to prevent the audience from seeing backstage on the sides).[16] The flat scenes were sometimes "cut scenes," parts having been cut out so that other scenery could be seen behind them. Occasionally varnished silk, or some similar material, was set into the openings cut in ordinary flats, providing "transparencies" and creating all sorts of effects from a bright moon to a complete heavenly vision.[17]

The idea of shutters came from the Jacobean court masque, and another legacy was the "relieve" (in Ben Jonson's time "relievo")—cutouts of wood or cardboard, or frames covered with cloth and painted to resemble rocks, bushes, statues, etc. Placed before the background, they created the illusion of perspective. Infrequently they were three-dimensional; usually they were merely painted to appear so. Long, low "relieves" were called "ground-rows." Representing distant hedgerows, grassy banks, ocean or other water, or objects on the horizon, they helped the perspective, hid the bottom of the background, and sometimes concealed the lamps employed to light it.

A full set of scenery might include shutters, wings, relieves, and ground-rows, as well as tables, chairs, and other furniture. All of this could be employed to create a large number of detailed scenes quickly and easily, and that is why the plays of Cibber and his contemporaries call for a number of different settings. These dramatists were not limited by a box set. They were nearly as free as the Elizabethans who, using hardly any scenery at all and having at their disposal multiple acting areas, could set their scenes in any place their imaginations (and those of the audience, inspired by the poetry) could furnish. But Cibber did not have to rely on descriptive poetry: he could order almost any kind of a set from the carpenters and the painters.[18] No wonder his plays ignore the Aristotelian unities of time and place.

These sets were expensive, but they could be used over and over, particularly the standard ones: an outdoor scene in a wood, a vista of a formal garden, a street, a drawing room, a great hall, and so on. Cibber knew his theater so well that he probably considered as he wrote what scenery he could use out of stock and what would have to be specially made. Certainly the stock pieces appeared frequently.[19] Many of Drury Lane's spectacular sets, which appeared with monotonous regularity, were originally designed for the opera, with which they now competed. They were often accompanied by thunder and lightning, and other special effects. One playwright's invention of a machine to make thunder (it used cannon balls rolling in a trough)—and his scream of fury from the pit when he discovered that the managers who had refused his play had "stolen his thunder"—is almost too familiar to bear repetition. Cibber was the sort of man who would steal anybody's thunder, and he must have attended other theaters and watched with a sharp eye for production ideas which he could build into his next play or employ to give new zest to an old one.

In these days almost no dramatist knows as he writes what the casting of his play will be. Only a few can say who will direct or design the finished work. Some have incredibly little familiarity with the most fundamental details of production and staging. But Colley Cibber worked in the theater all his life and his plays were written in the light of his experience. The worst of them was still stageable and playable.

Probably Cibber's worst work was written when he stressed theater at the expense of drama and produced expensive drama. Of course an emphasis on "scenes, machines, and dancing" was the province of the opera, but many plays, from Cibber's *Xerxes* to Shakespeare's *Tempest*, called for special effects. These brought in the crowds, and the advertisements of the period always played up any scenic novelty or unusual effect. Some of the authors of the period tried to bolster weak scripts by asking for effects that made Shadwell's *Psyche* (£800 for scenes and machines) or Shakespeare's *All's Well that Ends Well* ("Enter the Whole French Army") look easy.[20]

As Terence had done in ancient days, Cibber deplored excessive reliance upon scenes and machines. (They not only took the emphasis off the play, which is "the thing," but they cut into the profits too, if the play was not exceptionally successful.) But claptrap has always been a part of show business—and Cibber could always claim that he was just trying to keep up with such extravagant theaters as Lincoln's Inn Fields. Even Steele, who equally lamented such "non-rational" entertainment and had been instructed by Shrewsbury in his patent to "reform" the stage, grudgingly admitted that one could not stay in business without giving the public what it wanted. In 1716 Steele himself arranged, through his friend the Earl of Stair (then Minister Plenipotentiary in Paris), to import French entertainers for an afterpiece called *The Whimsical Death of Harlequin.* It was, like all other such spectacular pantomimes, a smash success. Pantomimes always caused jaded Londoners and sightseeing provincials to mob the theaters, to crowd backstage, to overflow from the pit and boxes onto the stage itself. It is amazing that Cibber, as a commercial playwright, did not include more of these trifles among his works. In our time, when splashy musicals threaten to take over Broadway completely and the wide screen of the cinema is filled with ever more colossal epics, we should be able to appreciate why Cibber produced masques and ballad opera and pastorals and a "Comical-Tragedy," *The Rival Queans, With the Humours of Alexander the Great.* Every producer would like to have to put extra seats on the stage.

The practice of selling admission "behind the scenes" and even seats on the stage died very slowly. It was as a sort of matter of course that *The Daily Courant* announced, when advertising Cibber's new play *She Wou'd and She Wou'd Not* (1702), "that no Gentleman may Interrupt the Action by standing on the Stage the First day." It was not until Garrick's day, when Cibber had retired from the theater, that the beaux were banished from the wings and the stage itself—and then Garrick made up for the lost revenue by foreshortening the apron and providing more seats in the pit.

Perhaps the proximity of these spectators was one of the reasons the properties used in Cibber's theater were not the imitations used today. In the modern theater silver plate can be cheap dishes disguised with aluminum paint, but for every performance

of *Volpone* Cibber hired silverplate from Mr. King, the under-
taker. Today, even in the professional theater (where "grips"
and propertymen often earn more than actors), an antique
throne may be chiefly plywood and Silastic "carving." The
Thanksgiving turkey (if it doesn't have to be carved) will be
artificial and a recent musical in which a lot of caviar had to
be consumed solved the problem by feeding the cast black-
cherry Jello forced through a sieve. Distance lends enchantment
to the modern "brocade" of cheap cotton with a design stenciled
on it with textile paint, to the "mossy bank" of artificial grass
mat, to the paper crown and the plastic tiara. But, even by
candlelight, the audience in Cibber's theater was not to be
fooled by too many imitations. Moreover, it was too much trouble
to make a cardboard sedan chair when one could be hired for
the night or to manufacture a fake roast chicken for a performance or two. The real thing was easier.[21] So, in addition
to sumptuous costume, elaborate scenery, and spectacular effects, the audience at Cibber's Drury Lane could expect a
certain degree of realism: real dirt thrown up from the grave
trap in *Hamlet*, real animal blood in *Richard III*, reality in everything from the large picture that plays a part in *The Rover* to
a handful of marbles in *The Fatal Marriage* to a few toothpicks
for *Epicœne*.

Cibber and his fellow managers supervised every detail of
every production, and every Monday they sat down in their
office and paid all the tradesmen and the workmen, all the actors
and musicians, all the crew and playhouse staff, all the creditors
of any sort. To the treasurer's snug office (decorated "compleat"
with red leather and floored with Dutch mat) no tradesman,
boasted Cibber, ever had to come twice with his bill. *The Daily
Courant* received its weekly guinea for running advertisements[22]
and the printers were sent ten shillings for every performance's
playbills—fifteen if there was something remarkable that called
for red ink. Every detail from printing tickets to paying land
taxes had to be attended to. It is amazing that Cibber found time
to act and to write, as well as to run this business. In addition,
he had to spend as a manager two or three hours at rehearsals
each morning. He attended performances, coached the actors,
oversaw the other employees of the house, and kept an eye on
expenses and standards. He also read new plays, though he
claims he did not particularly relish doing so because only one
in twenty was worth the trouble. But he had to be careful he
didn't miss a good one—as he had *The Beggar's Opera*— or his

carping critics would pounce on the fact as fresh evidence for
their continual assertions that Drury Lane, secure in a virtual
monopoly as they saw it, was not interested in new works.
Cibber was constantly being charged with failing to recognize
fresh talents when they appeared, "Fire in each eye, and papers
in each hand," at the door of Drury Lane.

Whatever plays, prologues, epilogues, farces, pantomimes,
afterpieces, and miscellaneous entertainments the managers
did accept, there were always plenty of disappointed authors
and their friends ready to cry that Cibber and his colleagues
were sitting enthroned in their office (resplendent in red
leather armchairs upholstered with brass nails) and turning
down the best submissions. Cibber, always to the fore in the
management, was the butt of most of the charges of high-
handedness, obtuseness, and lack of taste. Here is Marplay,
Junior (Theophilus Cibber) speaking in Act I, Scene 5, of
Fielding's *The Author's Farce* as an arrogant manager:

> Was you to see the plays when they are brought to us, a
> parcel of crude undigested stuff. We are the persons, sir,
> who lick them into form, that mould them into shape—
> The poet make the play indeed! the colourman might as
> well be said to make the picture, or the weaver the coat:
> my father and I, sir, are a couple of poetical tailors: when
> a play is brought to us, we consider it as a tailor does his
> coat; we cut it, sir, we cut it; and let me tell you, we have
> the exact measure of the town. . . .[23]

An author who had work accepted howled about it being "cut"
or altered. Those who had theirs rejected sometimes flung
about charges of plagiarism.[24] Such charges have been made
ever since Thespis first climbed up on a cart. There was no
more reason to suppose that all authors were betrayed or all
managers dishonest in Cibber's time than there is today. But
most modern managers or producers are not also playwrights,
forced to bring their own works before audiences which contain
the very enemies their own literary judgments have made. Cibber's plays were often received with hostility which cannot be
wholly attributed to their lack of merit: it was Cibber's very
success and power as a manager which made it on occasion
impossible for him to get a fair hearing for his dramatic works.
Audiences who ought to have been applauding the play sometimes hissed the author. Satire that was really prompted by
dislike of Cibber as a person was directed against Cibber's works.

It has been essential to explain Cibber's activities outside his writing to make clear not only why some of his work took the form it did but why some of it also had a reputation it did not deserve. The reception of *The Provok'd Husband* proves that Cibber's enemies sometimes had neither taste nor justice. *Love in a Riddle* was damned out of hand and *The Non-Juror* was excessively praised, both for reasons quite unconnected with their literary value.

Cibber produced his own plays with courage and conducted his business with efficiency. Pope paid his archenemy a left-handed compliment when he advised his friend Mallett (in a letter of December 29, 1730) to be shrewd in his affairs, contending that "to be well in it [the world], you must be a Cibber." While manager at Drury Lane, Cibber was indeed practical. Perhaps his only really impractical action was to turn author himself while in a position that made so many other authors his enemies, to expect justice where there was jealousy. But he wrote to please himself and—having acquired some of that base desire to please the public which he had previously deplored in old Christopher Rich—to earn money and public acclaim. He came to appreciate the hard facts of commerce, the competition of the other houses, the pressures brought to bear by the Lord Chamberlain and other officials, the fads and fashions in public taste, the recalcitrance and unpredictability of theatrical people, the vanity and venality of professional authors, the necessity of getting along with his partners and with the world. He was always the practical man of business "and had not virtue enough to starve, by opposing the Multitude." The people knew what they wanted, or they thought they did. They paid the piper, and they could call the tune. Cibber knew this: he was the public's servant at Drury Lane, just as he was the sovereign's servant when his actors played by royal command at rose-brick Hampton Court or before the Queen's Majesty at Bath. He undoubtedly aroused opposition by his arrogance toward officials, actors, and authors; but he succeeded as a manager and he succeeded as a playwright because he would listen to the public.

Though it was spoken by Garrick from Drury Lane's stage in 1747, and by then Cibber had retired from theatrical management, the old man must have given his characteristic slow nod of agreement as he sat out front and listened to these lines from Samuel Johnson's famous prologue:

Hard is his lot, that here by fortune placed
Must watch the wild vicissitudes of taste;
With every meteor of caprice must play,
And chase the new-born bubbles of the day.
Ah! let not censure term our fate our choice,
The stage but echoes back the public voice.
The drama's laws the drama's patrons give,
For we that live to please, must please to live.

CHAPTER 7

The Laureate

Salve, brassica virens corona
Et Lauro, Archipoeta, pampinoque,
Dignis principis auribus Leonis.

All hail, Arch-poet without peer!
Vine, Laurel, Cabbage fit to wear,
And worthy of thy Prince's ear.

—Grub-Street Journal, November 19, 1730

PERISH the thought—Cibber invented the phrase—that this chapter is going to be devoted to presenting Colley, with a quire of bad verses in one hand and a laurel in the other, as a misunderstood and unappreciated inditer of fine odes. For it must be conceded that the youthful productions that earned him odium at school and the official productions that brought him ridicule in later life were of much the same quality.

How bad his verse was, of course, has been exaggerated. *The Gentleman's Magazine* as early as August, 1742, was denouncing his odes as "unexceptionably the *worst* that ever was," and even when Cibber came to be entombed in that literary Westminster Abbey *The Dictionary of National Biography* Joseph Knight averred that "Cibber's 'Odes' are among the most contemptible things of literature." This statement is nonsense. The odes are not that bad. These judgments simply depart from accuracy for the sake of emphasis. On the other hand, the odes are certainly bad enough. It would be less than sensible to praise them and futile to excuse them. Perhaps it will be enough to explain how Cibber obtained the laureate sinecure, to note what it paid him (and what it cost him), to quote samples of his verse, and to clear up very briefly a few common misconceptions about the nature of the office Cibber held and the work that can legitimately be expected from an incumbent.

The temptation at the first is to vacillate between apology and accusation. This has been the most frequent approach, *vide* Walter Hamilton: "Although Cibber was not a good poet, he was persevering and consistent, and his integrity has never been questioned. . . . Wanting all the attributes of a poet, his Laureate Odes were never collected, simply because they were not worthy of preservation."[1] The next temptation is to grow belligerent and to present Cibber (and it can be done honestly) as the best Laureate England had had since Dryden—or, to come to modern times, to argue that Cibber's official verse was no worse than that Masefield has given us since 1930.[2]

A great deal of criticism of Cibber as Poet Laureate has been leveled at him by people who forget that the post is a sinecure in the gift of the government, not a literary prize, and that the Laureate, like the Archbishop of Canterbury, is appointed on political, not poetical, considerations. Cibber himself did not make this mistake. He claimed, and he was not far wrong, that the laurel was one of the rewards for *The Non-Juror.*[3]

By Cibber's time the Laureateship had come to mean compulsory praise of the monarch, but it was not unnatural (though it may have been un-English) for the son of a native of Flensborg to hymn the House of Hanover.[4] Cibber welcomed the appointment and was ready to discharge the duties as well as might be. He could console himself that, though his effusions were prompted by duty rather than by inspiration, they were at least no worse than the lickspittle odes of his recent predecessors. Also, if poor things, they were his own. Nicholas Rowe, an important playwright and editor of Shakespeare but an insignificant rhymester in this office, had frequently acted the absentee landlord while Laureate. Moreover, it would have been hard to find an easier poetaster to follow than the bathetic rector of Coningsby, the Reverend Laurence Eusden, who drank himself to death and whom Cibber succeeded as Laureate in 1730.

There came a time when Cibber heartily wished that his official odes had gone as unnoticed by the British public as they had gone unheeded by the Germanic Majesty to whom they were loyally addressed. But in 1730 the post was attractive to him. He campaigned for the honor, the money, and the annual tierce of canary wine, and used all the influence he had.[5] At the time of Eusden's appointment, there were many candidates but Cibber, though the least of them, was mentioned: "All came with full Confidence, flush'd with vain Hope,/From *Cibber* and *Durfey,* to *Prior* and *Pope.*"[6] At the time of Eusden's death, the competition was no less keen.

Despite Cibber's usual, oceanic self-confidence, he cannot have been very hopeful at first about his chances, for he was by no means the favorite. This position was filled, rather grotesquely, by a rudely self-educated thresher from Wiltshire, one Stephen Duck,[7] whose meteoric rise from rural "mute, inglorious Milton" to a royal pension of thirty pounds a year—and a rent-free cottage in Richmond Park, as a special mark of the Queen's favor—is a striking tale. His success spurred a whole gaggle of village versifiers and petty poetasters.[8] At the time of Eusden's demise, Duck had recently learned civilized English and his native wood notes wild threatened to drown the songs of more famous Whigs who were being spoken of as candidates for the office: John Dennis (already established as a major critic); namby-pamby Ambrose Phillips (active in politics, celebrated for *The Distress'd Mother*); Lewis Theobald (the erudite and, by the jealous Pope, much maligned editor of Shakespeare); and Mr. Cibber of Drury Lane.

Pope, who was out of the race,[9] ridiculed the whole contest and confided to the *Grub-Street Journal* for November 12, 1730, his conviction that *none* of the candidates should be selected:

> Shall royal praise be rimed by such a ribald,
> As fopling C[ibbe]r or attorney T[heobol]d?
> Let's rather wait one year for better luck;
> One year may make a singing swan of Duck.
> Great G[rafton]! such servants since thou well canst lack,
> Oh! save the salary and drink the sack!

Another, writing as "Bavius" in the same paper a week later, suggested that the laurel crown be mixed not only with the customary vine leaves but with brassica (symbolic of thievery) and ivy, "not only as it anciently belonged to Poets in general; but as it is emblematical of the three virtues of a Court Poet in particular, it is *creeping, dirty,* and *dangling.*" The writer went on to say that, if Cibber were elected, he could use theater props and ride in procession, not like the historic Laureate Camillo on an elephant but "on a *Dragon,* if he goes by land; or, if he chuse the water, upon one of his own *Swans* from *Caesar in Egypt.*" He concluded his frontpage article with this epigram:

> Behold! ambitious of the *British* bays,
> C[IBBE]R and DUCK contend in rival lays:
> But, gentle COLLEY, should thy verse prevail,
> Thou hast no sence, alas! against his flail:
> Wherefor thy claim resign, allow his right;
> For DUCK can *thresh,* you know, as well as *write.*

But Cibber would not withdraw and, despite Pope, one of the contestants had to win. In the third week of November, His Grace of Grafton announced his choice: in spite of competition, in spite of the rumors that the Queen herself had promised the post to Richard Savage,[10] the election fell on Colley Cibber. He was summoned to St. James's, granted the laurel crown, and permitted to kiss the pudgy royal hand. A royal warrant was duly issued on December 3, empowering and commanding Cibber to supply hyperbolical adulation to George II as occasion demanded. He was firmly installed for life, his enemy Mist bitterly charged, as a "Whig hackney."

The appointment was to some a disappointment; to others, a shock or an insult. A week after Pope's verses quoted above, the *Grub-Street Journal* was confessing: "I thought of Dennis, Theobald, Duck,/But never dreamt of Cibber." Pope said he was "sorry, not surprised" at the appointment. Taking but a month to polish it, he contributed this epigram:

> Tell, if you can, which did the worse,
>   Caligula or G[rafto]n's gr[a]ce?
> That made a consul of a horse,
>   And this a laureate of an ass.[11]

John Gay was credited with an ode for the New Year in which King George was made to remark:

> 'Then since I have a son, like you,
> May he Parnassus rule:
> So shall the Crown and Laurel too
> Descend from F[ool] to F[ool],'

and Dr. Johnson also equated the prince and the poetic pauper in dullness:

> Augustus still survives in Maro's strain,
> And Spenser's verse prolongs Eliza's reign;
> Great George's acts let tuneful Cibber sing,
> For Nature formed the Poet for the King.

These attacks seem as much directed against the House of Hanover and the Whigs as against Cibber. Their authors risked retaliation more at the hands of the government than at Cibber's, for he took them all in good humor. But then he was capable of smiling at the most devastating insult. Once, when Cibber wrote a poem with a diamond ring upon a pane of glass, a critic claimed that Cibber had at last created a work which

would escape the usual treatment; there was not a man alive
who would think of wiping his posterior with a pane of glass!
Cibber laughed as loudly as the rest. It must have been hard,
however, for him to take Henry Fielding's insults in his stride.
In *Pasquin* Fielding takes a crack at the Laureateship and official
odes in general when Lord Place speaks with a voter:

> *Second Voter.* I am a devilish lover of sack.
> *Lord Place.* Sack, say you? Odso, you shall be poet laureate.
> *Second Voter.* Poet! No, my lord, I am no poet, I can't
> make verses.
> *Lord Place.* No matter for that—you'll be able to make
> odes.
> *Second Voter.* Odes, my lord! What are those?
> *Lord Place.* Faith, sir, I can't tell you what they are; but
> I know you may be qualified for the place without
> being a poet.[12]

This is, really, more criticism of the office itself than it is
of Cibber, but the satire became more personal in Fielding's
Historical Register for the Year 1736. In it Medley (who seems
to be Fielding himself) comments that the New Year's ode
which begins the play is "the very quintessence and cream of
all the odes I have seen for several years late past," and it is,
in fact, a clever parody of Cibber's triteness and hobbled versi-
fication:

> This is the day, in days of yore,
> Our fathers never saw before;
> This is a day, 'tis one to ten,
> Our sons will never see again.
> > Then sing the day,
> > And sing the song,
> > And thus be merry
> > All day long.

There were other, more scurrilous attacks, but Cibber weathered the teacup storm very well.[13] If he did not notice a jibe
in a newspaper, he was sure to be handed a clipping by some
friend, but he was too confident to be crushed by criticism and
too realistic to be riled by "hackwriters." William Ayers tells us,
on what authority I know not, that from the beginning Cibber
took it all as a joke and even contributed anonymous verses
against himself, laughing to hear them praised as "palpable hits,
keen, things with spirit in them." This was the tactic Dean

Swift suggested. In his verses *On Poetry: A Rhapsody* (1733) he counseled the "young Beginner" to publish anonymously and then

> Be sure at *Will's* the following Day,
> Lie Snug, and hear what Criticks say.
> And if you find the general Vogue
> Pronounces you a stupid Rogue;
> Damns all your Thoughts as low and little,
> Sit still, and swallow down your Spittle.
> Be silent as a Politician,
> For talking may beget Suspicion:
> Or praise the Judgment of the Town,
> And help yourself to run it down.

Cibber's problem was that he could not be so cautious: his poetic labors were public ones. "Harmonious *Cibber* entertains/ The Court with annual Birth-day strains" noted Swift. Cibber's was the task to sing the royal praises—and to be taken to task for it by the many who thought as Swift did:

> O, what Indignity and Shame
> To prostitute the Muse's Name,
> By flatt'ring Kings whom Heaven design'd
> The Plagues and Scourges of Mankind.

Cibber had to laud what Swift could satirize:

> Fair Britain in thy Monarch blest,
> Whose Virtues bear the strictest Test;
> Whom never *Faction* cou'd bespatter,
> Nor *Minister,* nor *Poet* flatter.

Swift, safe in Dublin, got away with attacking the throne, but Cibber could not get away with defending it.[14] Thomas Gray was wise when, on Cibber's death, he refused the Laureateship on the grounds that in such a position a man was sure to write bad verse and to have it pilloried in the press. Cibber's experience proved this. It was bad enough to feel that, in spite of hard work, his verse was undistinguished; but to see it in cold print, devoid of the music and pageantry that bolstered its performance at court, all the defects as plain as a pikestaff—well, that was embarrassing and painful, even to a Cibber. It was not until Robert Southey's time[15] that the New Year's Ode ceased to be demanded of official poets, so Cibber's first act as Laureate was to compose a New Year's Ode for 1731. John Eccles set Cibber's limping lines to music and the ode was performed on New Year's Day before the King and the court by Hughes, Gates, the Children of the Chapel Royal, and a small orchestra. Cibber attended the royal levée that day and basked in his new honor—until one of the singers "leaked" a copy to the papers and the *Grub-Street Journal* printed this:

ODE *for* NEW-YEAR'S DAY

By C. CIBBER, *Esq;*

RECITATIVO.

Once more the ever circling sun
Thro' the caelestial signs has run,
Again old time inverts his glass,
And bids the annual seasons pass:
    The youthful spring shall call for birth,
And glad with op'ning flow'rs the earth:
Fair summer load with sheaves the field,
And golden fruit shall autumn yield:
Each to the winter's want their store shall bring
'Til warmer genial suns recall the spring.

AIR.

Ye grateful *Britons* bless the year,
    That kindly yields increase,
While plenty that might feed a war,
    Enjoys the guard of peace;
Your plenty to the skies you owe,
    Peace is your monarch's care;
Thus bounteous *Jove* and *George* below
    Divided empire share.

RECITATIVO.

Britannia pleas'd, looks round her realms to see
Your various causes of felicity!
(To glorious war, a glorious peace succeeds;
For most we triumph when the farmer feeds)
Then truly are we great when truth supplies
Our blood, our treasures drain'd by victories.
Turn, happy *Britons,* to the throne your eyes,
    And in the royal offspring see,
How amply bounteous providence supplies
    The source of your felicity.

AIR.

Behold in ev'ry face imperial graces shine
    All native to the race of *George* and *Caroline:*
In each young hero we admire
The blooming virtues of his fire;
In each maturing fair we find,
Maternal charms of softer kind.

RECITATIVO.

In vain thro' ages past has *Phœbus* roll'd,
'Ere such a sight blest *Albion* could behold.
Thrice happy mortals, if your state you knew,
Where can the globe so blest a nation shew?
All that of you indulgent heav'n requires,
Is loyal hearts, to reach your own desires.
Let faction then her self-born views lay down,
And hearts united, thus address the throne.

AIR.

Hail! royal *Caesar*, hail!
    Like thus may ev'ry annual sun
    Add brighter glories to thy crown,
'Til Suns themselves shall fail.

RECITATIVO.

May heav'n thy peaceful reign prolong,
Nor let, to thy great empires wrong,
Foreign or native foes prevail.
        Hail, &c.

Beside this incredible work appeared an *ODE humbly in-scrib'd to the Poet* LAUREAT, *taken from* LONDON EVENING POST, *Jan. 7. as there said By* STEPHEN DUCK, *Esq;* a parody which began in Cibber's praise and concluded:

RECITATIVO.

May heaven preserve thy genius clear,
For *Christmas* comes but once a year;
    Give the poet then some ale.
        Ale, &c.

The *Grub-Street Journal* for Thursday, January 21, picked Cibber's ode apart line by line for "elegance," "Propriety and Cadence," ending with the observation "that when a Song is good Sense, it must be made Nonsense before it is made Musick; so

when a Song is Nonsense, there's no other way but by singing it
to make it seem tolerable sense."

Though Cibber's ode on the page does unquestionably seem
to be proof of Addison's famous remark that nothing with any
sense in it is capable of being set to music, in all fairness one
must admit that Cibber's poetry probably sounded better than
it reads. Take for comparsion the celebrated ode set by Henry
Purcell, as composer to the court of William and Mary, for the
Queen's birthday in April, 1694. His magnificent music accompanied these words:

Counter-Tenor Solo and Chorus

> Come ye sons of Art, come away,
> Tune all your voices and instruments play,
> To celebrate this triumphant day.

It then went on to a duet (countertenors) and a grand "Come,
ye Sons of Art" chorus, and arrived at these verses, inescapably
reminiscent today of Sir W. S. Gilbert's Prince Agib:

Countertenor Solo

> Strike the viol, touch the lute,
> Wake the harp, inspire the flute,
> Sing your patroness's praise
> In cheerful and harmonious lays.

The ode continues to this insipid peroration and conclusion:

Soprano and Bass Soli and Chorus

> See, Nature rejoicing has shown us the way
> With innocent revels to welcome the day.
> The tuneful grove, the talking rill,
> The laughing vale, the replying hill,
> With charming harmony unite,
> The happy season to invite.
> What the Graces require,
> And the Muses inspire,
> Is at once our delight and our duty to pay.

I take the space to present the words to this Purcell ode for
it proves that Cibber was not alone in the creation of bad verse;
indeed, these verses are in some ways appreciably inferior to
Cibber's lines. But when Purcell adds to these words his wonder-
ful music (partly from *The Indian Queen*, but mostly new) the

poetry sounds impressive; and the whole piece, concluding with stirring trumpets ("See, Nature rejoicing") and brilliant orchestration reinforced by drums, ends on a note of triumph and, Westrup remarks, "the whole world seems to sing." Granted, Eccles was not Purcell; but, as we listen to the words and music of *Come, Ye Sons of Art* together, we cannot help thinking that the verses in the *Grub-Street Journal* unfairly represent Cibber's first official ode at court. Heard there, it was better, certainly adequate.

But, all demands for a fair appraisal being granted, a clammy suggestion of duty lingers miasmally around the edges of the ode and it could not have been a first-class performance. Criticism was not long in coming. We have already mentioned the parody purportedly by the disappointed Duck. *Fog's Journal* for January 9 carried another one. But on the same day an unexpected defense was seen in the *Whitehall and London Evening Post*.

A HYMN *to the* LAUREAT

Sir, *By giving a Place in your Paper to the following Unfashionable Hymn you will very much oblige, Sir, Your humbly Servant.*

> *Cibber,* accept these feeble lays
>   From an unskilful muse,
> Who tries with artless note, to praise
>   What *envious men* abuse.
>
> Nature and art in thee combine;
>   Thy comedies excell:
> With wit and sense replete, they shine,
>   And read politely well.
>
> Who see th'inconstant *Loveless* range,
>   But mourns *Amanda's* fate?
> Each female heart approves his change,
>   And pants for such a state.
>
> When *Lady Betty* treads the stage,
>   All *modish* prudes submit:
> What *Foppington* adorns our age,
>   With the same grace and Wit?
>
> In *Townley* see the *modern wife!*
>   How full of vice! how blam'd!
> How ruin'd by the *modern life!*
>   How valu'd, when reclaim'd!

May empty Journals weekly rail;
    May all dull bards repine:
If wit unequall'd should prevail,
    The *laurel's* justly thine.[16]

The paper pellets continued to fly back and forth in the
journals. Cibber continued to write. Keeping in mind that few
libretti can stand without music—and none were intended to
—we may read with slightly more tolerance the "execrable" ode
for the King's birthday (October 30, 1731). If for no other reason,
it is entertaining because it discharges pretty much every piece
in the armamentarium of official ode writers:

When Charles, from Anarchy's Retreat
    Resumed the Regal Seat;
When (hence by frantic Zealots driven)
    Our holy Church, our Laws,
Returning with the Royal Cause,
    Raised up their thankful Eyes to Heaven.
        Then Hand in Hand,
        To bless the Land,
Protection with Obedience came,
    And mild Oblivion wav'd Revenge,
    For Wrongs of Civil Flame.

Wild, and wanton, then, our Joys,
Loud as raging War before.
All was Triumph, tuneful Noise,
None, from Heaven, could hope for more.

Brother, Son, and Father Foes,
Now embracing, bless their Home:
Who so happy, could suppose
Happier days were still to come?

    But Providence, that better knows
        Our Wants, than we,
        Previous to those,
(Which human Wisdom could not, then, foresee)
Did, from the pregnant former Day
A Race of Happier reigns to come convey.

    The Sun [George I] we saw precede,
        Those mighty joys restored,
        Gave to our future Need,
From great PLANTAGENET a Lord.

From whose high Veins this greater day arose,

A second GEORGE, to fix our World's Repose.
From CHARLES restored, short was our Term of Bliss,
But GEORGE from GEORGE entails our Happiness.

From a heart that abhors the Abuse of high Pow'r
    Are our Liberties duly defended;
From a Courage, inflam'd by the Terrors of War
    With his Fame, is our Commerce extended.

Let our publick high spirits be raised to their Height,
    Yet our Prince, in that Virtue, will lead 'em.
From our Welfare, he knows, that his Glory's more bright,
    As Obedience enlarges our Freedom.

What ties can bind a grateful People more,
    Than such diffus'd Benevolence of Pow'r?

If private Views could more prevail,
    Than Ardour, for the Publick Weal,
Then had his native, Martial Heat,
    In Arms seduc'd him, to be Great.

But Godlike Virtue, more inclin'd
    To save than to destroy,
    Deems it inferior joy,
To lead, in Chains of Peace, the Mind.

With song, ye BRITONS, lead the Day!
Sing! sing the Morn, that gave him Breath,
Whose Virtues never shall decay,
No, never, never, taste of Death.

CHORUS.

When Tombs and Trophies shall be Dust,
Fame shall preserve the Great and Just.[17]

An ode on that lustful lout George II, a monarch whose bulbous eyes seemed to evidence the expanding vacuum of his brain! So much had seldom been made, so ineptly, of so little. Bad as this ode was, worse was yet to come. In 1732 the royal birthday was given as the purpose of the Creation—and a succession far more fearful than that with which the witches startled Macbeth was threatened from Farmer George and Caroline of Ansbach:

The word that formed the world
    In vain did make mankind;
Unless, his passions to restrain,
    Almighty wisdom has design'd

Sometimes a WILLIAM, or a GEORGE should reign.
Yet farther, *Britons,* cast your eyes,
  Behold a long succession rise
  Of future fair felicities.
  Around the royal table spread,
See how the beauteous branches shine!
  Sprung from the fertile genial bed
Of Glorious GEORGE and CAROLINE. . . .

Wyndham Lewis and Charles Lee in *The Stuffed Owl,* their anthology of bad verse, sympathize with Cibber and say that "one must needs admire the poet's tough struggle to get Seligenstadt, Klein-Ostein, Aschaffenburg, and Dettingen into an 'Air'." It is true that, say, Coleridge's problem with foreign words—he has three spelling errors in the first line of *Kubla Khan*—was nothing compared to those involved in this effusion of 1743:

Of fields, of forts, and floods unknown to fame,
That now demand of Caesar's arms a name,
  Sing, Britons, tho' uncouth the sound.

Air

Tho' rough Seligenstadt
The harmony defeat,
Tho' Klein-Ostein the verse confound,
  Yet, in the joyful strain,
  Aschaffenburgh or Dettingen
Shall charm the ear they seem to wound.

Strain, indeed. Consider also this fragment, previously unpublished:

Recitativo

First Voice: Remember, Europe, when thy Purple Lands
    With Blood of Hostile Bands,
    At once o'erflow'd, and fatten'd, to the Plough.
Second Voice: How Dismal, then, to see,
    Thy terrible Fertility!
    Where reaps the sword, in vain the wretched Son.
Third Voice: Delightfull Change! Blest Albion, now
    Outrides the Tempest, with a smiling Brow!

Air

No hopefull Harvest spoil'd
Deforms the Plenteous Field.

Nor Frighted Commerce dreads the Main.
While Earth, and seas Conspire,
To fill Mankinds desire,
Nor George, nor Phoebus, shines, in vain.

Recitativo

As Pleasing in the scene, from shore
To hear the Winds, and Billows Roar,
The Martial sounds, from Terror Free,
Assistant, to our Joys shall be.

Chorus

Awake the Trumpet! beat the Brown Drum.
And let the Jovial Noise
Give signal, to the Bomb,
And Cannons Voice,
The Thundering Cannon to the Skys,
Great GEORGE'S Fame
The Arbiter of Peace
And forever of Albions golden Days,
                    Proclaim.[18]

It would be kind to imagine that this sort of thing was carelessly dashed off, but it was bad, it appears, from lack of talent
rather than want of industry. Cibber was sincere and tireless,
as Dr. Johnson bore witness on June 25, 1763:

> His friends gave out that he *intended* his Birthday *Odes*
> should be bad: but that was not the case, Sir; for he kept
> them many months by him, and a few years before he
> died he shewed me one of them, with great solicitude to
> render it as perfect as might be, and I made some correc-
> tions, to which he was not very willing to submit. I re-
> member the following couplet in allusion to the King and
> himself:
>   'Perched on the eagle's soaring wing,
>   The lowly linnet loves to sing.'
> Sir, he had heard something of the fabulous tale of the
> wren sitting upon the eagle's wing, and he had applied it
> to a linnet. Cibber's familiar style, however, was better
> than that which Whitehead has assumed. *Grand* nonsense
> is insupportable.

It is hoped that the ordinary reader will not find the examples
of Cibber's verse quoted here "insupportable;" it is hoped that
they may amuse rather than appall, and that there is not enough

to permit Cibber, like Donellan, to poison us with laurel water. All will serve, indubitably, to acquit of us of the charge of infatuation with our subject and inability to see his flaws. This, and a desire for a certain completeness in the portrait, may justify the exhumation of the odes of Cibber in an age when even Wordsworth's single significant effort in this line may be left in decent obscurity.

Dr. Johnson was right—"Colley Cibber, Sir, was by no means a blockhead"—but so was Pope correct when he remarked that Cibber's poetry was "prose on stilts" and dismissed it as "poetry fallen lame."

CHAPTER 8

The Apology

ON April 7, 1740, a handsome, leather-bound volume was put on sale for a guinea by John Watts of London: *An Apology for the Life of Mr. Colley Cibber, Comedian, and Late Patentee of the Theatre-Royal. With an Historical View of the Stage during his Own Time. Written by Himself.* Cibber had been working on it for two or three years and it was to be the work, perhaps, by which he was best to be remembered.

The first edition sold briskly. It was the talk of the town, and few indeed shared the opinion of the anonymous enemy in *The Laureat* who damned it as a "long, dull, pert, injudicious laughing History; the work of a most undaunted Scribbler." Even he had to admit it had some entertainment value: "There are some good things in thy Book, old Colley,/But all the rest is, self-sufficient Folley."[1] The equivalent of a modern paperback (a cheaper edition at five shillings) appeared exactly a month later. Robert Walker tried to pirate it. The royalties rolled in,[2] and young Henry Fielding, observing all this, remarked that Cibber seemed to have lived his life just so that he could apologize for it.

It was not, however, an apology in the usual modern sense: indeed Cibber, as he sat down in Bath to write his memoirs, was smug about the successful career behind him, not apologetic. The dedication "To A Certain Gentleman" (probably Henry Pelham, brother of the Duke of Newcastle) was not really "most humble" at all. True, Cibber spoke in deprecating terms of his *opus*, asserting that "the Brat is now born, and rather than see it starve, upon the Bare Parish Provision, I chuse thus clandestinely, to drop it at your Door. . . ." But he also made it known to his readers that the dedicatee had heard the manuscript read with extreme enjoyment, and presumably he expected other readers to find it equally entertaining.

The word *Apology* meant simply "autobiography."[3] It was a somewhat impersonal history, for all that—a frothy, witty, chatty, gossipy history of forty years of the English theater. In his fine history of the art of biography—and there Cibber's book is a milestone—Edgar Johnson writes:

> Chattering away, the pert, lively creature, he gives us a glimpse of the sensible and warm-hearted man underneath the coxcomb and the rattle, lets us see a hardworking and penetrating technician in the art of the theatre, a generous appreciater of talent in his fellow actors, a frequently witty observer of life and manners. But all these are things that any reasonably keen spectator of his private life might have noticed—The curtain falls: And what of the man? we ask; the real, inner Cibber?—Ah, ladies and gentlemen, he has gone home.[4]

In Cibber's autobiography we find no scintilla of the dark night of the soul. Eighteenth-century autobiography dealt in facts and gossip, more or less intimate, not (at least until Rousseau) in agonizing self-appraisal. Cibber wrote, like Gibbon, his history as a public man. Of course he defended his character, but chiefly he sought to defend his career: to prove to the public that he had always had the best interests of the British theater at heart, that he had striven to bring it to the height of its achievement and the zenith of its prosperity.

He unabashedly recounts the follies of his youth.[5] Cibber was a self-satisfied man—indeed, a little less self-confidence and self-content might well have helped him along the road to greater art—and calmly confessed to being any kind of fool except an uncheerful one, to be lacking in any virtue except a sense of humor. So, in the early chapters of his autobiography, he cheerfully tells of his youthful indiscretions, making a joke of them, but he never gives us any real insights into his character. Perhaps he had none to give, or, more likely, it was not the fashion of the period.

By the fourth chapter Cibber has brought the narrative up to the point where he "look'd upon the Life of an Actor, when but eighteen Years of Age" and then he digresses into "A short View of the Stage, from the Year 1660" to 1690 and a notice of "theatrical Characters." In someone else's book this might be mere padding. In Cibber's, it constitutes one of the best parts. For two chapters (about fifty pages), he gives us a series of brilliant vignettes, portraits of all the leading actors of the time.

Here is the thundering Thomas Betterton—"an Actor, as *Shakespeare* was an Author, both without Competitors!" Pepys tells us that Betterton "did the Prince's part beyond imagina-

tion," that his Hamlet was "the best part, I believe, that ever man
acted," but Cibber's quick sketch in the Apology (60-61) brings
Betterton to life before our eyes:

> You have seen a *Hamlet* perhaps, who, on the first appear-
> ance of his Father's Spirit, has thrown himself into all
> the straining Vociferation requisite to express Rage and
> Fury, and the House has thunder'd with Applause; tho'
> the mis-guided Actor was all the while (as *Shakespear*
> terms it) tearing a Passion into Rage—I am the more bold
> to offer you this particular Instance, because the late Mr.
> *Addison,* while I sate by him, to see this Scene acted, made
> the same Observation, asking with some Surprize, if I
> thought *Hamlet* should be in so violent a Passion with the
> Ghost, which tho' it might have astonish'd it had not pro-
> vok'd him? for you may observe that in this beautiful
> Speech, the Passion never rises beyond an almost breath-
> less Astonishment, or an Impatience, limited by filial Re-
> verance, to enquire into the suspected Wrongs that may
> have rais'd him from his peaceful Tomb! and a Desire to
> know what a Spirit so seemingly distrest, might wish or
> enjoin a sorrowful Son to execute towards his future Quiet
> in the Grave? This was the Light into which *Betterton*
> threw this Scene; which he open'd with a Pause of mute
> Amazement! then rising slowly, to a solemn, trembling
> Voice, he made the Ghost equally terrible to the Specta-
> tor, as to himself! and in the descriptive Part of the natural
> Emotions which the ghastly Vision gave him, the boldness
> of his Expostulation was still govern'd by Decency, manly,
> but not braving; his Voice never rising into that seeming
> Outrage, or wild Defiance of what he naturally rever'd.
> But alas! to preserve this Medium, between mouthing,
> and meaning too little, to keep the Attention more pleas-
> ingly awake, by a temper'd Spirit, than by mere Vehe-
> mence of Voice, is of all the Master-strokes of an Actor
> the most difficult to reach. In this none yet have equall'd
> *Betterton.*

Cibber claims that with acting "you must have been present
at it! 'tis not to be told you!" but surely here he disproves his
own statement, as he does when he brings to life the "languid,
unaffecting" Estcourt or Nokes, so comically ridiculous in the
"plain and palpable Simplicity of Nature" that he was "enough
to have set a whole Bench of Bishops into a Titter":

> When he debated any matter by himself, he would shut up
> his Mouth with a dumb studious Powt, and roll his full

Eye, into such a vacant Amazement, such a palpable Ignorance of what to think of it, that his silent Perplexity
(which would sometimes hold him several Minutes) gave
your Imagination as full Content, as the most absurd thing
he could say upon it. In the Character of Sir *Martin Marr-
all* . . . what a copious, and distressful Harangue have I
seen him make, with his Looks (while the House has been
in one continued Roar, for several Minutes) before he could
prevail with his Courage to speak a Word. . . .[6]

The hilarity Nokes achieved by "this silent Eloquence, and
piteous Plight of his Features" in comedy, Cave Underhill also
managed with his wooden countenance. When he played "the
stiff, the heavy, and the stupid" characters—Obadiah in *The
Committee*, Lolpoop in *The Squire of Alsatia*—Cibber says that

he seem'd the immoveable Log he stood for! a Countenance of Wood could not be more fixt than his, when the
Blockhead of a Character required it: His Face was full
and long; from his Crown to the end of his Nose, was the
shorter half of it, so that the Disproportion of his lower
Features, when soberly compos'd, with an unwandering
Eye hanging over them, threw him into the most lumpish,
moping Mortal, that ever made Beholders merry![7]

But he excelled also in witty and more lively oafs, such as the
gravedigger in *Hamlet*.

Cibber quotes Dryden's praise of Mrs. Barry (from the Preface
to *Cleomenes*): "*Mrs. Barry, always excellent, has in Tragedy
excell'd herself, and gain'd a Reputation, beyond any Woman I
have ever seen in the Theatre*"—and then says that "I do not
only close with his Opinion" but

Mrs. *Barry*, in Characters of Greatness, had a Presence
of elevated Dignity, her Mien and Motion superb, and
gracefully majestick; her Voice full, clear, and strong, so
that no Violence of Passion could be too much for her:
And when Distress, or Tenderness possess'd her, she sub-
sided into the most affecting Melody, and Softness. In the
Art of exciting Pity, she had a Power beyond all the Actresses I have yet seen, or what your Imagination can con-
ceive. Of the former of these two great Excellencies, she
gave the most delightful Proofs in almost all the Heroic
Plays of *Dryden* and *Lee*; and of the latter, in the softer
Passions of *Otway's Monimia* and *Belvidera*. In Scenes of
Anger, Defiance, or Resentment, while she was impetuous,

and terrible, she pour'd out the Sentiment with an enchant-
ing Harmony; and it was this particular Excellence, for
which *Dryden* made her the above-recited Compliment,
upon her acting *Cassandra* in his *Cleomenes*. . . . She
was the first Person whose Merit was distinguish'd, by the
Indulgence of having an annual Benefit-Play, which was
granted to her alone, if I mistake not, first in King *James's*
time, and which became not common to others, 'till the
Division of this Company, after the Death of King *William's* Queen *Mary*.[8]

One of Cibber's liveliest portraits is the sketch of the scintillating Mrs. Monfort (sometimes known, after her second
marriage, as Mrs. Verbruggen). She played everything from the
fine lady to the comic drudge, from the vivacious ingenue to
Bayes in *The Rehearsal*:

But what found most Employment for her whole various
Excellence at once, was the Part of *Melantha,* in *Marriage-
A-la-Mode. Melantha* is as finish'd an Impertinent as ever
flutter'd in a Drawing-Room, and seems to contain the
most compleat System of Female Foppery, that could possibly be crowded into the tortur'd Form of a Fine Lady.
Her Language, Dress, Motion, Manners, Soul, and Body,
are in a continual Hurry to be something more, than is
necessary, or commendable. And tho' I doubt it will be a
vain Labour, to offer you a just Likeness of Mrs. *Monfort's*
Action, yet the fantastick Impression is still so strong in
my Memory, that I cannot help saying something, tho'
fantastically, about it. The first ridiculous Airs that break
from her, are, upon a Gallant, never seen before, who delivers her a Letter from her Father, recommending him to
her good Graces, as an honourable Lover. Here now, one
would think she might naturally shew a little of the Sex's
decent Reserve, though never so slightly cover'd! No, Sir;
not a Tittle of it; Modesty is the Virtue of a poor-foul'd
Country Gentlewoman; she is too much a Court Lady, to
be under so vulgar a Confusion; she reads the Letter, therefore, with a careless, dropping Lip, and an erected Brow,
humming it hastily over, as if she were impatient to outgo
her Father's Commands, by making a complete Conquest
of him at once; and, that the Letter might not embarrass
her Attack, crack! she crumbles it at once, into her Palm,
and pours upon him her whole Artillery of Airs, Eyes,
and Motion; down goes her dainty, diving Body, to the
Ground, as if she were sinking under the conscious Load
of her own Attractions; then launches into a Flood of

> Fine Language, and Compliment, still playing her Chest forward in fifty Falls and Risings, like a Swan upon waving Water; and, to complete her Impertinence, she is so rapidly fond of her own Wit, that she will not give her Lover leave to praise it: Silent assenting Bows, and vain Endeavours to speak, are all the share of the Conversation he is admitted to, which, at last, he is reliev'd from, by her Engagement to half a Score Visits, which she *swims* from him to make, with a Promise to return in a Twinkling.[9]

Cibber goes on to explain how Mrs. Bracegirdle, "the *Cara,* the Darling of the Theatre," contrived to make half the audience fall in love with her and half the playwrights to write parts in which she heard from the lips of the heroes protestations of love which really came from the hearts of the authors. *The Gentleman's Magazine* for February, 1745, when it mentioned the *Apology* "puffing" Cibber, singled out his "characters" of actors and actresses "as animated, as strongly mark'd, and as precisely individuated, as can be conceived."

These and other excellences flash from this diverting book— diverting in two senses, for Cibber can never resist a digression. It is the joyous account of a career happily lived among theater personalities and playwrights, of a life devoted to the stage. For that occupation Cibber offers no apology "As a good Play is certainly the most rational, and the highest Entertainment, that human Invention can produce. . . ."[10] He is proud of the English theater and of his substantial contribution to it. That, if not the man himself, certainly emerges from his book. That, if not the man himself, was just as certainly calculated to produce reactions to this popular book, but Cibber was content. He was not the man either to take advice against provoking attack nor to take attacks to heart. Pope (reading a Cibber pamphlet that crucified him) was observed in dire distress, but when Cibber's *Apology* brought forth waves of protest old Cibber calmly rode out the storm. Characteristically, he welcomed praise and ignored criticism.

Swift's publisher sent him a copy of the *Apology* when it first appeared, and Cibber wept tears of joy to learn that the Dean stayed up all night to read it.[11] It was less well received in more envious circles, closer to home. Pope wrote to the Earl of Orrery (January 13, 1743) an opinion that was shared by many: "And Cibber himself is the honestest Man I know, who has writ a book of his *Confessions*, not so much to his credit as St. Augustine's, but full as True & as open. Never had Impudence and Vanity so faithful a Professor."[12] The anonymous attack in *The Laureat, or the Right Side of Colley Cibber, Esq.*, which we have already noted, was much earlier (November 29, 1740) and much nastier than Pope's.

Perhaps the most consistent fusillades came from the tireless and vinegary Henry Fielding. Cibber had welcomed Fielding to Drury Lane, where he had been introduced by his cousin, Lady Mary Wortley Montagu; and Cibber had produced and acted in Fielding's first play, *Love in Several Masques* (1728). Fielding thanked Cibber effusively in the Preface to the published version for "kind behaviour previous to its presentation," but his affection cooled quickly when Cibber and his associates refused Fielding's next comedies.[13] Cibber had no dislike for Fielding, however—only for bad plays—and when Fielding's delightful burlesque *Tom Thumb* (soon expanded into *The Tragedy of Tragedies: or, The Life and Death of Tom Thumb the Great*) caught the popular fancy, Cibber patched up the quarrel with his special charm and invited the young author back to the Theatre-Royal in Drury Lane. Once again they were friends. In Cibber's last full season as a manager at Drury Lane (1732-1733), he seemed to favor Fielding and staged five of his plays;[14] but then Cibber retired from Drury Lane. Fielding remained, and, because Cibber began to appear occasionally at other theaters, the two men were once more working for rival companies. Fielding promptly dusted off *The Author's Tragedy* and revived it, putting in some new cracks at "Mr. What-d'ye-call-him, the gentleman that writes odes—so finely." Was this ungrateful of Fielding? Not really. Cibber had done much for Fielding's theatrical career, it is true; but Cibber was such a popular target that Fielding could not resist ignoring friendship for the fashion. His farces swiped at the Poet Laureate of Dullness in *Pasquin*. Cibber's son Theophilus was lampooned unmercifully in a number of sketches and made to refer to "Those glorious hisses, which from age to age,/Our family has born triumphant from the stage." Finally, in *The Historical Register for 1736*, Fielding combined in one play another attack on Colley Cibber (Ground-Ivy) with that famous portrait of Sir Robert Walpole (Quidam)—that "great man"—that brought down upon him and all his fellows the wrath of the government and the revenge of the Licensing Act.

It was this last act—Cibber aptly called it setting fire to the stage—that finally goaded the generally good-natured Cibber into retaliation for a decade of insults. Without naming Fielding, the *Apology* called him a broken wit and spoke slightingly of the numerous plays this "enterprising" young man had dashed off.[15] Cibber accused him of trying "to knock all Distinction of Mankind upon the Head," and dismissed him as a wild, irresponsible "Drawcansir of wit."

Fielding got wind of this even before it appeared. At the beginning of April he was writing in *The Champion* a prediction that Cibber would "end up as an author with a very bad Life." Throughout that month no issue of that periodical appeared without an attack on Cibber: as a cur ineffectually barking at a bear, as the author of "the saddest stuff that ever was writ," as an enemy of the King's English. And on this question of style Fielding was most voluble. In the April 15 issue of *The Champion* he accused Cibber of "writing as ill as possible"; in the April 29 issue he got down to cases. He had much earlier attacked Cibber's use of foreign languages—"the great laureate abounds with such a redundancy of Greek and Latin . . . he hath prefixed a Latin motto to every act of his *Caesar in Egypt*" —but now he picked at his English. Cibber not only misquoted Latin but used *adept* incorrectly, made "a verb active of *shine*," spoke of "a spectacle for vacancy of thought to gaze at," and so on. "I proceed to show the little advantage of learning, or grammar, to an author," wrote Fielding on April 29, "which I shall demonstrate in two ways: First, I shall show he is generally to be understood without, and Secondly, That he is sometimes not to be understood with it." Fielding set out to demolish "the ultra-sublime or Cibberian style" altogether. Cibber is granted the use of English—"whatever book is writ in no other language is writ in English. This book is writ in no other language, *ergo* it is writ in English"—but what English! An English which "ascends into the elevated and nervously pompous elements of the sublime"; a bastard English, devoid of grammar and sense; a "language [of which] the author shows himself an absolute master, for nobody except an absolute master of a language could trample its laws underfoot in the way done by Cibber!"

In May *The Champion* put Cibber on trial for the murder of the English tongue, making Cibber plead: "Sir, I am as innocent as the child which hath not yet entered into human nature of the fact laid to my charge. This accusation is the forward spring of envy of my laurel. It is impossible I should have any enmity to the English language, with which I am so

little acquainted. . . ." Cibber was let off with a verdict of
"chance-medley" in connection with the *Apology.* Just about this
time one "T. Johnson" picked up the idea for a scurrilous
pamphlet entitled *The Tryal of Colley Cibber,* and Cibber was
once again put into the dock for committing assault upon the
language with a goose quill, value one farthing. Perhaps Fielding
("Captain Hercules Vinegar") had a hand in this attack as
well; it is charitable to think him guiltless.

Another issue of *The Champion* found Fielding assigning Cibber to hell in a scene far wittier than anything in *The Tryal of
Colley Cibber.* Cibber is described as being searched before
being allowed to board Charon's ferry over the Styx and introduced as "an elderly gentleman with a piece of withered laurel
on his head."[16] Certainly Fielding strove to remove that laurel,
not only in ephemeral newspapers but in permanent monuments
of literature. Early in *Joseph Andrews* (1742), his incredibly
naïve hero encounters the quixotic parson Abram Adams, the
first and best of Fielding's portraits of "the good man." As he
describes Parson Adams, he cannot refrain from aiming another
shaft at Cibber:

> He was generous, friendly, and brave, to an excess; but
> simplicity was his characteristic: he did no more than Mr.
> Colley Cibber apprehend any such passions as malice and
> envy to exist in mankind; which was indeed less remark-
> able in a country parson, than in a gentleman who hath
> passed his life behind the scenes,—a place which hath
> been seldom thought the school of innocence, and which
> a very little observation would have convinced the great
> Apologist that those passions have a real existence in the
> human mind.[17]

In the same famous novel we read of "two books, lately published, which represent an admirable pattern of the amiable in
either sex." He means Cibber's *Apology* and Richardson's
Pamela,[18] the book that inspired Fielding to begin his novel:

> The former of these, which deals in male virtue, was writ-
> ten by the great person himself, who lived the life he hath
> recorded, and is by many thought to have lived such a life
> only in order to write it. . . . I mean . . . Colley Cibber.
> . . . How artfully doth the former, by insinuating that he
> escaped being promoted to the highest stations in church
> and state, teach us a contempt for worldly grandeur!

It is true that Cibber blithely suggests that he might have done well in church or state had his inclinations in youth run that way, but I do think that this opinion, though hardly modest, is tenable.[19] A man of his practical talents might well have succeeded in politics, the science of the possible. Certainly he had more than enough energy and perhaps too much intelligence to become an archbishop in the Established Church in that Age of Reason. With a great deal of luck and the right political connections he might very well have risen to that ecclesiastical eminence.

Barker summarizes Fielding's myriad attacks on Cibber and his autobiography:

> In *The Author's Farce* he shows us the manager; in *The Historical Register for 1736,* the laureate and the adapter of Shakespeare; in the *Champion,* the prose writer; and . . . finally [in *Joseph Andrews*], the apologist, the author of those hopelessly insincere and inaccurate chapters in the autobiography. Taken together these passages give an extremely amusing caricature of Cibber; much more amusing certainly than the somewhat muddled caricature in the first book of the *Dunciad.*[20]

Whether that be true or no, Pope must have a chapter to himself, for his relations with Cibber are a more important story. Though Cibber specifically disclaims envy of Pope in the *Apology,* we cannot believe him: his craving for fame was so exigent that he cannot have been without a trace of it. We shall, however, see him at his best in the literary war with Pope, even when bitter personal remarks are being exchanged, even in those carminative pamphlets which relieve the colics of jealousy, though not without griping accompanied by wind.

CHAPTER 9

The Literary Quarrel With Pope

THE literary quarrel between Cibber and Alexander Pope that flared into prominence after the publication of the *Apology* had been fitfully smouldering for many years. It began as far back as January 16, 1717, when John Gay's otherwise inconsequential farce *Three Hours after Marriage,* a trivial farrago on which Pope and Dr. Arbuthnot collaborated, premièred at Drury Lane. The play attacked Cibber, but that was not the cause of the quarrel. Though Dr. John Woodward (Fossile) and John Dennis (Sir Tremendous) were offended at the coarse caricatures of themselves in the play, Cibber (satirized as Plotwell) was more tolerant of the jibes at his dramaturgical and directorial skill. He played Plotwell himself, to great applause. Seemingly the audience never tired of laughing at Cibber—and besides, the satire was basically good humored though rather inept.

Though Cibber was a success, the play was a failure. Neither the lewdness of the lines nor the slapstick of the situations could save it:[1] it was hissed at the first performance and withdrawn on the seventh. But it was not the failure of the play that started the bickering. Cibber, as an experienced manager, knew that only an exceptional play enjoyed in those days a longer run and that *Three Hours after Marriage* had yielded more profit than could have been expected from such a script.

Perhaps Pope was disconcerted at the play's failure, but what really piqued him was that, a couple of weeks later, when Cibber revived *The Rehearsal* by royal command, he ad-libbed a few cracks about *Three Hours after Marriage.*[2] Pope flew into a rage, for he had none of Cibber's ability to laugh at himself, and stormed backstage. "His lips pale and his voice trembling," Cibber claimed, Pope ranted and raved and threatened to have Gay cane Cibber.[3] So abusive was Pope's language that Cibber calmly announced that he would repeat the offending line in every subsequent performance of *The Rehearsal,* a play whose sixty-year record of success (he might have added) was proof that it would be remembered long after the unfortunate farce had been forgotten which Gay, Arbuthnot, and Pope had been stupid enough to write and that Cibber himself had been foolish enough to inflict on the public. Pope, in a towering rage, hurled imprecations in all directions.

The next night, as promised, Cibber repeated the same feeble joke about mummies and crocodiles (which figure prominently in *Three Hours after Marriage*); and, as promised, John Gay came backstage afterwards to trounce him. Cibber hit Gay "a fillip on the nose" and the guards parted them before the skirmish could develop into a battle. Gay, who believed that "Life is a jest, and all things show it," was of a basically sunny disposition and soon forgot about the matter. Pope, characteristically, nursed his resentment. In December of the same year (1717) he wrote to Cibber, to whom he had apparently not spoken since the previous January, and enclosed six guineas for tickets to Cibber's *The Non-Juror*. He seemed to be seeking further differences with Cibber.[4] Having seen the play (and heard several mentions of his own work therein), he proceeded to damn *The Non-Juror* in an anonymous pamphlet, *The Plot Discovered, or a Clue to the Comedy of the Non-Juror*. With clumsy irony this silly piece attempted to demonstrate that Cibber's play was pro-Catholic and pro-Tory—actually an attack on the government and a defense of the Jacobites. Cibber, however, was either wise enough or tolerant enough to pretend he thought this idiocy funny, so nothing further came of it.[5]

Things might well have ended here, had Pope not been a truly irritable artist of the *genus irritabile vatum*. He wrote to his friends that Cibber's *Non-Juror* was a "damned" play, that Lady Scudamore ought to be praised for refusing to attend it, that Cibber was a fool. In a 1727 volume of miscellaneous works by Pope, Swift, Dr. Arbuthnot, and Gay, Pope included Cibber among those ridiculed in *Martinus Scriblerus* ΠΕΡΙ ΒΑΘΟΥΣ, *or the Art of Sinking in Poetry*. Cibber is labeled as a parrot-actor and as a plagiarist-playwright. He and Mrs. Old-field are attacked with spleen, and finally the whole management of Drury Lane is subjected to what is supposed to be withering irony:

HERE therefore, in the name of all our Brethren, let me re-turn our sincere and humble Thanks to the Most August Mr. *B[ar]t[o]n B[oo]th*, the Most Serene Mr. *W[i]ll[ia]m* [he means Robert] *Wilks*, and the Most Undaunted Mr. *C[o]ll[e]y C[i]bb[e]r*; of whom, let it be known when the *People of this Age shall be Ancestors*, and to all the *Suc-*

cession of our Successors, that to this present day they continue to *Out-do* even their *own Out-Doings*: And when the
inevitable Hand of sweeping *Time* shall have brush'd off all
the Works of *To-day,* may this Testimony of a *Co-temporary
Critick* to their Fame, be extended as far as *Tomorrow!*[6]

The sniping by Pope was greeted with silence. It continued.
In May, 1728, Cibber found himself attacked anonymously in
the first edition of *The Dunciad.* Pope wrote this major poem
chiefly to revenge himself upon Lewis Theobald,[7] but he found
room to mention Cibber as a plagiarist, as a tyrannical manager,
as an incompetent, and as the father of diverse abominations
from bad plays to Theophilus Cibber. The invective in *The
Dunciad* also went unanswered, but Cibber continued to be
the butt of Pope's snide remarks. When Cibber became Laureate,
there was a good deal of comment to the effect that the youngest
Laureate ever appointed (Eusden) had been succeeded by the
worst (Cibber); and Pope got in on it, contributing a few
squibs to the *Grub-Street Journal.* He took another swipe at
Cibber in the *First Satire of the Second Book of Horace* (1733).

The best of Pope's Horatian imitations was the *Epistle to Dr.
Arbuthnot* (1735) and it twice attacked Cibber, the most scald-
ing lines being these:

> Whom have I hurt? has poet yet, or peer,
> Lost the arched eyebrow or Parnassian sneer?
> And has not Colley still his lord and whore?

Cibber still maintained a dignified silence. Not even associating
him with patronage and prostitution could tempt him to reply
to Pope's nastiness. Cibber was as aware of Pope's talent as he
was of his waspish temper. He had subscribed to the very *Iliad*
translation—a poem, it was said, that had every merit but fidelity
to the original—that had made the moderately wealthy linen-
draper's son Pope immoderately wealthy, and thus independent
of patrons. Cibber admired Pope. He knew that Pope had genius
without geniality. He had no desire to give him cause for further
scrapping. When Pope praised *The Careless Husband,* Cibber
was pleased. When Pope attacked other works of his, Cibber was
silent.

At last Cibber had to reply. The time arrived when the reputation which Cibber had hoped to preserve by humoring Pope
began to be imperiled by Cibber's patience. Though Cibber
could not be "put out of Temper" by malicious and petty jibes,

no man as vain as he—and he was nearly as vain as Pope—could continue to suffer derogation with complete equanimity, nor any man as careful of his public image long allow public opinion to be deluded. When Cibber wrote his *Apology*, devoted in some measure to justifying the ways of Colley to man, Pope had to be mentioned; but Colley was magnanimous. He praised Pope unstintedly as the leading light of the literary profession. He assiduously avoided quoting the more painful things Pope had said about him: there was no need to give them greater currency, whether readers would think them worthy of Cibber or unworthy of Pope. Though severely critical of others, such as the lightweight journalist Nathaniel Mist,[8] when England's greatest living theatrical manager came to write of England's greatest living poet he almost seemed to make excuses for Pope.

After the *Apology*, Cibber was almost apologetic about his book, calling it "unequal, pert, and frothy, patch'd and parti-coloured, like a Coat of a Harlequin; frequently aiming at Wit, without ever hitting the Mark; a mere Ragout, tossed up from the Offals of other authors; my Subject below all Pens but my own." But in the *Apology* itself he sounded very confident; confident enough, at least, to excuse Pope, to pretend to be indifferent to "Censure and Invective," to admit his faults (shrewdly disarming his enemies), to decline to defend his failures or to puff his triumphs. He wrote of these that "When a work is apparently great, it will go without Crutches; all your Art and Anxiety to heighten the Fame of it, then becomes low and little."[9]

He had enough work "apparently great" to be able to stand secure, to ignore Pope's darts:

> When I therefore find my Name at length, in the Satyrical Works of our most celebrated living Author, I never look upon those Lines as Malice meant to me, (for he knows I never provok'd it) but Profit to himself: One of his Points must be, to have many Readers: He considers that my Face and Name are more known than those of many thousands of more consequence in the Kingdom: That, therefore, right or wrong, a Lick at the *Laureat* will always be a sure Bait, *ad captandum vulgus* to catch him little Readers: And that to gratify the Unlearned, by now and then interspersing those merry Sacrifices of an old Acquaintance to their Taste, is a piece of right Poetical Craft.[10]

Of course, this statement was hitting at Pope—who always

pretended to be motivated by nothing but a sense of social
justice and by the highest principles of poetic art—very fairly
but very hard. Having implied that the worst that could be said
of Pope was that he was only commercial, not malicious, aware
that "*Satyr* shall have a thousand Readers, where *Panegyric*
has one," Cibber asserted that he had to forgive him. After all,
was not Cibber's case the same? As Laureate he wrote odes
of merely "adjective merit" for what Burns would call a "wee
wee German lairdie," for money. Certainly these lame productions inflamed a true poet like Pope, but "as a little bad Poetry,
is the greatest Crime he lays to my charge, I am quite willing
to subscribe to his opinion of *it*."[11] Who ever said Poets Laureate
had to be good poets? How lucky Pope was to be able to write
when he pleased and not on order, and to be able to take for
his inspiration not something low such as the dull monarch but
something more sublime, such as personal vindictiveness! Cibber
concluded with a warning that wit as sharp as Pope's was a
dangerous weapon and expressed the hope that the poet's "happy Genius" might in future be employed in creating pleasure
rather than in inflicting pain.

Had Pope's soul been as great as his talent he might graciously have accepted the compliment and called a truce. But
he would not. He could not—insults and injuries, real or imag-
ined, were too often his stimuli for writing. Too often the pleasure his readers found in his works was the sadistic pleasure of
watching his victims, impaled by his wit, wriggling on the pin.
A life of peace and contentment might have meant the death
of Pope's art.

The war went on. The *New Dunciad* (1742) featured further
attacks on Cibber, and not entirely without the commercial
motives that Cibber had mentioned. Though rich, Pope always
needed money. Money was love to crippled little Pope. Cibber
had to reply sharply at last; for, though he could accept the
laurel being flung in his face by Pope, it was degrading to have
the olive branch flung back as well. But he did not reply in
rage. A letter of Friday, July 23, 1742, says that Cibber is
sending a friend "a printed letter of mine to Mr. Pope" and
that "I will not ask your Opinion, because if you like it, you will
have no very good one of Him. But I hope you will find I have
done him no injustice: for I like his Poetry, tho' that does not
like Me."[12] In this little work of what Habbema calls "quiet
argumentative tone and keen, though reserved, raillery," Cibber
struck Pope deliberately and decisively where it hurt most. The

pamphlet was called *A Letter from Mr. Cibber to Mr. Pope, Inquiring into the Motives that Might Induce Him in His Satyrical Works, to be so Frequently Fond of Mr. Cibber's Name.* Written (Cibber characteristically claimed) at the insistence of friends, it began in a tone generally mild and much less offensive than that in which Pope had couched his numerous attacks on Cibber. Then, suddenly, it lunged at Pope's weakest spot:

> He may remember then (or if he won't I will) when Button's Coffeehouse was in vogue, and so long ago he had not translated above two or three books of Homer [about 1715]; there was a young nobleman (as much his lord as mine) [an allusion to the line in the *Epistle to Dr. Arbuthnot*, in retaliation for which, apparently, this whole scandal is recounted] who had a good deal of wicked humor, and who, though he was fond of having wits in his company, was not so restrained by his conscience but that he loved to laugh at any merry mischief he could do them; this noble wag, I say, in his usual *gaieté de coeur,* with another gentleman still in being, one evening slyly seduced the celebrated Mr. Pope as a wit and myself as a laugher to a certain house of carnal recreation near the Haymarket, where his lordship's frolic proposed was to slip his little Homer, as he called him, at a girl of the game, that he might see what sort of figure a man of his size, sobriety, and vigor (in verse) would make when the frail fit of love had got into him; in which he so far succeeded that the smirking damsel who served us with tea happened to have charms sufficient to tempt the little-tiny manhood of Mr. Pope into the next room with her: at which you may imagine his lordship was in as much joy at what might happen within as our small friend could probably be in possession of it. But I (forgive me all ye mortified mortals whom his fell satire has since fallen upon) observing that he had stayed as long as without hazard of his health he might, I,
> > Pricked to it by foolish honesty and love,
> as Shakespeare says, without ceremony threw open the door upon him, where I found this little hasty hero, like a terrible tomtit, pertly perching on the mount of love! But such was my surprise that I fairly laid hold of his heels and actually drew him down safe and sound from his danger. My lord, who stood tittering without in hopes the sweet mischief he came for would have been completed, upon my giving an account of the action within, began to curse and call me an hundred silly puppies for my impertinently spoiling the sport; to which with great gravity I

replied, "Pray, my lord, consider what I have done was
in regard to the honor of our nation! For would you have
had so glorious a work as that of making Homer speak
elegant English cut short by laying up our little gentleman
of a malady which his thin body might never have been
cured of? No, my lord! Homer would have been too serious
a sacrifice to our evening merriment." Now as his Homer
has since been so happily completed, who can say that the
world may not have been obliged to the kindly care of
Colley that so great a work ever came to perfection?[13]

Pope's anguish was acute because of this story and the scurrilous and obscene cartoons, which circulated widely. The first
shot fired, other enemies assailed Pope and friends defended
him.[14] Pope himself was not idle. Vengeance inspired him
and he completed a new version of *The Dunciad,* desperately
revising his old attack on Theobald to enthrone Colley Cibber
as the King of the Dunces. He was, unwittingly, to immortalize
Cibber by it.

By the end of 1742 Pope was well on his way to completing
the revision, if indeed he had not finished it. If he needed any
further impetus, Cibber provided it. In January, 1743, appeared
The Egoist, or Colley upon Cibber and in February *A Second
Letter from Mr. Cibber to Mr. Pope. In Reply to Some Additional Verses in His Dunciad, Which He Has not yet Published.*[15]
This latter commented on the opening of Pope's poem and,
in equally good verse, made this telling rejoinder: "Still brazen,
brainless! still the same dull chime!/Is impudence in prose made
wit by rime?" If Pope has "a right to lay your satyrical Tail at
my Door, whenever your Muse has a Looseness, have I not,"
asks Cibber, "an equal Right to rub your Nose in it?"

The man that Lady Mary Wortley Montagu so aptly called
"the Wicked Wasp of Twickenham" fumed, full of what Dr.
Johnson later termed his "ambitious petulance"; and in October,
1743, the *New Dunciad* appeared, and Pope had launched his
popular, all-out assault in "the war of the Dunces."[16] He featured
Cibber in *The Dunciad,* and Warburton rewrote the accompany-
ing notes to fit. Obviously *The Dunciad* was written about Theobald. Cibber (as Pope said of the love scenes of *Cato*) was
"flung in after." Theobald had all but disappeared, surviving in
one couplet and a few scattered notes. For more than a year,
as Cibber had noted in his second letter to Pope, Pope had
been "as uneasy as a Rat in a hot Kettle." Now he had retaliated:
Cibber was crowned by the Goddess of Dullness and reigned

over Pope's satiric epic.[17] Attacking Cibber, after all, had become a sort of literary game; Pope had had more practice at it than most; and in any case Cibber was a likely target. For one thing, he was better known, both in literary circles and in the town, than Theobald; for another, he was a safer butt: the attack on Theobald only reminded Pope's readers that Theobald was right in making the inadequacy of Pope's slapdash edition of Shakespeare abundantly, painfully clear.

Perhaps Cibber was right in asserting that the "lord and whore" bit was "the flattest Piece of Satyr that ever fell from the formidable Pen of Mr. *Pope*," but in the *New Dunciad* was a barrage, and many of the shots hit home. Cibber's "New-year Odes" were lampooned, the Laureate being called one of those "pensive Poets" who go "Sleepless themselves to give their Readers sleep." His father's famous statues on the gates of Bedlam led to caustic comment:

> Close to those walls where Folly holds her throne,
> And laughs to think Monroe would take her down,
> Where o'er the gates, by his fam'd father's hand
> Great Cibber's brazen, brainless brothers stand.[18]

It did Cibber no good to counter that the statues were reclining and, though painted, made of stone: "First give me leave to observe that those figures do not *stand*, but *lye*. Do you observe, Sir? I say they are no more *upright* than you are when you *stand*, or write; nay, they *lye* as flat as you do sometimes when you write. . . ." Pope had made his point, and no pun could dull it. He went on to describe Cibber as "Bays, formed by nature Stage and Town to bless,/And act, and be, a Coxcomb with success."[19] He called Cibber a fop offstage and on, ridiculed his plays,[20] accused him of plagiarism: "he plundered snug/ And suck'd all o'er, like an industrious Bug."[21] And in pithy phrases Pope spoke of "prose on stilts," "poetry fall'n lame," and "Prose swell'd to verse, verse loit'ring into prose."[22] He coined a new term of opprobrium: "Cibberian." He mercilessly parodied Cibber's laureate versifying:

> Thou Cibber! thou his [Eusden's] Laurel shall support,
> Folly, my son, has still a Friend at Court.
> Lift up your gates, ye Princes, see him come!
> Sound, sound ye Viols, be the Cat-call dumb!
> Bring, bring the madding Bay, the drunken Vine;
> The creeping, dirty, courtly Ivy join.[23]

He called Cibber "the Antichrist of wit"; insulted Theophilus Cibber; denigrated the stage effects in Cibber's plays; made slurs on his English grammar and his Latin proficiency; deprecated his voice, his pertness, his face. He accused him of encouraging the "Chromatic tortures" of opera, of reclining in the lap of Dullness, of writing for hire. He rose to Miltonics in mock epic as Book II of the poem began:

> High on a gorgeous seat, that far out-shone
> Henley's gilt tub, or Fleckno's Irish throne . . .
> Great Cibber sate: The proud Parnassian sneer,
> The conscious simper, and the jealous leer,
> Mix in his look: All eyes direct their rays
> On him, and crowds turn Coxcombs as they gaze.

Such philippics Cibber could not ignore. He had earlier feared for his reputation. "A Disgrace from such a Pen might stick upon me to Posterity" he allowed, and it has. Now Pope had "run amuk" to such an extent that Cibber was compelled to attempt to win the battle from which he could not retreat. He did so with gusto, perhaps agreeing with Gwendolyn in *The Importance of Being Earnest*: "On an occasion of this kind it becomes more than a moral duty to speak one's mind. It becomes a pleasure." He addressed *Another Occasional Letter* to Pope. At last he seemed more angered than amazed at Pope's persistent sneers. His ire brought into play tactics he had previously avoided: he mentioned Pope's crooked body, his language grew less polite, he became threatening: "If you had not been a blinder Booby than myself you would have sat down quietly with the last Black Eye I gave you." He was most vehement about Warburton (whom he had never met but thought to have incited Pope), but he also found time to call Pope "an anxious, celebrated, miserable Man," equally devoid of both prudence and charity, spiteful and childish. Cibber himself claimed to remain "the same Laughing Fellow he was before thy Weakness was angry with him."

Pope would certainly have prolonged the fight, but he fell ill and was unable to reply. A friend of Cibber offered to print another attack on Pope, but Cibber personally dissuaded him, out of consideration for the poet's condition. When Pope died at Twickenham (May 30, 1744), Cibber joined the nation in mourning and *The Gentleman's Magazine* for June carried an epitaph for Pope ascribed to Colley Cibber:

> Our pious praise on tombstones runs so high,
> Readers might think, that none but good men die!
> If graves held only such: *Pope*, like his verse,
> Had still been breathing, and escap'd the hearse.
> Tho' fell to all men's failings, but his own, ⎫
> Yet to assert his vengeance, or renown,   ⎬
> None ever reach'd such heights of *Helicon!*   ⎭
> E'en death shall let his dust this truth enjoy,
> That not his errors can his fame destroy.

There follow Prince Henry's lines on the death of Hotspur and then these (signed "C. C."):

> VERSES *on occasion of* Mr P O P E ' *s Death.*
>
> *By the Author of a small Tract relating to moral*
>
> *virtue, lately inscrib'd to him.*

> How vainly we project! oh honour'd *Pope*
> Fruitless my labour, blasted all my hope!
> Long had I sought occasion to express
> My just regard, by no unfit address;
> Unknown and distant, yet I might attain
> My sole ambition, thy esteem to gain:
> Th' occasion found, flatter'd my fond desires,
> But oh! no sooner found, than Pope expires!

And so on, for twenty more limping lines. Among these sentiments, and the others printed in the same issue, Cibber's halting verses do not look so bad. The epitaph, if Cibber himself wrote it, may be said to have ended on an attractive note the long quarrel between the laureate poet and the Poet Laureate.

The critics Norman Ault and George Sherburn tend to make Pope's actions in this affair better than they were, and Miss Senior tries to make them appear worse. But whatever is debated, these facts are clear. Pope kept it going. Pope enjoyed the advantage of attack, but emotion robbed him of moderation and personal animus deprived him of restraint. Cibber, on the whole, maintained an admirable good humor throughout the whole unfortunate business, and we must respect him more. Cibber's calm, of course, only increased Pope's fury and made him nastier and shriller. It was a stupid dog fight in which Cibber, a large and somewhat less nervous mutt, was more amused than injured by the yapping and snapping of a purebred but puny lapdog.[24]

Pope suffered intensely from Cibber's attacks. They made him fretful and petty in his last days and drove him to take Malice for his muse. They caused him to mar an important work, *The Dunciad*, with a hero who did not fit, to stain the final pages of his life with rash and ill-founded words and actions. Pope, who had much of the power of the young Horace (as well as his fiery temper), demolished Addison, Lord Hervey, Dennis, Phillips, Curll, Budgell, Welsted, Moore, Theobald, and even Bentley (perhaps the greatest classical scholar of his century); but he met more than his match when he tried to enthrone Cibber as "Dullness's Laureate Son." *The Dunciad* became a monument of spite as well as genius; a work which not only justly castigated offenses, but sometimes flung baseless charges at the innocent; a work which, now and then, when it should have dispensed justice, enshrined revenge. But, though Pope was not a great soul, he had produced a great poem. Cibber himself realized *The Dunciad*'s merit—and its value to him. After all, he preferred ridicule to being ignored. Notoriety was nearly as useful to him as fame. He was annoyed by Pope's pettiness but fully conscious of his greatness: "I grant the Dunciad a better Poem of its kind than ever was writ." He was aware that he would be remembered as the grindstone that sharpened the wit of Pope—Pope, who despised, envied, assailed, insulted, and immortalized Cibber.

CHAPTER 10

Old Age

THE *Apology*, which appeared when he was sixty-eight, could
have capped the career of any man; but Cibber lived to a
ripe old age, postponing, like any actor, his farewell appearance.
He was occasionally beset by ill health, but his was generally a
happy and active life to its end. Colley's main worries in his
later years were his two incorrigible children. In the *Apology*
Cibber joked about his having produced plays and children in
equal profusion. Fortunately for his fame, his dramatic productions were more admirable and more moral than his two
disreputable offspring, Theophilus Cibber and Mrs. Charlotte
Cibber Charke, whose harebrained escapades must have caused
him acute embarrassment in his declining years.

Fairly early in his marriage Cibber received some legacies
from the more affluent members of the family of his wife,
Katherine Shore. On these, and his own salaries as actor and
manager, he raised a brood of ten, writing plays to augment
his income. Perhaps without the pinch of penury he might never
have written *Love's Last Shift*, a play designed chiefly to give
him a good role and advancement in the theater. Somehow he
contrived to feed his large brood and to settle them during the
summers at Twickenham and Hampton.[1] Cibber as a young man,
rising penniless from the gaming table, used to exit with "Now
I must go home and eat a Child!" Had he devoured either
Theophilus or Charlotte in their infancy, we modestly propose
that he would thereafter have spared himself and others a great
deal of pain, though we should have lost thereby two of that
century's most intriguing, most improbable eccentrics.

On November 26, 1703, a "violent and destructive" storm
raged "over the greatest part of Europe" and almost as if he had
chosen, in his exhibitionistic way, to arrange this dramatic beginning for his picaresque career, Theophilus Cibber was born.
After attempts to educate this recalcitrant boy, Cibber allowed
him to go on the stage, though he had inherited his father's
slight physique and shrill voice.[2] His "effronterie" made him a

place. His extravagant, grimacing style made him a great success as the swaggering Ancient Pistol. He appeared with his father as a fop in *The Rival Modes* (Colley was the Earl of Late-Airs) and later took over some of his father's roles—Sir Francis Wronghead in *The Provok'd Husband*, Lord Foppington in *The Careless Husband*, and Abel Drugger in *The Committee*.

Theophilus played the fool offstage as well as on. He ran up debts (until he was thrown into prison) and led a life that scandalized his father. His second wife (1734) was Susannah Maria Arne, sister of Dr. Thomas Arne, the composer.[3] Colley was against the match, which Susannah's father (an upholsterer) and Theophilus (eleven years her senior) seem to have arranged between them. Colley foresaw having to write a lot more plays to support this pair for, though Susannah had appeared with some success as a singer, Colley insisted "she had no fortune." His roistering, reckless son was enough of a financial drain upon his father's resources. Colley Cibber could not afford to worry about Theophilus' wife and family as well. But Susannah succeeded in captivating the old man, who is said to have retained to the last an eye for a pretty face and a trim figure. He liked her saucy manner and quick wit. Perhaps it inspired some of the clever ladies he created in his plays, for Cibber liked to draw from life; moreover he discovered Susannah had possibilities for the stage. In those days a singing voice was really required to cope with the fashion for chanted tragedy. As he had with so many fledgling actors at the theater, Cibber took her under his wing.[4] In 1731 she sang in the first complete public performance of Händel's *Acis and Galatea*[5] and her rendition of the contralto part in the first performance of Händel's *Messiah* (in Dublin, 1741) so moved Dr. Patrick Delany, whom Swift called "the most eminent preacher we have," that he rose in his seat and cried: "Woman, for this be all thy sins forgiven thee!"[6]

Music's loss was the theater's gain, for Cibber made his daughter-in-law into a great actress. In 1731 she delighted audiences as Ethelinda in *Aethelwold* and on Twelfth Night in 1736 she starred as Zara in Aaron Hill's version of Voltaire's *Zaïre*.[7] Later she starred with Quin, Macklin, and (for a dozen years) with Garrick, who said at her death that tragedy had passed away with her.[8]

The same dishonesty that made Susannah's life with Theophilus hectic and humiliating—he was as frequently in bagnios as at home, as often drunk as sober, jealous of her success and extravagant and selfish with her money, heartless about their two children (who died in infancy), and heedless about notoriety—was seen in his dealings with his father, whom he subjected to a great deal of adverse publicity and guilt by association. Surely Cibber would not have been such a figure of fun, such a butt for satire, had all the old man's children been "kind and natural."

Theophilus was constantly embarrassing old Colley. In 1732, for example, Cibber and the other managers at Drury Lane received a royal patent to last for twenty-one years. Almost immediately the management dissolved. Wilks died in 1732 (leaving a certain John Ellis to handle his share for the benefit of his widow), and Booth, then suffering his final illness, sold half of his share to John Highmore. Cibber, left in charge with two tyros, Ellis and Highmore, decided to quit the business. First he delegated his authority to Theophilus, but nobody could get along with him and Cibber finally sold out to Highmore for three thousand guineas. Theophilus immediately betrayed his father's successor, led an actors' revolt which deprived him of almost all his stars (except the reliable Kitty Clive), and set up in competition at the Little (or French) Theatre in the Haymarket. This ruined Highmore and forced him to sell out Drury Lane to Charles Fleetwood for half its value. Theophilus Cibber and the other actors then returned to Drury Lane! The whole sordid story is the subject of a Covent Garden play of 1733 called *The Stage-Mutineers: or, A Play-House to be Lett.*[9]

But this was not the end of Theophilus' career. He continued to bring opprobrium on his father and brickbats about his own ears, as this report of 1740 of one of his appearances indicates:

> The house was very early crowded, and the harmonious discordant concert of catcalls, whistles, etc., etc., began to play before the curtain drew up. Well, though the actors were all frightened, the play began with calmness and applause; but this was only a prelude to the battle. When the scene came in which he was to appear [Theophilus as Lord Foppington in Act I, Scene 3 of *The Relapse*], there was a dead silence, till he popped his poor head from behind the scenes; then at once the hurly-burly began, volleys of apples and potatoes and such vile trash flew about his ears. He retired, the storm subsided; he advanced, it began again. In the most humble gesture and address he made a motion to be heard; it was all in vain and he was once more pelted off. . . . But determined to go through with the play, he went through it amidst the greatest uproar that

ever was heard so long a space in the theatre, and by a
confident heart he surmounted what many of less resolution
would have sunk under.[10]

"A confident heart" and "resolution" are kind terms indeed
for a man of Theophilus' unmitigated gall. He seems to have
inherited a good deal of his father's brass, if not his gold. Pope's
Dunciad ticked Theophilus off as a brash fool "who takes the
foremost place/And thrusts his person full into your face," and
we can only guess at how much of the satire of Colley Cibber in
that poem was occasioned by Pope's dislike of his son. Satirists
certainly tended to link them. When Theophilus, always scribb-
ling to pay his debts,[11] offered to write an autobiography, someone (probably Henry Fielding) beat him to it and published a
scurrilous attack in a pamphlet that pretended to be Theophilus'
Apology. It is certainly not so entertaining as a frank confession
of that rowdy rascal Theophilus would have been, but then he
probably would have lied anyway. The writer soon shows his
hand when he admits that "the Life of no Man stood in more
need of Apology than mine." Colley Cibber is also blamed in
this publication, not only indirectly (as the father of such a
blockhead) but specifically (for the discursive and peculiar
style of his *Apology*). Would this and other attacks have been
avoided had Cibber's son not brought him such frequent and
unpleasant publicity?[12] The public never really liked Theophilus.
He found it difficult to stay out of debt even when he was
making a regular salary in the theater. For several seasons he
did not work at all, partly through his own fault and partly
because of his estranged wife Susannah *"privately agreeing, that
whatever Manager she played with, should by no Means receive
me into the same Company."* He tells us further: "I was banished
Drury-Lane Stage, because she acted there. And a Cartel sub-
sisting between the then Managers of the Theatres, I could not
be received at *Covent-Garden*, being on the *Drury-Lane* List."
Probably the managers of both theaters welcomed the excuse
to exclude such a troublemaker and the public seems to have
been well able to do without his mugging mummery for a while.
Even theaters where he had once been among the managers—
perhaps we should say, especially such theaters (Drury Lane
and the Haymarket)—were pleased to do without him. The
swaggering that distinguished his performance as Ancient Pistol,
when carried over into real life, was exceedingly unattractive.
His father, the perfect fop onstage, was never legitimately accused of being one offstage.

The public that took Susannah Maria Cibber to its heart grew tired of Theophilus. As the memory of his father's performances grew dim, the novelty wore thin of seeing the younger Cibber in the older Cibber's parts. Theophilus' exaggerated style of acting, suitable perhaps in the older farces, struck the wrong note in modern plays, influenced as they were by the elder Cibber's natural, easy style of comedy. The hack writing to which Theophilus turned when his stage career fell apart brought in but little. He alternately tried to make something out of being his father's son and fought with the old man as he did with everyone else. There was no help to be expected from Colley Cibber. Theophilus began to drink more. He sank into degradation in the same Covent Garden dives in which he had squandered his youth. Though Colley, too, had a taste for liquor and a penchant for gambling (as his father had had before him), at least the elder Cibber in his declining years had managed a little dignity. Colley was neither foolish nor generous enough to supply his reckless son with money; but, on the other hand, he was too vain to observe with equanimity the spectacle of a Cibber in disgrace.

When his father died (in December, 1757), Theophilus capitalized on public sympathy and obtained the permission of the Lord Chamberlain (who "consider'd the unfortunate, extraordinary condition of a Comedian") to "try his fortune, awhile, at the Little Theatre in the Hay-market." In Aaron Hill's *The Insolvent; or, Filial Piety* he stepped before the curtain, in full mourning, and delivered this lugubrious Prologue:

> Our scenes, to night, would Nature's pangs impart;
>   True filial piety should reach the heart.
> I feel it now—that thought the tear shall claim;
> To merit sacred, and immortal fame.
>   Now sleeps the honour'd dust, which gave me birth;
> Recent in death, but newly lodg'd in earth;
> Forgive the heart-felt grief! the filial lay!
> The public tear might drop o'er CIBBER's clay!
>   His comic force—for more than half an age!
> His well wrote moral scene, his manly page,
> Your fathers fathers pleas'd—His scenes shall live;
> And to your childrens children, equal pleasure give.

Theophilus then inserted a few more praises of his famous father (whom we might imagine spinning in his crypt), dropped a few more tears over his sad demise, and then made what moderns would call his "pitch":

Now for the father's sake, the son endure;
Let his paternal worth your Smile secure.
    Let his rich merit my poor wants atone;
His high desert I plead—boast none my own.
Let then this tribute, to the father due,
This public tribute, be approv'd by you.

It is nice to know that these benefit performances were "flops,"
—despite the fact that Theophilus was desperate for money.
Finally Thomas Sheridan, looking for some novelty to counter-
act the competition of the new theater in Crow Street, invited
Theophilus to make a few appearances at the Theatre-Royal in
Dublin. It was rather like accepting "a split week in the pro-
vinces," but Theophilus was in no position to refuse. Accordingly
he boarded the *Dublin Trader*—it was October, 1758—and,
with about sixty other passengers, set sail for Ireland. His
exit from the world's stage was to be as dramatic as his entrance:
a violent storm cast up the ship on the rocky coast of Scotland
and Theophilus Cibber was drowned.

Theophilus was not the only child to vex Cibber's old age.
There was also his youngest daughter, Charlotte, who arrived
when her mother was forty-five years old and who was "not
only an unexpected," she said, "but an unwelcome guest into
the family." If she was "regarded as an impertinent intruder"
at birth, Charlotte certainly devoted the rest of her incredible
life to being a wild buckeen, making sure that, if she were not
wanted, she at least would not be ignored.[13] The desire to be
noticed that had led her father to make a career on the stage,
that drove her brother Theophilus to the most preposterous
extravagances, assumed in Charlotte the form of a mania for
exhibitionism. At the age of four she dressed up ("that by dint
of a wig and a waistcoat I should be the perfect representative
of my sire") and paraded in the streets. This transvestitism and
exhibitionism were more than a child's play; they prefigured
Charlotte's later rebellion against her station and her sex. One
critic who kindly called it "a whimsical disregard for conventional
decorum" put it much too mildly.

As the youngest child she remained at home with her mother
long after her brothers and sisters had left, but she was proud
of being undomestic. She excelled instead in Latin, Italian, geo-
graphy, music, and dancing. She trained herself to act like a
boy, turned to shooting, gardening, grooming horses, and riding.[14]
Sent to live in a doctor's house to learn domestic duties,
she dressed herself in men's clothes and doctored the credulous

old women of the neighborhood, impressing them with sesqui-
pedalian Latin words and unpalatable concoctions. (Cibber was
amused—until he got the apothecary's bill.)

Colley, glad to relieve himself of such a burden as Charlotte,
rejoiced when he married her off to a young violinist at Drury
Lane, Richard Charke, even though it was clear that this flighty
young man was at least as interested in Colley Cibber's fortune
as he was in Colley Cibber's daughter. Charlotte was tempera-
mentally quite unsuited to be a wife, as was Richard to be a
husband. The marriage didn't last very long. Charlotte was left
with an infant child and Richard took off for parts unknown.[15]
Charlotte took up with another man—there was the baby to
think of—but, like her husband, he failed to support her. Colley's
patience ran out: there was no money from home, only letters
like this one:

Dear Charlotte:

I am sorry I am not in a position to assist you further. You
have made your own bed and therein you must lie. Why
do you not disassociate yourself from that worthless scoun-
drel, and *then* your relatives *might* try and aid you. You
will never be any good while you adhere to him, and you
most certainly will not receive what otherwise you might
from your Father

COLLEY CIBBER.[16]

Her lover died and Charlotte wound up in jail for debt.
She was bailed out by a disreputable woman who frequented
Drury Lane. To avoid being recognized, Charlotte left the jail
disguised as a man—and wearing the hat of the officer who had
detained her. She had to find some employment and, much to
her father's chagrin, she decided to go on the stage. She made
her debut (about 1730) as the ingenue in *The Provok'd Wife*
and played a number of roles, including some "breeches parts"
which called for male attire.[17] Then she turned, as her father
had done, from acting to playwriting. *The Art of Management: or, Tragedy Expell'd* Charlotte wrote as an attack on
Charles Fleetwood, the manager of Drury Lane, who had fired
her for immorality. The farce is set in Drury Lane after Colley
Cibber's time, and the characters include Brainless (Fleetwood),
Bloodbolt (Charles Macklin), Headpiece (Theophilus Cibber), and Mrs. Tragic (Charlotte). It tells of a monstrously
mismanaged theater, of hopelessly imcompetent directors, and

of a repertory that is about to give way to rope dancers. The actors split into two factions and contrive, in a way no less confusing than the squabbles of Cibber's time, to oust Brainless. When Fleetwood threatened to sue her, Colley Cibber intervened and convinced him to reinstate Charlotte at his theater, which was quite a triumph for a man whose enemies labeled him tactless, bumbling, and unpersuasive.[18] But Charlotte went on battling, tangled with Fleetwood again and John Rich, and finally gave up the stage. She wrote another play for Rich (*The Carnival; or, Harlequin Blunderer*, 1735) and much later her entertainment called *Tit for Tat; or, The Comedy and Tragedy of War* was produced at the New Theatre in St. James's Street, Haymarket. It was done several times at Drury Lane in 1749. The *Narrative* of her life gives still another theater piece of hers, a Prologue to *The Recruiting Officer* which is so lamentable that I would forbear to reproduce even a bit of it here did it not, in substance and in skill, recall the work of her father as Poet Laureate:

> May gracious heav'n the youthful hero give
> Long smiling years of happiness to live:
> And Britons, with united voices, sing
> The noblest praises of their glorious king;
> Who, to defend his country and its rights,
> Parted from him in whom his soul delights.
> Then with a grateful joy Britannia own,
> None but great George should fill the British throne.

Having left the theater, Charlotte took to wearing men's clothes all the time (for "substantial reasons," unspecified).[19] It never brought her to the point of facing her lover in a duel (as happens to one woman in a Cibber play), but it did enable her to engage in a whole series of improbable occupations and adventures. She opened a greengrocer's shop in Long Acre but she went bankrupt. She kept a public house in Drury Lane and was a waiter at another, The King's Head in Marleybone, until one of the women fell in love with "this young man." She was a strolling player in men's parts, under the name of Mr. Brown. She sold sausages in the street, was a printer's devil, and failed as a farmer. She was a pastry cook in Wales, a conjuror's assistant in Petticoat Lane, a performer at fairs. She was suitor to a young heiress (with £60,000) until a sudden twinge of honor obliged her to reveal her sex. (The girl refused to believe the story until offered ocular proof and, receiving it, fled tearfully into the country.) She was a valet to a lord (who knew of her sex) until his friends objected. She set up a grand puppet show over the tennis court in St. James's Street, near the Haymarket, "the most elegant ever exhibited," and opened to great success in 1737. But within the year she had worked herself to exhaustion and came down with a violent fever that forced her to take to her bed.[20] She took a house in Masham Street, Westminster, and nursed herself back to health. Then she rented a large hall owned by a Mr. Ashley and showed her puppets again but, unable to hire other manipulators, she had to sell them. She got about one twenty-fifth of their value.

Charlotte was constantly on the brink of starvation, but the rest of the Cibbers were fairly comfortable. Theophilus, though a wastrel, somehow always managed to find more cash to squander. Anne, another of Colley's daughters, ran a "Siam" shop for a while and then married John Boultby and left trade.[21] Elizabeth Cibber married Dawson Brett and then Joseph Marples and ran a restaurant in Fullwood's Rent, near Gray's Inn.[22] Charlotte's great enemy was her eldest sister, Catherine, who married a Colonel Brown and who, during Colley's last years, kept house for him (and Theophilus' two children by his first wife) in Berkeley Square, near Bruton Street. Charlotte felt that it was Catherine who turned old Colley against her and deprived her of his financial help, out of sheer malice. Perhaps that was true—perhaps, though Miss Senior's suggestion doesn't seem very convincing, Colley was angry because Charlotte had dared to play *his* role of Sir Fopling Flutter—but Charlotte was indeed cut off by the family. On March 8, 1755, she attempted a reconciliation.[23] Perhaps Colley never saw her letter, Catherine having intercepted it. In any case, the answer was merely her own letter, returned in a piece of blank paper which "might well have been filled up with blessing and pardon, the only boon I hoped for, wished, or expected." Might not Cibber's strict morality in his plays, what Theophilus called his "well wrote moral scene," have been quite sincere—and his knowledge of the world shrewd enough to enable him to see that in real life not every rake reforms, despite what sentimental comedies preach?

Her hopes of assistance from her father thus dashed, Charlotte became a strolling player to support herself and her child, an infant unwelcome (as a corrupting influence on Jane and Elizabeth) in the household of Colley and Catherine. She performed at a fair booth in the driving rain; found that she could then not speak above a whisper; and, deprived thereby of her means of livelihood, was reduced to having to pawn most of her own and the child's clothes. Then she somehow got money enough to rent a large house at Chepstow and determined to return to one of her many trades, that of pastry cook. A widow lent her money to set up in business, but she failed. She tried farming, but her sow was barren and her vegetables would not grow. She sold the furniture and left Chepstow. This must have been a great relief to Colley Cibber, who lived nearby and whom she had been unsuccessful in embarrassing into helping her. There is even a story that she tried more drastic measures; infuriated at parental parsimony, "the amazing Mrs. Charke equipped herself with a horse, mask and pistols, made herself up as a highwayman and waylaid her father in Epping Forest. Poor Cibber handed over his money, making only the rueful reproof: 'Young man, young man! This is a sorry trade. Take heed in time.' 'And so I would,' replied his disguised daughter, 'but I've a wicked hunks of a father, who rolls in money, yet denies me a guinea. And so a worthy gentleman like you, sir, has to pay for it!' "²⁴

Probably Charlotte, though quite capable of such an escapade, confined herself to putting on her "mercantile face," as she called it. This was not always a completely honest one either. One of her last dodges was refurbishing a shady pub in Drury Lane, borrowing money from an uncle a little more long-suffering— and a little less sensible—than Colley. This venture failed too, for Charlotte seems to have been alarmingly deficient in that business sense that brought her father the fortune with which he was now so distressingly loath to part.

Charlotte's last appearance on the stage was in 1759 and also rather unprofitable. Notoriety, though in those days it might obtain one an engagement or two (as it did in nineteenth- and twentieth-century American vaudeville), was no sound basis for a theatrical career. Theophilus Cibber may have courted it but Colley Cibber built his acting career without it. His plays suffered from the opposition to him as a manager rather than benefited by the fact that his name was a household word.

Charlotte also toyed with the idea of setting up a theater school for aspiring youngsters, though of course she had no hope of raising the necessary capital. The idea was, presumably, that young hopefuls could be trained in London under her cultured, refined aegis, rather than gain experience in the disreputable bands of strolling players who caravaned about the countryside, picking up jobs at fairs and laundry from hedgerows. She herself had traveled with these rogues and vagabonds and thought little of them.[25] She complained that the acting profession was being invaded by "barbers' prentices, tailors, and journeyman weavers" who "impudently style themselves players" despite the fact that they had no training, no talent, and "a dissonancy of voice which conveyed to me a strong idea of a cat in labour."

Indeed the provincial theaters, the road companies, the strolling mountebanks and players to be found in jerrybuilt booths at May Fair, Bartholomew Fair, Tottenham Court Fair, Southwark Fair, as well as at similar gatherings all around the country—all these must have been rather like the theatricals of the King and the Duke in Mark Twain's *Huckleberry Finn*. It was only in such theaters as Drury Lane, where Cibber had helped to establish the traditions of carefully supervised rehearsals and apprenticeship in the craft, that actors had the opportunity to learn their trade thoroughly. Without Cibber's help and encouragement such stars as Mrs. Oldfield, Catherine Raftor (Mrs. Kitty Clive), and Susannah Maria Cibber might have been no better than Charlotte Charke and her gypsy mummers, and might have perished in the same pitiful penury. Cibber had not only written a number of good plays for the theater of his time; he had contributed largely to creating the actors who brought them to life. Few dramatists have had such control as he over so many aspects of the production and acting of their works.

One day in 1755 Samuel Whyte and a friend, a bookseller, waded through the mud to "a wretched thatched hovel where it was usual at that time for the scavengers to deposit the sweepings of the streets." There they found the "tall, meagre, ragged figure" of Charlotte Charke (accompanied by a mangy dog named Fidele and a pet magpie) in whose new novel *The History of Henry Dumont* they had an interest.[26] She read them the book and asked thirty guineas for it. She settled gratefully for ten. Whether she ever received even that amount is not certain, but she died a pauper on April 6, 1760. What happened to her daughter, Cibber's grandchild, is not known.[27]

But Cibber ended his days in affluence. He was to be heard swearing like a trooper at the gaming tables of White's and other clubs; seen at the theater and the fashionable assemblies of London and Bath, Tunbridge and Scarborough; noted at court as Laureate, mingling with the great; observed, chattering gaily, on the arms of young beauties; received as a guest in the houses

of the great—entertained, it is said, by the Earl of Chesterfield
while Dr. Johnson, forgotten, fumed in an anteroom.

Perhaps it was the memory of that occasion that irked Dr.
Johnson, as late as October, 1783, into asserting: "I once talked
with Colley Cibber and thought him ignorant of the principles of
his art." Johnson also condemned Cibber for his immoderate
language and said that Cibber (who enjoyed access to social
circles from which the Litchfield lexicographer was clearly barred) had learned but little from "the great and the witty"
with whom he associated. Johnson forgot, apparently, how much
of what Cibber had learned of society went into his plays. He
laughingly told Boswell in a belittling tone that Cibber was a
"great man."

Perhaps Cibber did strut, affect to know more than he did,
and spice his conversation as highly with *demme*'s as Dr. Johnson
did with *Sir*'s; but what annoyed Johnson most was, despite
all, Cibber was well received and content in the glittering sets
of the Dukes of Grafton and Richmond, the Earl of Chesterfield, Samuel Richardson, and Giles Earl (First Lord of the
Treasury and inseparable crony of Walpole).

Cibber courted ladies as well as lords. The actor Macklin
described Cibber's "predominant tendency to be considered
among the men as a leader of fashion, among the women as a
beau garçon," With Owen Swiney he used to tag along after
Peg Woffington, who was no doubt amused by the antics of these
aged gallants and entranced by Cibber's conversation and theatrical gossip.[28] Benjamin Victor, who conducted a literary correspondence with Cibber during these years, reported that
Cibber "did not fail to transmit to me exact accounts of the
surprising improvements of *Woofington;* but as that very happy,
singular old Gentleman retained the Air of the Lover long after
the Age of Seventy, I attributed his encomiums on this Lady's
perfections in Tragedy, to the excess of his passion."[29] Cibber
met Peg Woffington before she became the darling of the town.
He was interested in her as an actress—too. He coached her in
roles, taught her the old-fashioned elocution of tragedy, and returned to the stage to play opposite her in *The Old Bachelor.*
He became jealous when other men started to take an
interest in her. His inability to appreciate Garrick may at least
partially be explained by the fact that the younger man stole
her away.[30] Sheridan described Peg Woffington's "great influence over all men that lived with her" and ticked her off as
"a most willing bitch, artful, dissembling, lewd and malicious."

Cibber took the loss of Woffington lightly, however, and apparently went on in dalliance. Victor described him as "the gay, blooming Colley" as Cibber continued to flirt at Bath with such as Miss Banks and Miss Howe. The novelist Richardson was moved to censure the old man: "What figures do Mr. Beau Nash and Mr. Cibber make hunting after new beauties and with faces of high importance traversing the walks!"[31] Richardson was also at Tunbridge to record Cibber's brief passion ("over head and ears" in love) with the much sought after Miss Chudleigh, the belle of the season, and to describe the pleasure that everyone took in hearing and repeating their twinkling conversations. Why it was just like the verbal fencing in a play! Cibber was smitten like a boy, but he was more the actor than the adolescent in his articulate wit.[32]

Silly as this may seem at his age—unless, of course, he had discovered some aphrodisiac comparable to the "balsamic corrorborant" advertised widely in the 1760's as a miraculous "restorer of nature"—it would be wrong of us to be overcritical. To ask dignity of senility is sometimes as foolish as to expect wisdom of youth. Even greater men—Yeats with his "parish of rich women" and embarrassing gland operations—have been ridiculous in old age.

More important than his fling with Miss Chudleigh was Cibber's relationship with the incredible Mrs. Pilkington, an adventuress who had just fled a scandal in Dublin that had involved—of all people!—Jonathan Swift.[33] She set up house in London right across the street from White's, a highly respectable gentlemen's club; and she soon had Cibber dancing attendance on her.[34] Partly with Cibber's assistance, it appears, she began to add to the income that was assured an attractive, enterprising woman residing in St. James's Street, opposite White's—she addressed poems to various patrons, who responded with a few guineas now and then. Summer came. The social season at the spas emptied the salons of the capital. Mrs. Pilkington was obliged to move to a cheaper part of town and, eventually, to take to the streets. On one occasion, it is related, starvation brought her to the brink of suicide, but a well-dressed gentleman came along at the opportune moment and she went to dinner instead of to her Maker.

Some of Mrs. Pilkington's verses were addressed to Cibber. When she was thrown into Marshalsea Prison (for debt), Cibber raised the money for her release.[35] She rewarded him with a New Year's Ode—how appropriate!—in 1743 which contained so

many superlatives, said Cibber, that it might well have been
addressed to an archbishop. Whatever benefits, poetical or otherwise, Cibber reaped at this time from this talented and industrious woman, he did in fact receive a substantial reward later
for his kindness to her. After Mrs. Pilkington had retired to Ireland, she published her *Memoirs* (1748), and, while Dean
Swift was naturally the principal figure in her first volume, she
made Cibber the sterling hero of her second. Even Cibber must
have blushed at this: "The Almighty raised me one worthy
friend—good old Mr. Cibber, to whose humanity I am, under
God, indebted both for liberty and life." One cannot guess his
reaction to her emphatic denial that Cibber had been prompted
by any but the most altruistic of motives: "I dare say nobody will
imagine that he served me from any carnal views, since

> If truth in spite of manners must be told,
> Why really seventy-six is something old."

How much truth there was in these popular memoirs of an
Irish adventuress is difficult to tell; how much pleasure old
Cibber felt in being coupled with Swift, even by so weak a link,
is easy to imagine.

Another great name in English literature that was coupled
with Cibber's at this time was that of Samuel Richardson. Cibber met him about the time that Richardson was writing *Clarissa*,
found the story very moving, and begged the novelist not
to let his heroine die. Mrs. Pilkington wrote to Richardson to
say that an untimely end for Clarissa, that paragon of virtue,
was too painful to contemplate: "Spare her virgin purity, dear
sir, spare it! Consider if this wounds both Mr. Cibber and me
(who neither of us set up for immaculate chastity) what must
it do for those who possess that inestimable treasure?"[36] That
was a fine touch ("who neither of us set up for immaculate
chastity"); but Clarissa, it was clear, ruined by Lovelace (a
profligate, though an earl's nephew), was too good for this
naughty world and had to be sent elsewhere for her virtue's
reward. In the earlier period, when Cibber was writing plays,
the matter would have been handled differently, but the century
and the bourgeois were progressing.

In 1747 Cibber published a fat quarto, virtually unreadable
today, on *The Character and Conduct of Cicero*, a pastiche of
somber history and flighty irrelevancies, jokes and snatches of
song in among the sober stuff like flowers peeping up among

imposing ancient ruins. But it pleased Richardson, who called it "spirited and pretty," "candid and impartial."[37] The next year Cibber's *The Lady's Lecture, a Theatrical Dialogue between Sir Charles Easy and His Marriageable Daughter* was less happily received by Richardson and his circle. They thought it tended to encourage children to be heedless of the advice of their elders, too "chearful," and not at all respectful enough of parental authority. They might have added that Cibber, who had such trouble with his own offspring, was scarcely the one to give instruction. Cibber and Richardson were always politely debating such points, Richardson being inflexibly upright and Cibber more liberal, as befitted his conduct and reputation. Cibber even suggested that somewhere in his dilated novel of *Sir Charles Grandison* Richardson find room to give his hero a little humanity. Grant him, said Cibber, one or two redeeming vices. Cibber laughed at the idea of a "male virgin"—Fielding had got enough fun out of that—and suggested that Sir Charles (already bedeviled by having to choose between Lady Clementina della Porretta and Harriet Byron) should also have a mistress, if only to provide him with the opportunity of virtuously renouncing her. This was the plot-making dramatist speaking. Cibber claimed it was possible that there could be "moderate rakes" and that men might be "criminal without being censurable." This was the writer of sentimental comedy's opinion; he could not convince the writer of sentimental novels. The trend that Cibber's *Love's Last Shift* had begun had now outstripped its originator.

But Cibber and Richardson had things in common. Cibber enjoyed Richardson's generous hospitality, and Richardson, the son of a Derbyshire joiner, was not above tuft-hunting and rejoicing to see his table graced by the Poet Laureate. Despite their differences over moral questions, they admired each other's work. (Cibber, always an astute critic, had consistently recognized the best, even when it was that of an enemy like Pope.) They must have had many lively debates at Berkeley Square and North End, for both men were voluble, opinionated, and dogmatic. But the times had passed Cibber by: when he contributed a letter to the epistolary novel *Clarissa,* Richardson thought it quite unsuitable. It made his Miss Harlowe act more passionately and think less mawkishly than he liked.

Cibber's literary friendships also included a bricklayer named Henry Jones, whom Chesterfield had picked up in Ireland and whom Cibber hailed as a poet in that era when the "natural" and the "untutored" were the rage. Cibber encouraged Jones

‌‌‌‌‌‌‌‌‌‌‌‌‌‌‌‌‌‌‌‌‌‌‌41

to publish his *Poems on Several Occasions* (1749) and the next year, his health failing, Cibber tried to promise the laurel to Jones, writing his own patron, the Duke of Grafton:

> May it please your Grace,
>
> I know no nearer way of repaying your favour for these last twenty years than by recommending the bearer, Mr. Henry Jones, for the vacant laurel; Lord Chesterfield will tell you more of him. I don't know the day of my death, but while I live, I cease not to be your Grace's etc: etc:
>
> COLLEY CIBBER

Chesterfield approved of this arrangement, wittily commenting that "a better poet would not take the post, and a worse ought not to have it." But Jones was not to step that easily into a vacancy. Cibber though aged, was of a sturdy constitution. He wrote on Christmas Day, 1750, to Richardson: "Though Death has been cooling his heels at my door these three weeks, I have not had time to see him. The daily conversation of my friends has kept me so agreeably alive that I have not passed my time better a great while."[38]

Death was to wait much longer. Cibber recovered completely. Unable to bequeath Jones the laurel, Cibber assisted him to finish a tragedy, *The Earl of Essex*,[39] which brought Jones some public notice, but he began to run about London with rake-hells (Cibber's son Theophilus among them), ran up debts, frequented the lowest dives which advertised "Drunk for a Penny. Dead Drunk for Tuppence," and lost both his reputation and his meager talent. Chesterfield dropped him.[40] Eventually Cibber did too. Jones disappeared into the slums which are found in any city of 700,000. In 1770 he went on a three-day binge and staggered into the way of a wagon in St. Martin's Lane. Henry Jones died in the poorhouse of his injuries.

Cibber, having recovered and robbed Jones of his "great expectation," went on hale and hearty and in 1753 he was as vigorous as ever. He sent his Birthday Ode as Laureate to the Duke of Newcastle (the Lord Chamberlain) with some lively remarks, though signing himself "in the completed eighty-second year of my puerility." In the same year he made his will, signing it with a flourish in the presence of a distinguished group of titled witnesses. He left £1000 each to Jane and Elizabeth, granddaughters by his son Theophilus, and to Theophilus and

his sister Anne he bequeathed fifty pounds each. His daughter
Elizabeth he remembered with a mere five pounds, for she was
now Mrs. Joseph Marples and comfortably well off. Charlotte,
who was destitute, however, he dismissed with a like amount—
"£5 and no more"—to make his disapproval abundantly
clear. The bulk of his estate was to go to Charlotte's bitter
enemy, Colley's eldest daughter Catherine Brown, with whom
(and a grandchild Elizabeth) Cibber lived at 20 Berkeley Square.

His will was not his last production. Occasionally he published
some little work. In 1751 it had been *A Rhapsody upon the
Marvellous, Arising from the First Odes of Horace and Pindar,*
an unimportant discourse on ancient poets and modern standards, and about 1754 he addressed to a friend of many years'
standing (the Duke of Newcastle) some *Verses to the Memory
of Mr. [Henry] Pelham.* He also published in miscellanies a
good deal of pedestrian verse. One of the best of these poems
is from the first volume of *The British Musical Miscellany*
(1734). It also appeared as a broadside:

THE BLIND BOY

O say! what is that Thing call'd Light,
    Which I can ne'er enjoy;
What is the Blessing of the Sight,
    O tell your poor Blind Boy?

You talk of wond'rous things you see,
    You say the Sun shines bright:
I feel him warm, but how can he
    Then make it Day, or Night.

My Day, or Night my self I make,
    Whene'er I wake, or play;
And cou'd I ever keep awake,
    It wou'd be always Day.

With heavy sighs, I often hear,
    You mourn my helpless woe;
But sure with patience I may bear,
    A loss I ne'er can know.

Then let not what I cannot have,
    My cheer of Mind destroy,
Whilst thus I sing, I am a King,
    Altho' a poor Blind Boy!

This poem was admired. His odes continued to be ridiculed in the periodicals:

On seeing tobacco-pipes lit with one of the Laureate's Odes
While the soft song that warbles George's praise
From pipe to pipe the living flame conveys,
Critics who long have scorned must now admire,
For who can say his ode now wants its fire?

But now Cibber spent little time at his desk and more at his club. In 1755 Horace Walpole noted him at White's, as vivacious and garrulous as ever, and recalled that twenty years before Lord Mountfort bet Sir John Blount that Beau Nash would outlive Cibber. In 1755 Lord Mountfort and Sir John Blount were both dead, and Cibber still flourished.[41] "How odd," confided Walpole to his diary, "that these two old creatures, selected for their antiquity, should live to see both their wagerers put an end to their own lives! Cibber is within a few days of eighty-four, still hearty, and clear, and well. I told him I was glad to see him look so well. 'Faith,' said he, 'it is very well that I look at all!'"

A member of White's since its earliest days, perhaps a charter member, Cibber was a fixture at the club. He was to be observed chatting with animation, playing a hand of whist, perhaps recounting in hushed tones his adventures with some girl he encountered in the Ranelegh Gardens. The old man seems to have been welcomed and respected at the club, despite Thomas Davies' comments to the contrary.[42] Perhaps it is understandable why a partisan of Garrick, from whom Cibber (as we have said) withheld due praise, might make fun of him; but it is difficult to understand the more serious attacks on Cibber from Edmund Bellchambers who, considering his lack of appreciation for his subject, was the rather surprising editor of Cibber's *Apology* in 1822. Bellchambers prefaced his edition with moralizing *de haut en bas* on Cibber's frailties and was willing to grant him no more than that he was "no hypocrite in his turpitude," which was damning with faint praise indeed. Bellchambers, I think, vitiates the force of his attack by his prejudice for Pope and his unwarranted exaggeration. The descent of a famous man into senility should be described with more sympathy. *Peu des gens savent être vieux.* To demand of a character as passionate, vain, and impudent as Cibber's that it mellow to a grand old age and totter with decorum to the grave is to expect white hairs to become a fool and jester.

The old age of Cibber certainly limits his claim to be considered as a beautiful soul, but I would not claim that title for him any more than I would claim it for Pope. Cibber's latter years, however morally reprehensible, cannot detract from his importance in literary history, where greatness and goodness have seldom been found in conjunction. Had moral perfection the decisive voice in literary fame, we should have lost many a man of genius (like Pope) and many a man of talent (like Cibber). Cibber lived, if you will, licentious and laureate: his official odes numbered thirty in all, and those who alleged he conducted affairs left them uncounted.

On Sunday morning, December 11, 1757, his servant looked in at Cibber's bedroom at six o'clock. The old man was sitting up in bed, in bubbling good spirits. At nine o'clock he was found dead. He had passed away full of years and of peace. He was laid to rest beside his father and mother under the monument Caius Gabriel Cibber had erected in the Danish Church he had built in Wellclose Square.[43] The monument and the church itself were demolished in 1869 to make room for some buildings for St. Paul's schools,[44] but Cibber lives in his literary remains.

Colley Cibber's importance must not be overemphasized by an enthusiastic scholar, but neither need one apologize for his life. Cibber was a superb actor and, in a career that lasted from 1691 (when he made his debut in a bit part in *Sir Anthony Love*) to 1745 (when he starred in ten performances of his own *Papal Tyranny in the Reign of King John*), he created an army of coxcombs "first in all foppery" and a host of sneering villains. I find that he played about 130 different parts. He was more than a famous actor, for he was equally active in both the literary realms of gold and the brazen world of commerce. He was one of the foremost theatrical managers in English stage history, running the leading theater over a very long period and with a success that belied his assertion that "a giddy negligence always possess'd me."

Cibber was a playwright of considerable talent and popularity. Besides writing tragedies, ballad operas, and many other stage pieces, he may be credited with launching the vogue of sentimental comedy. That alone would earn him a secure place in English literary history. He adapted, with great success, plays from the French and (boldly following Dryden's example and shrewdly assessing the taste of his own time) even Shakespeare. Cibber produced no *All for Love,* it is true, but his *Richard III* banished the Bard's version from the boards until the nineteenth century.

Moreover, Cibber was Poet Laureate, though his odes were as notorious as his other offspring—the obstreperous Theophilus Cibber and the incredible Charlotte Charke. He fought with Dennis and Mist, Fielding and Pope, and generally acquitted himself pretty well. He trained a generation of actresses and gave Kitty Clive her start. He knew Händel, worked closely with Steele, helped Richardson. He moved in the most glittering circles socially. He was an uncommonly just critic of playwrights and an acute observer of such theatrical luminaries as Betterton, "Nurse" Nokes, Sandford, Mrs. Barry, Mrs. Bracegirdle, Mrs. Verbruggen, Wilks, Booth, and others.

Of these and other personalities he gave us, as one critic has said, "a series of stage portraits which no lover of theatrical history would willingly let die," and these vignettes comprise only one of the features of a brilliant, honest autobiography which is also a scintillating and valuable history of forty years of the English theater, 1690-1730. It is not too much to say that Cibber is one of the most significant theatrical personalities of the late seventeenth and early eighteenth centuries.

Cibber deserves a better reputation than Pope's *Dunciad* would give him. Though Pope immortalized him, he slandered him too. Cibber was anything but dull. He was no stupid mountebank, no forgotten figure of fun. He was a lot more than the drunkard and fornicator Edmund Bellchambers described when he edited Cibber's *Apology* in 1822. Pope's portrait and Bellchamber's are false. It is better to look at Roubillac's colored bust of Cibber in the National Gallery in London; to study the cheerful, shrewd, frank, and ruddy face, the humorous expression of the thin lips that seem about to speak, probably with a little vanity and with more than a little determination. There is the man whose best work is well worth attention, a man who occupies a small but significant niche in the edifice of English literature. Let Warburton pronounce his epitaph:

> Cibber, with a great stock of levity, vanity, and affectation, had sense, and wit, and humour.

Notes and References

Chapter One

1. Caius Gabriel Cibber was born in Flensborg, Schleswig, in 1630; Jane Colley in Glaston, Rutlandshire, in 1646.
2. The Cibò family had produced Pope Innocent VIII (a Genoese named Giovanni Battisa Cibò, 1432-1492, elected successor to Sixtus IV in 1484), a man whom Savonarola attacked for his worldliness but whose descendants were still prominent in Cibber's time.
3. Throughout this chapter I am indebted for information on Cibber's father to Harald Faber, *Caius Gabriel Cibber, 1630-1700*, Oxford, 1926. Colley's father may have studied with Bernini in Rome. He then seems to have worked in the Low Countries, perhaps with de Keyser. I see in his work less of Bernini than Faber does, more of the exuberant Flemish baroque style of sculpture epitomized in the work of Artus Quellinus the Elder.
4. The warrant of this creation was signed by the Earl of Dorset, May 30, 1693. Caius Gabriel produced decorations for the royal palaces at Hampton Court and Windsor, for the City of London (the Monument, the Royal Exchange, the Steel Yard, etc.); for the Devonshires' country seat at Chatsworth (1687-1690); for Trinity College at Cambridge; and for Sir Christopher Wren's new cathedral, St. Paul's. Between 1694 and 1696 he built the Danish Church in Wellclose Square, served it as elder for the rest of his life, and erected there the memorial under which his wife, himself, and his famous son were all buried. It bore the arms of Cibber (Cibò) and his wife (Colley: Argent a cross wavy Sable), arms which Colley Cibber bore impaled throughout his life.
5. Lewis was a rake—even Colley used to scold him—but he did manage to get into Winchester (as Colley did not) and died (in 1711) a Fellow of New College, Oxford, soon after the Bishop of London had ordained him in holy orders. This is probably the direction Colley would have taken had he not been stagestruck at an early age.
6. Throughout I quote the first (1740) edition of *An Apology for the Life of Mr. Colley Cibber* . . . .

7. Faber, *op.cit.*, pp. 20-21. Caius Gabriel was forced to borrow money from his brother-in-law Edward Colley and from others to discharge his debts.

8. They were portraits of two of the inmates of the asylum, one of them Daniel, Oliver Cromwell's mad porter.

9. *Apology*, pp. 19-20.

10. *Ibid.*, p. 20.

11. *Ibid.*, pp. 21-22.

12. His descent was, presumably, indirect, for William of Wykeham was a priest under a vow of celibacy.

13. *Apology*, pp. 35-36.

14. Caius Gabriel was assisting William Talman and other architects in "raising that Seat from a *Gothick*, to a *Grecian*, Magnificence." The Earl belonged to a family famous for its patronage of the arts—his son was later to become one of the major collectors of Rembrandt drawings—and he considered it incumbent upon himself to transform his ancient country house from the Gothic style (then thought to be barbarous) to the newly fashionable Classical mode. Cibber's son later renovated old theater pieces and brought them up to date; he prided himself on his understanding of the current public taste, the latest fashions in dramatic art.

15. So glittering was the occasion, though, and so ravishing was Sarah Churchill, who was later to grace London society as the Duchess of Marlborough, that fifty years later Cibber was to remember that banquet in his autobiography as the high point of his brief military career. For information about the extraordinary friendship between Anne and Sarah Churchill, *cf.* Maurice Ashley, *The Stuarts in Love*, New York: Macmillan, 1964, pp. 251-52.

16. Pepys describes a time when Betterton and Harris, so overcome with giggles at some misadventure in a scene, doubled up with laughter and were unable to continue the play.

17. Thomas Davies, *Dramatic Miscellanies*, III, 417-18.

Chapter Two

1. He first appeared on the stage as a servant to Sir Gentle in Thomas Southerne's new comedy *Sir Anthony Love, or the Rambling Lady*. That year he also played Sigismond (seventeen lines) in *Alphonso, King of Naples* and Pyrrhot (a courtier, nine lines) in a revised version of Chapman's *Bussy d'Ambois*. In 1692 he was Albimer in *The Rape*, Splutter in *The Marriage-Hater Match'd*, and Pisano in *The Traitor*.

2. Cardell Goodman began his career in 1677 in *The Rival Queens*.

3. *Apology*, pp. 107-08. Command performances on short notice were not uncommon, for "His Majesty's Servants" were treated as such. On November 22, 1718, for example, though Drury Lane had posted bills and distributed flyers all over town announcing

The Orphan, the program was changed at the last minute to Cibber's *Love Makes a Man,* by the King's command. Even for a repertory company, this sort of thing must have been a strain.

4. Barker, who examined Shore's will in Somerset House, points out (*Mr. Cibber of Drury Lane,* New York, 1939, p. 18) that in it he still insisted on referring to Mrs. Cibber as Katherine Shore.

5. She played Hillaria in *Love's Last Shift* and Olivia in *Womans Wit,* both by Cibber; Galatea in Elkanah Settle's *Philaster;* Orinda in Mrs. Mary Manley's *The Lost Lover;* Biancha in John Lacy's *Sauny the Scot.*

6. *Apology,* p. 59.

7. *The Laureat: or, The Right Side of Colley Cibber, Esq.* (London, 1740) p. 103.

8. The style in tragic acting then, recalled Aaron Hill years later, demanded a sort of recitative in which "recitation was a kind of singing." Cibber decided to make an actress out of his son Theophilus' wife Susannah Maria Arne because she had a good singing voice. *Cf.* Alan S. Downer, "Nature to Advantage Dressed: Eighteenth-Century Acting," *Publications of the Modern Language Association,* LVIII (1943), 1002-37; Helen Ormsbee, *Backstage with Actors,* (New York, 1938); William Archer, *Masks or Faces?* (London, 1888).

9. Dr. Johnson talked with Cibber about this and there was a tinge of envy in his wry remark that Cibber had been only an outsider then, "had perhaps one leg only in the room, and durst not draw in the other." Such reticence on Cibber's part, outsider or no, might well have been appropriate, but Johnson ought to have known better than to have expected this uncharacteristic shyness of Cibber.

10. *Apology,* p. 119.

11. A. T. Bartholomew in "The Restoration Drama: III", *Cambridge History of English English Literature,* VIII, 192.

12. *Apology,* p. 124.

13. *Loc. cit.*

14. *Memoirs,* II, 201.

15. This is part of the opening soliloquy of Sir John Vanbrugh's play (1697).

16. In 1741 Cibber came out of retirement to play a benefit and grossed £182, a sum much above average then, in *The Provok'd Husband;* Garrick (in Cibber's *Richard III*) could draw only £171 of business.

17. These self-mitigating roles included, said Steele, Sir Fopling Flutter, Sir Courtly Nice, Sir Novelty Fashion, and Lord Foppington; Sparkish (*The Country Wife*), Witwould (*The Way of the World*), and Atall (*The Double Gallant*); Captain Brazen (*The Recruiting Officer*), and Gibbet (*The Beaux' Stratagem*); and such tragic villains as Richard III, Iago, Syphax (*Cato*).

Burleigh (*The Earl of Essex*), and Cardinal Wolsey (*Henry VIII*).

18. *Eutrephilia*, or well-bred arrogance, was an ideal of the Greeks.

19. The historical Richard, of course, was basely denigrated by Tudor hirelings. I deplore this treatment of him, for I concur in the judgement of Miss Jane Austen, who wrote charmingly at the age of fifteen: "I am rather inclined to suppose him a very respectable man." Read Josephine Tey's *Daughter of Time* or Taylor Littleton and Robert R. Rea's *To Prove a Villain*.

20. *The Laureat*, p. 35.

21. I am throughout indebted not only to Barker, Senior, and Habbema, but to De Witt C. Croissant's "Studies in the Work of Colley Cibber," *Bulletin of the University of Kansas, Humanistic Studies*, I, 1.

22. This is in Act II, Scene 1, of Vanbrugh's play.

23. He was briefly at the Haymarket for Owen Swiney and, after his retirement from Drury Lane, appeared now and then at various other theaters.

24. In July, 1709 Christopher Rich's arguments with his actors at Drury Lane caused him to have Zachary Baggs, the theater's "receiver and treasurer," publish an *Advertisement concerning the Poor Actors, who under Pretence of Hard Usage from the the Patentees, are about to Desert their Service*. We learn that Cibber received 5 pounds a week during a season of twenty-two weeks and a half, six acting days a week. (The season was shortened by the death of Queen Anne's consort, Prince George of Denmark. This closed the theaters between October 26 and December 14, 1708.) The season opened October 12, 1708. The theater was closed by the officials on June 4, 1709, and in between there had been 135 days of performance. For his work during this period Cibber received £111 in salary, £51.10.10 as proceeds from a benefit performance, and about fifty guineas more in tips at benefit time: total (according to Baggs) £162.10.10. Betterton, Estcourt, and Mills were getting £112.10., basic salary, only a pittance more than Cibber. Wilks, who conducted rehearsals as well as acting in almost every production, got £168.6.8, plus benefit proceeds.

25. He was able to purchase a tidy country house—the site of Walpole's famous Strawberry Hill later in the century, one writer asserts—and to risk very considerable sums in the popular speculation of the time, the South Sea Company. His London house was in Berkeley Square, and he eventually belonged to the best clubs and relaxed at all the fashionable spas.

26. On June 8, 1710, the Thursday *Tatler* carried a notice that, even when we remember that Steele was in effect trying to advertise a performance at Drury Lane, much commended Cibber's acting: "The first of the present stage are Wilks and Cib-

ber, perfect actors in their different kinds. Wilks has a singular
talent in representing the graces of nature, Cibber the deform-
ity in affectation of them. Were I a writer of plays [Steele was,
having written *The Funeral: or, Grief à-la-Mode* as early as
1701], I should never employ either of them in parts which
had not their bent this way. This is seen in the inimitable strain
and run of good humour which is kept up in the character of
Wildair, and in the nice and delicate abuse of understanding
in that of Sir Novelty. Cibber, in another light, hits exquisitely
the *flat* civility of an affected gentleman-usher, and Wilks
the easy frankness of a gentleman . . . . To beseech gracefully,
to approach respectfully, to pity, to mourn, to love are the
places wherein Wilks may be made to shine with the utmost
beauty. To rally pleasantly, to scorn artfully, to flatter, to ridicule, and to neglect, are what Cibber would perform with no
less excellence. . . . I have prevailed with the house to let the
'Careless Husband' be acted on Tuesday next, that my young
author may have a view of the play, which is acted to perfection both by them and all concerned in it; as being born within
the walls of the theatre, and written with an exact knowledge
of the abilities of the Performers. [This is an important comment on Cibber's dramaturgy.] Mr. Wilks will do his best in this
play, because it is for his own benefit; and Mr. Cibber, because
he writ it. Besides which, all the great beauties we have left in
town, or within call of it, will be present, because it is the last
play of the season."

27. Horace Walpole wrote a friend, December 3, 1741: "Cibber
plays to-night and all the world will be there."

28. The desecration planned on the corpse of Shakespeare aroused
so much opposition that Cibber canceled the 1736 performances
himself. In those days rehearsals for new plays went on for two
or three weeks—meanwhile the company played its repertoire—and Cibber's *King John* was nearing opening night when
one day the author, stung by coffeehouse quips, stamped on
stage during a rehearsal, snatched the manuscript off the prompter's desk, and, cramming it into his capacious pocket, walked
off without uttering a word.

29. Cibber brought forth his *Papal Tyranny* the more hesitantly
after it transpired that Garrick intended to present, at Drury
Lane, himself and Mrs. Susannah Cibber in competition,
in Shakespeare's *King John*. Colley Cibber was not the only
theatrical entrepreneur with a shrewd eye for the commercial
possibilites of mediocre old plays.

30. Quin and Pritchard were applauded for their bravura performances, Theophilus and Mrs. Bellamy hissed for their old-fashioned acting and dated, marionettelike gestures.

31. Thomas Davies, *Dramatic Miscellanies*, I, 14.

Chapter Three

1. *The Drama: Its History, Literature, and Influence on Civilization.* Victorian Edition. London, 1903, XV, 4.
2. Quoted in D. M. E. Habbema, *An Appreciation of Colley Cibber, Actor and Dramatist* (Amsterdam, 1928), p. 58.
3. Cibber wittily suggested in the Prologue to *Ximena* that Collier's crabbed pages were scanned by readers who wanted "But to be pointed to the bawdy plays."
4. Preface to *Ximena.*
5. *Spectator*, No. 10, March 11, 1711.
6. "Doubtless, it is unnecessary to find fault with the term 'sentimental comedy,' which is sanctioned by contemporary usage and actually adopted by Goldsmith in his attack upon sentimental drama. But it is important to recognize that the wave of sentiment swept over a wider field than that of English comedy, or even of English drama." The *Cambridge History of English Literature* X, 68 then mentions Destouches, Marivaux, Nivelle de Chaussée, Voltaire, and Diderot, concluding that in France the term *drame* "suggests the obliteration of the rigid line between comedy and tragedy. In England and on the continent alike, sentiment tended to break down the barriers of dramatic convention." Cibber's decision to make virtue and order triumph in comedy (as it had done in tragedy), if only at the last, made comedy's laughter less of "a distorted passion", more "serious," more moral.
7. *Dramatic Miscellanies*, III, 441.
8. *Rhetor. ad Herenn.*, Book I. Steele uses the Latin as the epigraph to *The Conscious Lovers.*
9. "In short, madam, the cravat string, the garter, the sword knot, the centurine, the burdash, the steenkirk, the large button, the long sleeve, the plume and the full peruke were all created, cried down, or revived by me."
10. "We may hope that Cibber had the grace to smile, if not blush, when he wrote those words, for in their conscienceless pandering they are surely among the most indecent ever written. And they are among the most permanently offensive—the very spirit of what is meretricious, and calculating, and mercenary, the epitome of all the crocodile tears and sanctimonious headshakes that crowd fast upon four acts of titillation and suggestiveness. After two or three such sentimental comedies, we sigh for the wholesome decency of Shadwell or Wycherley."—Louis Kronenberger, *The Thread of Laughter* (New York, 1952), p. 149.
11. *Critical Works*, p. 408.
12. Preface to *Womans Wit.* Another "hindrance" is that the play contains no character like Sir Novelty Fashion, the fop so unconscious of his hilarious foolishness that he can modestly and

sincerely turn aside a compliment on his popularity with "Stap my vitals, I don't believe there are five hundred women in town that ever took any notice of me." Not only is Cibber trying harder to write *Womans Wit,* but his characters are trying harder to be funny. When Cibber *strains* at wit, he always fails.

13. Corneille had come to England as early as 1637, when Joseph Rutter's *Cid* was played "before their Majesties at Court and on the Cockpitt Stage in Drury Lane." Sir William Lower, Mrs. Katherine Philips, John Dancer, and others all translated and adapted Corneille. John Crowne and Ambrose Philips both did versions of Racine's *Andromaque,* and Thomas Otway (*Titus and Berenice*) was only one of the other playwrights who made English successes out of Racine's works.

14. Our later comments on the theater and scenery in Cibber's time will make it clear that "unity of place" was dictated by some appreciation of "Classical" rules and not, as is the case in the modern Broadway theater, by financial considerations.

15. *The Laureat,* p. 102.

16. *Tatler,* No. 42, July 16, 1709.

17. *Shakespeare Without Tears* (New York, 1942), p. 62.

18. Richard III was seen in the Restoration in John Caryl's *The English Princess, or the Death of Richard III* (1667) and in "little starch'd Johnny" Crowne's *The Misery of Civil War* (1681).

19. *Shakespeare from Betterton to Irving* (New York, 1920), II, 153.

20. Garrick was first seen at Goodman's Fields in 1741. Pope saw the production three times and said Garrick would "never have a rival." London went "horn-mad" about him, said Thomas Gray.

21. Edmund Kean reintroduced the small, nervous character that Cibber had played, so brilliantly and so jerkily that Coleridge said watching Kean as Richard III was like "reading Shakespeare by flashes of lightning."

22. Hazlitt speaks in his *Characters of Shakespeare's Plays* (Vol. IV, pp. 165, 364, of the Centenary Edition of the *Complete Works,* 21 vols., London and Toronto, 1930) of "perverse consistency" and "vulgar caricature."

23. As for America, Cibber's *Richard III* (played in New York in 1750) was the first "Shakespearian" production seen in this country. Edwin Forrest's tours made it mean "culture" (and entertainment) all across the land.

24. Genest said Cibber was "wanton" and made more changes than anyone would believe. If Cibber did so, as was the case with Shakespeare himself, his success was his excuse. Furness' *Variorum* edition details all the changes.

25. William Gillette (born in Hartford, Connecticut in 1855) took

Conan Doyle's Sherlock Holmes, Dr. Watson, and Professor Moriarity, added eight characters and a main plot of his own, and created *Sherlock Holmes* (London, 1922). Première Buffalo, New York, October 24, 1899; in New York, November 6, 1899; in London, September 2, 1901.

26. Hazelton Spencer's *Shakespeare Improved* (Cambridge, Mass., 1927), analyses and compares the Shakespeare and Cibber versions in detail.

27. Cibber put in the death of Henry VI, undoubtedly, for sensationalism and with no political reason in mind.

28. Cibber last revived the play himself in 1739.

29. Cibber himself, as Richard, provided the "low, mincing curtails of magnaminity" required by the role, yet the third night (the author's benefit) yielded him a paltry five pounds. For recent comments see: Eleanor Prosser, "Colley Cibber at San Diego," *Shakespeare Quarterly,* XIV (1963), 253-61; Albert E. Kalson, "The Chronicles in Cibber's *Richard III,*" *Studies in English Literature, 1500-1900,* XIV (1963), 253-57.

30. *The British Theatre: Its Repertory and Practice* (London, 1960), p. 159.

31. Quoted in Barker, *op. cit.,* p. 46.

32. *Ibid.,* p. 47.

33. Susanna Percival (born 1667) made her debut at fourteen in D'Urfey's *Sir Barnaby Whigg.* In 1686 she married the comedian William Mountfort (killed by a Captain Hill in 1692). She appeared in Southerne's *Sir Anthony Love* (1690), in which Cibber made his debut, and (as Mrs. John Verbruggen, the wife of the actor who had been Cibber's closest friend at the time he joined the Drury Lane company) she appeared in many plays with and by Cibber: as Narcissa in *Love's Last Shift,* Berinthia in Vanbrugh's *The Relapse,* Louisa in *Love Makes a Man,* and Hypolita in *She Wou'd and She Wou'd Not.* Her daughter, Susanna Mountfort, had an affair with Barton Booth. Her acting career (1703-1718) was cut short by insanity. Cibber found Mrs. Verbruggen "Mistress of more variety of Humour than I ever knew in any one Woman Actress," and her death would have been a very great loss to him had not Mrs. Oldfield come along, rather unexpectedly. (Only a year before Mrs. Verbruggen's death *A Comparison Between the Two Stages* was hailing her as "a Miracle" while dismissing Mrs. Oldfield and Mrs. Rogers as "mere Rubbish that ought to be swept off the stage with the Filth and Dust.")

34. *Apology,* p. 177.

35. Before her roving eye lit on Brett and she married him to save him from the bailiffs, she had a lively career. She had once been Countess of Macclesfield, and it was rumored that the famous Richard Savage was her illegitimate child by the Earl Rivers. Her daughter elevated Mrs. Brett to the highest circles

when the young lady became the first English mistress of King George I.
36. Introduction (p. x), *Six Restoration Plays*, (New York, 1959).
37. *A History of English Dramatic Literature to the Death of Queen Anne*. 2 vols. (London, 1875), II, 597.
38. Sir George Etherege is characterizing his *Sir Fopling Flutter, or The Man of Mode*.
39. *The Careless Husband* had a long acting history; it influenced Steele's *The Tender Husband* (1705); it was translated into German as *Der sorglose Ehemann* (Göttingen, 1750); it was modified by Sheridan to make *A Trip to Scarborough* (1777). Barker, *op.cit.*, pp. 52-53, comments on various critical pronouncements on *The Careless Husband* and Habbema, *op.cit.*, devotes most of his study to a painstaking analysis. *Cf.* Harry Glicksman, "The Stage History of Colley Cibber's *The Careless Husband*," *Publications of the Modern Langauge Association*, XXXVI (19-21), 244-50.
40. *Critical Works*, p. 407.
41. Dennis was something of a pedant in this work of 1725. In his other sometimes abusive, sometimes judicious criticism, he was the sort of man who found Shakespeare lacking in "art and learning," who believed that "the end of poetry" was solely "to instruct and reform the world, that is, to bring mankind from irregularity, extravagance and confusion, to rule and order."
42. F. W. Bateson, "The *Double Gallant* of Colley Cibber," *Review of English Studies*, I (1925), 343-46.
43. A. H. Thorndike, *English Comedy* (New York, 1929), p. 357. A very useful book.
44. *Biographia Dramatica*, II, 173.
45. Mrs. Bracegirdle's last regular appearance was on February 20, 1707, in a revival of Banks' *The Unhappy Favorite*. She appeared on a later occasion in a single performance of *Love for Love* as a special favor to Thomas Betterton. (She had been brought up in Betterton's family, "whose Tenderness she always acknowledges," reported Edmund Curll, "to have been Paternal.")
46. Henry Dell (*fl.* 1756-1766) revamped Cibber's *Comical Lovers* in 1757 (for Covent Garden) as *The Frenchified Lady Never in Paris*, but Cibber's "original" remained unsurpassed.
47. Ernest Bernbaum, *The Drama of Sensibility* (Harvard University Press, 1915), p. 107.
48. Thorndike, *op. cit.*, p. 358.
49. Mrs. Centlivre, who wrote nearly a play a year from 1700 to 1722, had touched on this subject and so had James Shirley in *The Gamester* (1633). Edward Moore (1712-1757) produced an excellent bourgeois tragedy of this title in 1753. One of the most famous scenes of the century was in Mrs. Centlivre's *The Gamester* (1705) in the fourth act, when the gambling lover

loses his fortune to his mistress, who is disguised as a man.

50. James Miller, a clergyman, writing in the Dedication to *The Man of Taste* (1735).

51. Among the adaptations from Molière were Dryden's *Sir Martin Mar-all* (from *L'Étourdi*), Wycherley's *The Plain Dealer* (from *Le Misanthrope*), Vanbrugh's *The Mistake* (from *Le Depit amoreux*) and *The Cuckold in Conceit* (from *Sganarelle*), and Fielding's *The Mock Doctor* (from *Le Médecin malgré lui*) and *The Miser* (from *L'Avare*).

52. For this Dedication the dramatist received not only permission but £ 200 as well.

53. These lines are from the Epilogue to Dr. George Sewell's *Tragedy of Sir Walter Raleigh* (1719).

54. *Apology*, pp. 302-03.

55. The nonjurors were those English and Scottish clergymen who remained loyal to James II and would not swear allegiance (hence the name) to William and Mary in 1689. The archbishop of Canterbury, some bishops, and about 400 other clergymen in England thus lost their positions. They were joined by most of the Church of Scotland when Episcopalianism was there disestablished (1689) in favor of Presbyterianism. Though nonjurors theoretically were nonresisters of established authority, many were active in the Old Pretender's rebellion of 1715, and nonjuring took on political as well as theological implications. The "Bangorian Controversy," involving the nonjurors, began in 1717 when Benjamin Hoadley, Bishop of Bangor (Wales) preached a sermon before the King in which he asserted that Jesus Christ had delegated no authority to the Church. William Law, a Fellow of Emmanuel College, Cambridge, answered him for the nonjurors in several public letters which defended ecclesiastical authority and touched off a literary battle in which more than fifty writers and two hundred works were involved. It was against the background of this massive controversy that Cibber's *Non-Juror* was seen and argued. Among many articles relevant here are: W. B. Gardner, "George Hicks and the Origin of the Bangorian Controversy," *Studies in Philology*, XXXIX(1942), 65-78; three articles by D. H. Miles: "A Forgotten Hit: *The Non-Juror*," *Studies in Philology*, XVI (1919), 67-77, and "The Original of *The Non-Juror*," *Publications of the Modern Language Association*, XXIII (1915), 195-214; and "The Political Satire of *The Non-Juror*," *Modern Philology*, XIII (1915), 281-304; W. M. Peterson, "Pope and Cibber's *The Non-Juror*," *Modern Language Notes*, LXX (1955), 332-35.

56. Cibber probably got the idea from history: King George I granted such a pardon to the son of the Duke of Atholl after the Rebellion of 1715 had failed.

57. Laurent, Charles' opposite number in the Molière play, remains offstage throughout.

58. D. H. Miles, "The Relation of *The Non-Juror* to *Le Tartuffe*," Master's Thesis, University of Chicago, 1908, p. 12. Since we know that Cibber visited France several times (and was fond of putting French phrases into the mouths of his dandies) we may hazard a guess that Cibber translated his French sources himself.

59. Pope's "key" was *The Plot Discovered.* Pope's father had been a nonjuror who "never dar'd an oath, or hazarded a lie," and Pope himself was a devout Roman Catholic—as well as an enemy of Cibber. See Chapter Nine.

60. Barker, *op.cit.*, p. 108.

61. Bickerstaffe had already retouched *The Plain Dealer.*

62. Pierre Corneille's tragicomedy caused a great controversy in its time because the Academicians objected to the way it violated their ideas of Neoclassical unities (and seemed to condone dueling, prohibited by Cardinal Richelieu). The Academy condemned its story, style, and dénouement, but it has since been recognized as one of the glories of French literature.

63. *Corneille and Racine in England* (New York, 1904), p. 176.

64. The story was that Pope had offered to put finishing touches on Cibber's *Ximena* in exchange for Cibber's cooperation in producing *Three Hours after Marriage* at Drury Lane.

65. Molière was, in Cibber's time, only rivaled by John Fletcher as a quarry for dramatic materials. Altogether Molière influenced more than sixty surviving plays, from those by D'Avenant to those by Sheridan. Even *Les Femmes savantes* had already suffered a sea change to something called *The Female Virtuosoes* (1693) by the time Cibber got around to it.

66. Cibber himself was only one of thousands who speculated in the South Sea Company, formed by Robert Harley in 1711, a bubble which burst disastrously in 1720, ruining banks and individuals who had bought inflated stock—it went from 128½ to 1000 when the government got behind the company. It destroyed confidence in the unlimited expansion of credit. The government fell when the bubble burst. Sir Robert Walpole was appointed First Lord of the Treasury and Chancellor of the Exchequer to straighten out the tangle. To Cibber this meant the return of Walpole's friend Steele to power at Drury Lane and, eventually, Cibber's preferment at court under the Walpole administration (1721-1742). In writing a play about the South Sea Company, Cibber was once again dealing with a widely discussed political and social situation of his day.

67. *Cf.* G. W. Whiting, "Colley Cibber and 'Paradise Lost'," *Notes and Queries*, CLXIV (1933), 171-72.

68. William Wycherley in *The Double Dealer*, another play excessively heavy in plot, defines a "humour" as "some distinguishing quality."

69. Croissant, *op. cit.*, p. 25.

70. *"Une époque n'est bien connue que si l'on connait bien les choses que cette époque a particulièrement aimées."*—Louis Petit de Julleville.

71. Fletcher wrote more than a dozen plays with Massinger before 1623. This is one of the best of them.

72. Dorothy Fisher, *op. cit.*, p. 223.

73. H. W. Pedicord, *The Theatrical Public in the Time of Garrick* (New York, 1954), *passim.*

74. Barker, *op.cit.*, p. 142. Barker devotes some pages to detailing the "tricks of Cibber's trade" revealed by these changes.

75. "A Discourse upon Comedy in Reference to the English Stage: in a letter to a friend (1702)" as edited by Barrett H. Clark, *European Theories of the Drama*, (Revised Edition, New York, 1945), p. 221.

76. Cibber's play appeared in France in 1761 as *Le Mari poussé à bout.*

77. Thomas Davies, *op. cit.*, I, 108-09.

78. E. J. Burton, *op. cit.*, p. 160: "A simple plot, a gay or satiric delineation of the more or less accepted life of the period, could be made attractive and exciting by the selection of popular song tunes to which fresh words were fitted. The 'releasing' power of music which seems to strengthen every gesture and movement, and to sanction that theatrical enlargement of character and situation which most people find attractive (music removes the play from the conventions of naturalism), gave the new age its true and freer expression."

79. Actually *Polly* was suppressed by Walpole's government for purely political reasons. Cibber had nothing to do with it. *Polly* was not seen, however, for fity years.

80. The standard book here is E. McA. Gagey's *Ballad Opera*, New York, 1937. Gagey reports (p. 36): "In a record run of sixty-two performances, interrupted only by a few benefit nights, *The Beggar's Opera* proved to be the sensation of the age, reaching all parts of England, traveling to Ireland, Scotland, Wales, and Minorca, and bringing great profit to all concerned. [Gagey means to say that the sixty-two performances were in London. The "road companies," of course, brought the total number of performances much higher, and they did not star the London actors.] Gay netted £693 13s 6d from the four author's nights and sold the copyright of the play and the *Fables* for ninety guineas. His total proceeds have been variously computed from £2000 down."

81. Porpora was a Neapolitan singing teacher and composer well known in Italy. He had collaborated with the great Domenico Scarlatti and others. He wrote forty-four operas in all, five of them in England, where he became a Fellow of the Royal Society.

82. Pepusch was a learned German who joined the Drury Lane

orchestra as a violinist, became a cembalist, then a composer and organist to the Duke of Chandos (a post in which he preceded Händel). In addition to writing the pieces listed for Lincoln's Inn Fields, he also arranged *The Beggar's Opera, Polly,* and *The Wedding.*

83. Croissant, *op. cit.,* p. 5.
84. John Nicols, *Literary Anecdotes of the Eighteenth Century,* VIII, 294-95.
85. This advertisement appeared at the end of Thomas Parnell's *Poems on Several Occasions* (1726).
86. *Cf.* Leo Hughes and A. H. Scouten, *Ten English Farces,* Austin, Texas, 1948, p. 123.
87. Barker, *op. cit.,* p. 219n.
88. G. W. Whiting, *"The Temple of Dullness* and Other Interludes," *Review of English Studies,* X (1934), 206-11.
89. I date this piece from the fact that Thomas Arne was awarded the Mus. Doc. degree by Oxford University in 1759.
90. *Cf.* Croissant, p. 2, and Whincop's *Complete List of all the English Dramatic Poets,* p. 199.

Chapter Four

1. The patents granted by the King were "for the presentation of tragydies, comedyes, plays operas, and all other entertainments of that nature," and, though women's parts had previously been played by boys, each theater had permission to employ actresses as well as actors. The two patents remained in effect for more than one hundred and eighty years.
2. Killigrew's King's Company played temporarily in the Red Bull, an inferior theater in Clerkenwell which had been made over from an old bear-baiting pit. The company then moved into an old rectangular building in Vere Street. It had once been a tennis court, but they pompously styled it the Theatre-Royal.
3. D'Avenant's company began in 1660 in two surviving buildings in which the old drama had been presented, the Cockpit (Drury Lane) and Salisbury Court. Then they removed to Lisle's converted tennis courts in Lincoln's Inn Fields.
4. The theater has always been a perilous enterprise. As Sir Max Beerbohm observed some three hundred years later:

> The Theatre's in a parlous state,
> I readily admit;
> It almost is exanimate—
> But then, when wasn't it?

5. Charles Gildon's *Comparison between the Two Stages* described Rich as "a waspish, ignorant pettifogger." Gildon gives a good picture of the time in his *Life of Mr. Thomas Betterton* (London, 1710).

6. Leading actors such as Powell and Verbruggen were lucky to get their meager two pounds a week from Rich. In the *Apology,* p. 146, Cibber explained that "he kept them poor that they might not be able to rebel." So destitute were Goodman and Griffin, for example, that they had but one shirt and one bed between them. Once they quarreled over the shirt and Goodman (who had been expelled from college for rowdiness and had been a highwayman before he turned actor) offered to settle the ownership at sword's point. The two actors nearly killed each other in a duel.

7. They financed it by selling life subscriptions at one hundred pounds each to thirty affluent citizens.

8. Years later in his *Apology,* p. 183, Cibber demanded: "For what could their vast Columns, their gilded Cornices, their immoderate high Roofs avail, when scarce one Word in ten, could be distinctly heard in it? . . . This extraordinary, and superfluous Space occasioned such an Undulation, from the Voice of every Actor, that generally what they said sounded like the Gabbling of so many People, in the lofty Isles of a Cathedral—The Tone of a Trumpet, or the Swell of an Eunuch's holding Note, 'tis true, might be sweeten'd by it; but the articulate Sounds of a speaking Voice were drown'd, by the hollow Reverberations of one Word upon another."

9. *Cf.* Cibber's Preface to *Womans Wit.* Betterton got away with it; but when Doggett attempted to join Betterton in 1697 Rich had a warrant issued for Doggett's arrest, almost as if he had been a runaway slave.

10. Barker, *op. cit.,* p. 58, discusses *Visits from the Shades,* a little satire of 1704. Nathaniel Lee (born about 1653) was the "shade" in this case. He had drunk himself to death in 1692.

11. Cibber altered Steele's arrangement of scenes in *The Conscious Lovers,* doctored it as he thought fit, and demanded that Steele insert the subplot of Phyllis and Tom lest the whole be too grave for an English audience. He was right.

12. Charles Hart, the grandson of Shakespeare's sister Joan, spoke these lines in the Prologue to William Wycherley's *The Country Wife.*

13. Playwrights did not always get their benefit money. George Villiers, the great Duke of Buckingham, stood up and heckled an actress right off the stage on one occasion, ruining a play on the second night and thus depriving John Dryden, whom he disliked—see the merciless lampoon in *The Rehearsal*—of his third performance and his payment for the play.

14. Quoted in *Plays about the Theatre in England . . . 1671 . . . 1737 . . .,* D. F. Smith (London and New York, 1936), p. 207.

15. Charles Boadens' sentimental drama *The Modish Couple* was itself attacked in the Fielding farce, *Pasquin,* mentioned above.

16. *The Modish Couple,* Act IV.

17. A *History of Early Eighteenth Century Drama, 1700-1750*, Allardyce Nicoll, (London, 1929), p. 25. Students will also find a standard reference book in *A History of Restoration Drama, 1660-1700* (London, 1928), also by Nicoll. There is no work on Cibber's audience comparable to *The Theatrical Public in the Time of Garrick*, H. W. Pedicord, New York, 1954.

18. No one is sure of the date of Wilks' birth, but it cannot have been far from 1665, so he was a few years older than Cibber.

19. Farquhar's *Complete Works* were edited by C. A. Stonehill in two volumes (London, 1930). If Farquhar gave Wilks one of his best parts, Wilks repaid the debt, for it was a gift of twenty guineas from his close friend Wilks that enabled Farquhar to write his last (and in many ways his best) play, *The Beaux' Stratagem* (1707). When Farquhar died soon after, Wilks became the guardian of his orphaned daughters.

20. Curll also handled Betterton's famous *History of the Stage* and many other books by and about theater personalities. He was not overly honest.

21. William Prynne (1600-1669) was an enthusiastic moralist, or a moral enthusiast. His fat, fanatic *Histriomastix*, with all its notes and references, runs to about eleven hundred pages and is the *locus classicus* of Puritan railing against the stage.

22. John Evelyn and others had already deplored the immorality of the Restoration stage, but it took Jeremey Collier (armed with "good sense" of the Thomas Rymer variety) to pillory the immodest, the licentious, and the profane. His *Short View of the Immorality and Profaneness of the English Stage* (1698) was chiefly directed at others, but Cibber was touched on at least once, when Collier denounced Lord Foppington for saying that Sunday was "a vile day" and raved about *The Relapse:* "I almost wonder the smoke of it has not darkened the sun, and turned the air to plague and poison." The reaction produced by Collier's book was immediate but not long lasting. "Congreve," said Cibber, "seemed too much hurt to be able to defend himself," but Vanbrugh, for instance, expressed the hope that "nobody will mind" what Collier said. Cibber's comedies and other plays that followed Collier's fireworks, says the *Cambridge History of English Literature* (VIII, 168), "afford no evidence of a chastened spirit." Cibber was never obscene, though he sometimes confesses to being "lewd," but I doubt very much if he could have heard without a smile the advice of Maecenas, the patron of Dramatick, in *The Author's Triumph: or, The Manager Manag'd* (1737):

> I need not warn you, Sir, that no Obscenity must stain your Page: That virtue and Religion must ever be sacred, and Majesty rever'd: That your Satyr must be levell'd at Vice alone, for personal Abuse is Cruelty: That Wit must be ever Attendant on good Manners: And that the Thirst of Fame must

give Way to the Satisfaction of deserving it.
The World's Applause affords but little Rest.
'Tis conscious Merit makes the Mortal blest.

Chapter Five

1. Swiney was promised a hundred guineas a year in salary, Rich's complete cooperation, the use of any of Rich's actors he needed, and half the profits. In exchange Rich was to exercise control over all theatrical production and have both theaters under his aegis.
2. Rich sued actors who left him for breach of contract.
3. He had bought a fairly large interest in Drury Lane from Sir William D'Avenant's son Alexander, but he had long retained it quietly, content to allow Rich to exercise the patent.
4. *Apology*, p. 216.
5. *Ibid.*, p. 219.
6. As the authors in those days relied on their "benefits" (the receipts of the third night's performance), so the actors had "benefits" (gala performances at which the star of the night usually played his most popular role and collected the takings and tips). These bonuses formed a significant part of the actor's income.
7. Swiney's lease on the theater from Vanbrugh still had fourteen years to go. An unpublished manuscript in the Harvard Theatre Collection summarizes the eight points of Swiney's agreement with Wilks, Doggett, and Cibber, the major article being (abbreviations expanded): "That after all Charges thus paid and clear'd Mr. Swiney Shall Receive £300 a Year out of the Profits in consideration of his pains and care in the government &c. That Mr Wilks Mr Dogget and Mr Cibber Shall for their care in Managing and for their Acting on ye Stage receive each £200 a year and Mr Wilks £50 more for Attending and taking care of Rehearsals. And After these payments [are] made, the clear Profits Shall be divided into two equall parts, one of which to be detained by Mr. Swiney and the other to be Equally divided between Mr Wilks Mr Dogget and Mr Cibber, The Losses if any to be allow'd for after the Same proportion." This document is in Owen Swiney's hand and was addressed to the Lord Chamberlain as "Mr Swiney's Case" at the time when he argued with his partners.
8. *Henry VIII*, Act III, Scene 2.
9. Collier's only real success in the 1709-1710 season was when Mrs. Santlow drew crowds for Shadwell's *The Fair Quaker of Deal*. The Haymarket lost money.
10. This letter is among the unpublished papers of Owen Swiney in the Harvard Theatre Collection. It sounds a trifle more desperate or defiant than "Mr Swiney's Case, humbly Offerd to ye Consideration of my Lord Chamberlain," already quoted in

part, which concludes: "Mr Swiny therefore most humbly prays that my Lord Chamberlain will please by his authority to Compell the Said Mr Wilks Mr Dogget and Mr Cibber to proceed According to ye true tenure and meaning of the above Receited Contract, And that it may be enter'd in the Books of his Grace's Office That by inserting their Names in the License, there was nothing intended to Annull or Invalidate their former Agreements but only to give them an Equall power in the Management."

11. Twenty years later he returned. Old quarrels were forgotten. Cibber played a benefit for Swiney at Drury Lane in 1735 and the two were such cronies that one could scarcely believe that they had ever bickered. Indeed, they were rivals by that time only for the attention of the actress Peg Woffington.

12. Considering all that his *Tatler* had done for the theater in the way of free advertising, Steele was entitled to his share.

13. In the 1714-1715 season, when the competition from the theater in Lincoln's Inn Fields reduced Drury Lane's profits by two-thirds, Steele obligingly accepted the managers' offer of an equal share in lieu of his seven hundred pounds.

14. Cibber's date in the *Apology* is in error. There are a number of places where the *Apology* requires correction or explanation. (R. W. Lowe's editions are very helpful in this respect.) The patent was to remain in effect during Steele's life—he died in 1729—and for three years after for the benefit of his heirs.

15. Barton Booth (1681-1733) spent six years at Westminster School and then appeared on the stage as the noble Oroonoko at Smock Alley, Dublin, making his debut at the age of seventeen. Thomas Betterton engaged him to play at Lincoln's Inn Fields (1700-1704) and took him to the newly erected theater in the Haymarket (1705), where he remained for about four years. Then he came to Drury Lane, playing the Ghost to Wilks' Hamlet and a number of other roles, mostly bravura roles for which his handsome face, sonorous declamation, and commanding bearing fitted him. He soared to fame as Pyrrhus in Ambrose Phillips' *The Distressed Mother*, a version of Racine's *Andromaque* for which Steele wrote the Prologue and to which his Will Honeycomb takes Mr. Spectator in *Spectator* 290.

16. *Apology*, p. 268.

17. *Ximena*, though first acted in 1712, had been published only two months before.

18. This was a Dryden play of 1680 then still popular. Very few modern readers have read past its Preface on tragi-comedy.

19. Steele held strong political views—he had been expelled from Queen Anne's Parliament for them—and had opposed the Duke of Newcastle on both political and private issues. He had written to Newcastle to protest the suspension of Cibber ("a Principall

Actor") and this apparently had brought the Duke's temper to a boil.

20. The seventh issue discusses Cibber's "address and capacity," particularly in self-mitigating roles.
21. The appointment of Steele's friend Sir Robert Walpole to the Exchequer brought Steele back into a position of power.
22. Steele's *Correspondence,* Rae Blanchard, *ed.*, London, 1941, p. 172.
23. *Cf.* John Loftis, *Steele at Drury Lane,* Berkeley, California, 1952.
24. On April 12, 1722, they made an agreement with John Rich of Lincoln's Inn Fields that no actor employed by one house could play at the other (under penalty of twenty pounds) without the consent of both managements. On September 22, 1722, they agreed how many "house seats" each partner would get at Drury Lane: each of the four partners was to receive weekly a sealed envelope containing twelve free tickets to the week's performances, and no more.
25. Steele's *Dramatic Works* were edited by G. A. Aitken, London, 1894.
26. *Apology,* p. 307.
27. Cibber, Booth, and Wilks countered effectively: since they had three pockets out of which to pay lawyers, and Doggett had but one, the triumvirate deliberately dragged out the litigation as long and as expensively as possible.
28. He drew full houses in such roles as Othello, Lear, Brutus, Hotspur, and Henry VIII, to mention only his Shakespearian successes.
29. *Apology,* p. 262.

Chapter Six

1. Throughout this chapter I draw on such theater histories as Allardyce Nicoll's *History of Restoration Drama* and *History of Early Eighteenth Century Drama;* Montague Summers' *The Restoration Theatre* (New York, 1934) and *The Playhouse of Pepys* (New York, 1935); and my own doctoral dissertation, "The Management of The Theatre-Royal in Drury Lane under Cibber, Booth and Wilks," Princeton University, 1956. On the basis of the unpublished manuscripts in the latter (bills, receipts, letters, etc., of the managers of Drury Lane 1713-1716), we can say that the Drury Lane company in that period listed three managers (Cibber, Booth, Wilks), thirty-eight actors, twenty-six actresses, and a child. Of the dancers employed during the period the names of five are known. The "front of the house" and stage crews included a stage manager, a treasurer, box-keepers, stagehands, a house tailor, a propertyman, a script clerk, seamstresses, and laundresses. Four different music clerks and copyists were hired from time to time and, although we know

the name of but one musician (Mr. Sorine—guitar), the size of
the regular orchestra can be guessed from the fact that the copyists usually charged for preparing twelve parts. The payroll also
included the constable, the watch, the sweeper, and Mrs. Struke
(the cook).

2. Cibber's *Apology* tells us that in 1712-1713 the managers made
£4000, in 1713-1714 about £3600, and in the autumn of 1714
alone £1700.

3. Steele described the patent as "a lasting Authority" in his petition to "the King's Most Excellent Majesty."

4. By modern standards Garrick, who mouthed rather than mum-
bled, would be regarded as "hammy," but in 1774, in *The Retaliation*, Oliver Goldsmith celebrated Garrick's easy, natural style
on stage: "On the stage he was natural, simple, affecting;/
'Twas only that, when he was off, he was acting."

5. Wilks' fortes were grief, tenderness, and resignation, in addition
to his natural bents toward amiability and arrogance.

6. Cibber tried to keep ad-libbing in check, but it was common.
"You are never to perplex the drama with speeches extempore,"
warns Clinket in Hamletlike admonition in *Three Hours after
Marriage* (1717). "Madame," replies Plotwell (Cibber), " 'tis
what the top players often do." It was ad-libbing in this very play
that earned Cibber the enmity of Pope.

7. Summers, *Restoration Theatre*, p. 270: "Throughout the eighteenth century, and later, well-nigh innumerable references to the
traditional green carpet, which playgoers loved to see, might be
cited from prose and poem."

8. Garrick's epilogue to Home's *Alfred*.

9. A newspaper of 1723 questioned the need for it: "King Duncan
has not had a new habit for the last century, Julius Caesar was
as ragged as a colt, and his guards were a ragged regiment; only
the parts played by the managers were well dressed."

10. The tragic actress was attended by a page at all times, even
when the playwright made a necessary point of secret trysts
or loneliness. Mrs. Oldfield complained: "I hate to have a Page
dragging my Tail about."

11. Addison's *Spectator* for April 18, 1711, exaggerated very little
when it said:

> The ordinary Method of making a Hero, is to clap a huge
> Plume of Feathers upon his Head, which rises so very
> high, that there is often a greater length from his Chin
> to the Top of his Head, than to the sole of his Foot. One
> would believe, that we thought a great Man and a tall
> Man the same thing. This very much embarrasses the Actor,
> who is forced to hold his Neck extremely stiff and steady
> all the while he speaks; and notwithstanding any Anxie-
> ties which he pretends for his Mistress, his Country or his

Friends, one may see by his Action, that his greatest Care
and Concern is to keep the Plume of Feathers from falling off his Head. For my own part, when I see a Man uttering
his Complaints under such a Mountain of Feathers, I am
apt to look upon him rather as an unfortunate Lunatick,
than a Distressed Hero.

It was true that the hero and his panache were as inevitably
at cross-purposes in plays of this sort as were love and honor,
love and country, or love and friendship. All these headdresses
were expensive to purchase and startlingly costly to have cleaned. In
one bill (November 16, 1714) there is a charge of one pound
for dyeing a "Roman feather" scarlet for Mr. Mills. The managers balked at the cost—they were in the habit of discounting
bills, paying round numbers and ignoring odd pence—but in
this case the dyer received the full amount for he "wou'd not
abate one farthing." Mills had to have the feather. He no sooner
could have gone on without it than he could have dispensed
with his truncheon or his Tarquin stride.

12. Nicholas Rowe, author of *Tamerlane, Jane Shore,* and *The
Fair Penitent* (three of the six most frequently acted tragedies
of the period 1702-1776), was Poet Laureate from 1715 to
1718. He edited Shakespeare's *Works* (6 vols.) in 1709, with
illustrations. Gertrude, in the same picture, might have stepped
without arousing comment (except for her facial expression) into
"the court of good Queen Anne."

13. Philip Henslowe's *Diary,* edited by Sir Walter W. Greg (2 vols.,
1904-1908), supplemented by *Henslowe Papers* (1907) and a
couple of fragments published since, records many expensive
items of apparel which he (a Tudor and Stuart theater manager)
bought for actors.

14. His "first Entry" was a "Lantdchap of the West-*Indes,*" very
detailed, with flora, fauna, and "Natives, in feather'd Habits
and Bonnets."

15. *Apology,* p. 297.

16. Failure to change the wings to match the shutters or backdrop
sometimes led to an incongruous avenue of trees in a drawing
room or impressive colonnades in a supposedly virgin forest.
Cibber's production of *The Tempest* required six sets of wings,
and they caused some trouble.

17. Phillipe Jacques de Loutherbourg (who came to London from
Strasbourg in 1771 and was soon after employed as scene de-
signer at Drury Lane) is popularly supposed to have introduced
transparent scenery and made possible spectacular effects such
as moonlight, cities on fire, volcanoes in eruption, etc. But
students of theater history know that such "petty wonderments"
were (with painting and carpentry) "the soul of masque" in
Ben Jonson's time and that he used transparencies in his *Oberon,*

The Fairy Prince, a New Year's masque of 1611. A manuscript of December 23, 1714 records Cibber's Drury Lane using 2000 "small Nayles that Mr Howard had to nayle the Caleco for ye transparent figures in the Haven" and another speaks of "Transparients: in Oyle Varnished and ye fronts New Colourd" for *The Tempest.*

18. Perhaps as late as Cibber's age the Restoration backdrops survived on which human figures were depicted. It must have required a Zeuxis to achieve the willing suspension of disbelief demanded of an audience asked to view actors rushing about the stage before a backdrop on which static figures were painted, frozen in attitudes of horror and flight. In the nineteenth century furniture was still occasionally painted on the backdrop.

19. Steele in *The Tatler* for July 16, 1709, gave a mock inventory for Drury Lane which included "Groves, Woods, Forrests, Fountains, and Country Seats, with very pleasant Prospects on all Sides of them. . . ."

20. Steele reported in *The Spectator* for Saturday, August 11, 1711, that Johnson and Bullock, Jr., narrowly escaped serious injury in Sir Francis Fane's *Love in the Dark,* a satire on *Psyche.* As the players attempted this:

> Players turn Puppets now at your desire,
> In their Mouth's Nonsense, in their Tail's a Wire,
> They fly through Clouds of Clouts, and Showers of Fire.

Predictably they got tangled in the wires.

21. Moreover, the real thing did not look unreal under the lights they had, as it sometimes does under our more brilliant illumination, for the "glare" of which Gainsborough complained in Garrick's time had not yet come in.

22. Later these advertisements seem to have been carried free, as a public service.

23. Fielding in *The Historical Register for 1736* denied Cibber and the other managers even this excuse for their disrespectful handling of dramatic offspring, making Ground-Ivy (Cibber) say that "it was a maxim of mine, when I was at the head of theatrical affairs, that no play, though ever so good, would do without alteration" and, when the Prompter speaks of public opinion and taste, Cibber and Charles Fleetwood say:

> *Ground-Ivy.* Damn me, I'll write to the town and desire them to be civil, and that in so modest a manner, that an army of Cossacks shall be melted . . . I tell you, Mr. Prompter, I have seen things carried in the house against the voice of the people before today.
> *Apollo.* Let them hiss, let them hiss, and grumble as much as they please, as long as we get their money.

24. John Genest, *Some Account of the English Stage* (Bath, 1832), II, 390, quotes this story from Cibber's time: "A lady offered a play to the perusal of Cibber, in which she had drawn the char-

acter of an impudent fellow who acted under his own appearance
two different persons . . . [and] this character Cibber scouted
extremely—the poor lady was beat out of her design; but as
Cibber had the play for some time in his hand, he culled out
this very character, and had it acted as his own [creation]."

Chapter Seven

1. Walter Hamilton, *The Poets Laureate of England* (London,
   1879), p. 172.
2. Mr. Masefield has now occupied the post longer than Cibber,
   who held the record for longevity as Laureate before this.
3. *The Non-Juror* firmly established Cibber on the side of the Hano-
   vrians, and so pleased the King that he graciously permitted
   Cibber to dedicate the play to him (in the blackest type) and
   rewarded the author with a purse of £200. The Laureateship followed.
4. *Cf. Ballads and Songs Loyal to the Hanoverian Succession
   1703-1761*, edited with an introduction by John J. McAleer.
   Augustan Reprint Society, 96. Los Angeles: Clark Memorial Library, University of California at Los Angeles, 1962.
5. Miss Senior, *op. cit.*, says (p. 116n), that Cibber was the last to
   enjoy the traditional payment in wine as well as in money. Cibber was a friend of the Duke of Grafton, the grandson of one
   of the bastard children of Charles II. In 1724 he had become
   Lord Chamberlain and as such held the post of Laureate in his
   gift. Eusden had capitalized on his friendship with the Duke of
   Newcastle in 1717 in a similar way.
6. The couplet is from the satire "The Election of a Poet Laureate
   in 1719" by John Sheffield, Earl of Mulgrave (and later Duke
   of Buckinghamshire).
7. London newspapers (such as *The Daily Post*) and Dean Swift
   (as far away as Ireland) considered Duck as good as appointed
   almost before Eusden was cold.
8. One poor weaver of Spittlefields was inspired to address the
   Queen in a miscellany of verse that included the deathless line:
   "*Thy fortune*, DUCK, *affects my kindred mind.*" Joseph Spence
   claimed Duck learned English "just as we get Latin."
9. For one thing, Pope was a Catholic.
10. Richard Savage was born in London about 1697. He main-
    tained he was the illegitimate son of Earl Rivers and the Countess
    of Macclesfield, and wrote a poem *The Bastard* (1728) about
    it. He died in debtors' prison in Bristol on August 1, 1743. Dr.
    Johnson wrote a *Life of Savage* and included it, slightly revised,
    in his *Lives of the Poets*. It records vividly the dismal existence
    of the Grub-Street hackwriter, a life Cibber's success in the
    theater and the court spared him.
11. Caligula, Roman emperor 37-41 A.D., "is reported to have

made his horse a consul and a member of a priestly college."
Columbia Encyclopedia, Third Edition (Columbia University
Press, 1963), p. 319.

12. This must have taken on special significance on that occasion
when Cibber's tomboy daughter, the arrant Charlotte Charke,
played Lord Place.

13. Harry Carey ridiculed Cibber's appointment in *Of Stage Tyrants*
(1735), printed in Wood's edition of his *Poems* (p. 104), in
verses so scathing that Wilks denied Carey "the liberty of the
scenes" (access backstage) at Drury Lane. Thomas Davies reports (*Dramatic Miscellanies,* II, 255) that Wilks was "surprised
at his impertinence, in behaving so improperly to a man of
such great merit." Wilks clearly spoke as a friend of Cibber
rather than as a friend of literature. Carey's satire *Chrononhoton-
thologos* (1734), billed at the Little Theatre in the Haymarket
as "Being the Most Tragical Tragedy, that ever was Trage-
diz'd," had already earned him the ire of the Drury Lane management for his outspoken satire.

14. Had Swift been in London his fate might have been different.
Motte, who printed Swift's poem in London, and Mary Barber,
a friend of Swift who had brought the manuscript over from
Ireland, each went to jail for a year for their part in the publication.

15. Robert Southey was Poet Laureate from 1813 to 1843. He
wrote some successful short poems, but his larger works were
largely failures. "While his acorns mouldered in the ground,
these small seeds took root," says Samuel C. Chew in *A
Literary History of England,* edited by Albert C. Baugh (New
York, 1948), p. 1162. (Students will find this one of the very
best standard histories.)

16. The characters referred to in stanzas 3-5 are respectively from
Love's Last Shift, The Careless Husband, and *The Provok'd
Husband.*

17. Miss Senior, *op. cit.,* prints this ode as Appendix C.

18. I found this in the uncatalogued papers of the Folger Shakespeare Library in Washington, D.C., and have expanded some
abbreviations and corrected a few spelling errors. Final judgment on Cibber's bad verse should not be pronounced until that
of other Poets Laureate has been examined. E. S. Turner in
The Court of St. James's (London, 1959), devotes a whole chapter to the subject ("The Clown of Parnassus") and quotes numerous examples of official odes that vie with Cibber's or surpass
his in incompetence.

Chapter Eight

1. *The Laureat: or, The Right Side of Colley Cibber, Esq.* was
published anonymously in London, 1740. Once again it seems
to have been a case of personal criticism of the author rather than

aesthetic objection to the work, which has always and justly been praised. Blanch M. Baker's standard bibliography on *Theatre and Allied Arts* (New York, 1952) says of the *Apology* (p. 232): "This famous work has gone through six or more editions, being revised and expanded from time to time. . . . Cibber's work is considered a valuable theatrical document of a remarkable period in stage history, being a description and criticism of the art of the theatre, the actors, acting, management, productions, and of the social life and manners of that day."

2. Cibber made about £1500 out of it in the next decade and then sold the copyright to Robert Dodsley for £52/10/—. It was reprinted throughout the eighteenth century—Edmund Bellchambers' "new edition, with many critical and explanatory notices" (London, 1822) was the fifth edition—and R. W. Lowe edited it in limited editions ("with notes and supplement," London, 1889, 510 copies, and in a "Connoisseur Edition" of 150 copies for the Grolier Society, London, 190-?). The edition of 1756 "with modern modifications of spelling and punctuation" was issued in a limited edition of 450 copies in two volumes by the Golden Cockerel Press, London, 1925. I quote the first edition thoughout.

3. The word "autobiography" was not to be used in English, as far as I can tell, until Robert Southey employed it in a review in the nineteenth century.

4. Edgar Johnson, *One Mighty Torrent: The Drama of Biography* (New York, 1955), p. 107.

5. Apparently Cibber believed with Roger North that "a Life should be a Picture; which cannot be good, if the peculiar Features, whereby the subject is distinguish'd from all others, are left out. Nay, Scars and Blemishes as well as Beauties, ought to be express'd; otherwise it is but an outline fill'd up with Lillies and Roses."

6. *Apology*, p. 86.

7. *Ibid.*, p. 92.

8. *Ibid.*, pp. 95-96.

9. *Ibid.*, pp. 99-100.

10. *Ibid.*, p. 104.

11. Thomas Davies, *Dramatic Miscellanies*, III: 477.

12. *Pope's Correspondence* has been edited by George Sherburn, 5 vols. (Oxford, 1956).

13. These were *Don Quixote in England* and *The Temple Beau*. Refusing them was to Cibber's credit. He did not allow friendship to blind him to literary deficiencies. Furious, Fielding took them to Goodman's Fields and began complaining about the high-handedness of Cibber and Wilks at Drury Lane, satirizing them as Marplay and Sparkish in *The Author's Farce* (1730). The rejection of two mediocre pieces had inspired a good one.

14. These were *The Lottery, The Old Debauchee, The Covent Gar-*

den Tragedy, The Mock Doctor, and *The Modern Husband.*
For the last Cibber even wrote an epilogue, but it was so pedestrian that it had to be replaced after four performances. The next season Cibber wrote a slightly better epilogue for Fielding's *The Miser.*

15. It was, in fact, Fielding's habit to dash off farces overnight, sometimes on the backs of pieces of paper in which he had bought tobacco.

16. Fielding adds: "As soon as he was stripped, we observed a little book which he had bound very close to his heart. I read the words Love in a Riddle very plain, but he was obliged after many entreaties to leave it behind him. I was surprised to see him pass examination with his laurel on, and was assured by standers by, that Mercury would have taken it off, had he seen it."

17. *Joseph Andrews,* (London and New York, [1929]).

18. Fielding also attacked *Pamela* as *Shamela,* under the pseudonym "Conny Keyber."

19. *Cf.* Edgar Johnson, *op. cit.,* which refers to "a few speculations about how he [Cibber] might have entered Cambridge and become a celebrated preacher, or joined the army during the revolution of 1688 and become a great soldier (for Cibber infuriated the prosaic-minded by his bland assumption that he would have shone in these professions as well as his own)."

20. *Mr. Cibber of Drury Lane,* p. 231. Other comments on the *Apology* will be found in Henry Brodribb Irving, *Occasional Papers, Dramatic and Historical* (London, 1906), pp. 91-121; and Edward Robins, Jr., *Echoes of the Playhouse* (New York and London, 1895), Chapter 6.

Chapter Nine

1. At one point Plotwell, to escape Fossile, leaves a room concealed under the voluminous skirts of Townly.

2. Since *The Rehearsal* (1671), by the Duke of Buckingham and some of his friends, was a satire on plays and contained some rather caustic comments, the ad-libs were not especially out of place. Emmett L. Avery, "The Stage Popularity *of The Rehearsal,* 1671-1777," *Research Studies of the State College of Washington,* VII (1939), 201-204, states that there were 291 performances of the play during the period covered. Both Cibber and his son were frequently seen as Bayes.

3. Pope himself could not do it, being practically a dwarf, held together by corsets, and incapable even of dressing by himself.

4. It was common knowledge what the subject of the play was and Pope, a Catholic and a Tory, was certain to find offense in its politics, if nothing else.

5. Edmund Curll, the disreputable publisher of Rose Street, tried to

promote a profitable pamphlet war. He revealed Pope's authorship and goaded him: "Go on the frauds of Cibber to explain."

6. It is only fair to say that ΠΕΡΙ ΒΑΘΟΥΣ is important for the
critical remarks it makes about the affected diction of some of
Pope's contemporaries. This clumsy passage, however, is a gauche
attempt at recalling some of the errors made by Cibber. He
wrote of Mrs. Oldfield that she *"outdid* her usual *outdoing"* and
referred to her possessing "in all respects the *paraphonalia* of
a woman of quality." Later he corrected these mistakes, but not
before his enemies had seized upon them and laughed at them.
References to his errors in grammar and spelling, etc., plagued
Colley: he was forever being accused of knowing no English.
An attack by one, however, who made his fortune "translating"
Homer while knowing much less Greek than he ought to have
known does lose some of its effect.

7. Theobald (1688-1744) was one of the more pedantic of the five
editors of Shakespeare in the 1709-1747 period. In 1726 he was
incautious enough to publish *Shakespeare Restored: or, a Specimen of the Many Errors, as well Committed as Unamended,
by Mr. Pope,* a detailed exposé of the lamentable inadequacies
of Pope's hack edition of Shakespeare.

8. Newspapers of the period were necessarily careful about offending government officials—John Matthews was hanged, drawn,
and quartered in 1719 for publishing treasonable remarks—but
libel of private individuals was common. The minor journalist
Nathaniel Mist ran a weekly Jacobite journal which, after
The Non-Juror was performed, repeatedly assailed Cibber.

9. *Apology,* p. 33.

10. *Ibid.,* p. 22.

11. *Ibid.,* p. 23.

12. H. P. Vincent, "Two Letters of Colley Cibber," *Notes and
Queries,* CLXVIII (1935), 3-4. This letter was found among the
papers of the Pennsylvania Historical Society.

13. Modernized, as quoted by Barker, *op. cit.,* p. 213. Even before
it was printed rumor of the force of this attack reached Pope,
but friends reported that he was quite unprepared for what he
received, that his face was "writhen with anguish" as he read
this passage.

14. Lord Hervey (whom Pope had forever branded as Sporus, a
"mere white curd of asses' milk" in the *Arbuthnot* satire)
entered the lists with two pamphlets: *The Difference between
Verbal and Practical Virtue, with a Prefatory Epistle from Mr
C[ib]b[e]r to Mr P[ope]* and a *Letter to Mr C[ib]b[e]r on His
Letter to Mr P[ope].* Others supported Cibber in *Blast upon
Blast and Lick for Lick, or a New Lesson for P[ope]* and
Sawney and Colley. ("Sawney" is a Scottish nickname for
"Alexander.") Pope's defenders got into the fray with *A Blast*

upon *Bays, or a New Lick at the Laureat* and *The Scribleriad.
Being an Epistle to the Dunces. On Renewing their Attack upon
Mr Pope under Their Leader the Laureat.* All were dated
1742.

15. Someone—could it have been Pope himself?—sent a pre-pub-
lication copy of at least part of the forthcoming *Dunciad* to
Cibber, in reply to *The Egoist.*
16. Replacing Theobald with Cibber caused some clumsiness, as
when Pope puts Cibber incongruously in the midst of Theobald's
scholarly library or when he describes Cibber, who always dined
not wisely but too well, as going "supperless" from poverty.
17. Pope may have taken his cue for this coronation from a parody
of Cibber's Birthday Ode of 1732.
18. The best edition of *The Dunciad* is that edited by James
Sutherland, Vol. V of the Twickenham edition of Pope's works.
London, 1956. This passage is Book I, lines 29-32.
19. *Dunciad,* I, 110-11.
20. Pope recalled painful memories of *Perolla and Izadora, Ximena,
Caesar in Aegypt,* and the version of *Papal Tyranny* withdrawn in 1736.
21. *Dunciad,* I, 129-30.
22. *Ibid.,* I, 190.
23. *Ibid.,* I, 299-304.
24. Cibber's friend Mrs. Barry died from the bite of a lapdog suddenly gone rabid. Cibber did not: it was the dog that died.

Chapter Ten

1. When Mrs. Cibber's asthma forced her to leave the stinging fogs
of London, Colley rented a house for her at Uxbridge, near
Hillington, and there (their daughter Charlotte says) she lived
happily for years. Cibber never discusses his wife, and we know
practically nothing about her.
2. His father sent him while still very young to Winchester (the
school where Colley himself had once been refused but which
Colley's brother Lewis had attended—after Caius Gabriel Cibber
had made a gift to the school of a statue of the founder which
is to be seen there to this day). While still in his teens Theophilus
made his stage debut at Drury Lane as Daniel ("a country boy,
servant to Indiana") in *The Conscious Lovers.* Baker's *Biographia
Dramatica* (I, 126) tells us the lad had "an apparent good understanding and quickness of parts; a perfect knowledge of what he
ought to represent; together with a vivacity in his manner, and a
kind of effronterie. . . ." Like father, like son.
3. The first was Jane Johnson, an actress whom William Rufus Chetwood hailed as a "rising genius," but she died at twenty-six of
puerperal fever, leaving two daughters, Jane and Elizabeth. Dr.
Arne was at one time conductor of the orchestra at Drury Lane.

He is known today for having written—for a forgotten play called *Alfred*—the stirring "Rule, Britannia."

4. Colley decided to make her an actress. Theophilus had taken one William Sloper to court, charging "criminal conversation" with Susannah, though actually he had sold his wife to Sloper, forcing her to submit to his attentions at the point of a pistol. Colley Cibber's deposition testified: "When they married she was a singer, but there were better voices. I thought her voice not the best; and if not the best 'tis nothing. I thought it might possibly do better for speaking." He found her an apt pupil: "I believe I was the person who chiefly instructed her; I spent a good deal of time and took great delight in it for she was very capable of receiving instruction. In forty years' experience that I have known the stage, I never knew a woman at the beginning so capable of the business or to improve so fast." It was the same knowledge of acting and dialogue that made Cibber both a good drama teacher and a good dramatist.

5. Susannah's father, an amateur impressario, got hold of this masque, Händel's first dramatic work in English (written and performed for the Duke of Chandos in 1718) and papered London with bills announcing: "At the New Theatre in the Hay-market this present Wednesday being the 17th Day of May will be perform'd in English, a Pastoral Opera, call'd *Acis and Galatea*. Composed by Mr. Handel. With all the Grand Chorus's, Scenes, Machines, and other Decorations; being the first time it ever was perform'd in a Theatrical Way. The Part of *Acis* by Mr. Mountier, being the first Time of his appearing in Character on any Stage; *Galatea*, Miss Arne. . . ." It was just such musical extravaganzas as these, "perform'd in a Theatrical Way" with "Scenes, Machines, and other Decorations" that gave Cibber and the other managers of Drury Lane such unwelcome competition for their plays.

6. Senior, *op. cit.*, p. 26.

7. Alexander Pope to Aaron Hill on "Sat. Morn. Nov. 14, 1731": She seemed "to be Mistress of her Part" and it was "a Pity that Mrs. *Cibber's* Voice and Person were not a little higher; she speaks extremely justly." Hill later gave her her "big break." In the Preface to his *Zara* he inveighed against the artificial style of acting then current and announced that he had deliberately assigned the two main roles in the tragedy to performers unknown as actors. Mrs. Cibber, coming from the operatic stage, well repaid his confidence. She was natural, moving, and irresistible. Her brilliant career is chronicled in *An Account of the Life of That Celebrated Actress, Mrs. Susannah Maria Cibber. Also the Two Remarkable and Romantic Trials Between Theophilus Cibber and William Sloper*. The two scandalous trials were in 1738 and 1739. The first trial netted Theophilus only ten pounds and

a lot of ruinous publicity; the second got him £500 of the
£10,000 damages he had demanded from Sloper—and caused
him to be booed vociferously at Drury Lane. Cibber returned
from a vacation in France to testify at the first trial and was
mortified by the second.

8. She was buried (February 6, 1766) in the cloisters of Westminster Abbey and many people placed her likeness, as a *vivan-
dière* in Chelsea Derby pottery, on their mantels.

9. Theophilus is satirized under the name of Mr. Pistol and there is
much pseudo-Shakespearian stuff in his speech which is a parody
of Othello's magniloquent outburst:

> Now, for e'er farewel,
> Rough-rumbling Verses and theatric Rage;
> Farewel the plumed Crest and the big Buskin
> That constitute the Hero—O farewel!—
> Farewel the shrill-crak'd Trump, and slacken'd Drum,
> The gilded Truncheons and the clashing Swords,
> Pride, Pomp, Embellishments of peaceful Warrs.
> And, O ye Iron Bowls! whose massy Balls
> The thundring *Jove's* great Clamours counterfeit;
> Farewel,—For *Pistol's* Occupation's gone.

This is also a convenient summary of some of the accoutrements
of tragedy in those days, the properties and effects that accompanied Cibber's *Xerxes* and such.

10. Barker, *op. cit.*, p. 191, quotes this passage from *An Apology
for the Life of Mr T . . . C . . ., Comedian. Supposed to be Written by Himself.*

11. Theophilus not only had the nerve to play Othello, he altered
*An Historical Tragedy of the Civil Wars In the Reign of Henry
VI* from Shakespeare and, with greater brazenness, "Revis'd and
Alter'd" *Romeo and Juliet*, in which he appeared with his daughter. Beside these effronteries Colley Cibber's *Richard III* looks
like a devout tribute to the Bard. Theophilus was also responsible
for gallimaufries such as *Patie and Peggie* (ballad opera), *The
Lover* (comedy), *The Harlot's Progress* (grotesque pantomime),
and *The Auction* (farce). None is worth further comment.

12. In 1753 Theophilus, who had twice been imprisoned for six
months at a time in the Rules of the Fleet (for debt), painfully reminding Cibber of Caius Gabriel's soujourn in the Marshalsea for a like reason, made a little money by publishing
the first part of *The Lives and Characters of Eminent Actors
and Actresses of Great Britain and Ireland* (1753), an interesting bit of theatrical memorabilia. Then he earned thirty guineas reworking *An Account of the Lives of the Poets of Great
Britain and Ireland*, in five volumes (1753). Dr. Johnson asserted
that the work was done chiefly by Robert Shiels, a Scotsman

he himself had employed as an amanuensis. The authorship is unimportant, the point here being that the Cibber family name, the publisher must have thought, would sell a lot of copies of almost anything. Other works by Theophilus, the very titles of which hint at his bellicose personality, are: *A Letter from Theophilus Cibber to John Highmore* (1733); *A Lick at a Liar: or Calumny Detected. Being an Occasional Letter to a Friend* (1752); *An Epistle from Mr. Theophilus Cibber to David Garrick, esq.* (1755); and Cibber's *Two Dissertations on the Theatres* (1756), in three parts. Not only did he trade on the family name but he kept it on people's tongues in connection with contention.

13. *A Narrative of the Life of Mrs. Charlotte Charke* . . . was first published in 1755. There is a modern edition, London, [1829], and an article by Helen Waddell, "Eccentric Englishwomen: viii Mrs Charke," *Spectator*, June 4, 1937, 1047-48. Mrs. Charke's autobiography is one of the most fascinating of this whole colorful century, rivaling Defoe's *Moll Flanders*, Fielding's *Jonathan Wild*, and Smollett's *Ferdinand, Count Fathom* in interest—and it is true.

14. Colley, looking out a window one day, is said to have perceived his youngest, preceded by a child with a fiddle and trailed by a crowd of street urchins, mounted on a donkey, in triumph. "Gad demme!" cried her father, "an ass upon an ass!"

15. Some time later news arrived that he had died in Jamaica, so she said.

16. H. P. Vincent, "Two Letters of Colley Cibber," 3-4.

17. Advertised as "a young gentlewoman, who had never appeared on any stage before," she made her debut on the same night as Mrs. Oldfield's last appearance on the stage. To avoid being overshadowed, she arrived at the theater in a sumptuous, hired coach, though her father begged her to be less conspicuous until she had proved herself. She acquitted herself well, probably more because of confidence than ability, and her next appearance was heralded by playbills which carried her name in capital letters, which she beheld with undisguised pride. Senior, *op. cit.*, p. 65, says Charlotte played Aurora in *The Jovial Crew*, Macheath in *The Beggar's Opera*, Alicia in *Jane Shore*, Fairlove in *The Tender Husband*, Lucy in *The Old Bachelor*, Millwood in *The London Merchant*, Charlotte Weldon in *Oroonoko*, and Mrs. Tragic in her own farce *The Art of Management*.

18. There may have been some other cause as well, for though she was undeniably immoral in her private life it was difficult for an actress to distinguish herself by vice in a company in which Charles Macklin had murdered another actor for wearing his wig. As Charlotte wrote in introducing her libelous play (ironically dedicated to Mr. Fleetwood): "While my Follies only are hurtful to my self, I know no Right that any Persons, unless Relations, or very good Friends, have to call me to Account."

The play was presented at the York Buildings in September, 1735, but soon closed by a threat that Charlotte "was to suffer from Civil Power for exhibiting a Satyr on the Managers of Drury Lane." The play was published but Fleetwood bought up and destroyed all the copies of it.

19. This sort of deception was apparently rather easy in the eighteenth century. Mrs. Centlivre, before her marriage to the King's cook, lived, disguised as a boy, with Anthony Hammond, sometime commissioner of the Navy.

20. A Mr. Yeates ran the marionette show there from 1739 to 1740 and made money at it.

21. Barker, *op. cit.*, p. 177, quotes her advertisement from *The Daily Post* of November 1, 1727, for "all sorts of China and Japan ware; the best tea, as pekoe, congon, bohea, hyson, green, and imperial; likewise coffee, sago, and chocolate; also fine hollands, cambrics, and most sorts of millinery goods." Such shops had, in those days, bad reputations as places of assignation. Perhaps Anne's was respectable.

22. Charlotte says that Elizabeth led a singularly unfortunate life. What could have happened to her to elicit this comment from a woman who suffered all that Charlotte did is hard to imagine.

23.   Honoured, Sir, I doubt not but you are sensible I last Saturday published the first number of a Narrative of my Life, in which I made a proper concession in regard to those unhappy miscarriages which have for many years justly deprived me of a father's fondness. As I am conscious of my errors, I thought I could not be too public in sueing for your blessing and pardon; and only blush to think my youthful follies should draw so strong a compunction on my mind in the meridian of my days, which I might so easily have avoided. Be assured, Sir, I am perfectly convinced I was more than to blame, and that the hours of anguish I have felt have bitterly repaid me for the commission of every indiscretion, which was the unhappy motive of being so many years estranged from the happiness I now, as in duty bound, most earnestly deplore. I shall with your permission, Sir, send again, to know if I may be admitted to throw myself at your feet; and with sincere and filial transport, endeavour to convince you that I am, Honoured sir, Your truly penitent and dutiful daughter,
CHARLOTTE CHARKE
In a sentimental comedy by Cibber such a petition would have lead to a grand reconciliation scene, but in life it did not.

24. The source of this newspaper clipping, pasted in one of Robinson Locke's scrapbooks in the Theatre Collection of The New York Public Library, is unknown.

25. She asserted that "going strolling is engaging in a little dirty kind of war," that she was "not only sick, but heartily ashamed

of it, as I have had nine years' experience of its being a very contemptible life; rendered so through the impudent and ignorant behaviour of the generality of those who pursue it; and I think it would be more reputable to earn a groat a day in cinder-sifting at Tottenham court, than to be concerned with them."

26. The success of her 1755 autobiography, published first in parts and then in book form, encouraged them to believe that money might be made out of her writing.

27. We can hope that she fared better than Elizabeth's daughter who, in an undated letter now among the Cibber papers in the Harvard Theatre Collection, addressed some forgotten nobleman in these pitiful and nearly illiterate terms:

> May it please your Grace[,] I am an unfortunate grand daughter of the Late Colley Cibber whose unhapines was never to feell for the distress of his own family otherwise then by a Partiall Judgement the aflictions of his Children was greatly owing to his unfeelingnes my Mother My Lord never Commited She Could Say it on her Death Bed an Act of Disobeadeince: to her and my Aunt [Charlotte] Charke he Left but five pound Each to there Children nothing but the bulk of his fortune my Aunt [Catherine] Brown had and my uncle Theophilus Daughters [Jane and Elizabeth] had a thousand pound Each Worn down by Affliction and growing in years not brought up to Earn my Bread by Servile Business a wrong Judgement in Parents who flatters us with Hopes we never Tast[e] the old Nobility all dead who usd thro pity to Aleavate the Distresses of my family inforces me to plead to your pity in this hope that my Aunt Charke Shard in your Compassion I never and please your grace Intreated your Assistance before but as I am informed your Benevolence at this to be in the Number as my distress is great and all I am Capable to do is with my Needle and there is no imploy all Publick Charity. taking it in that Heaven with its Choisest Blessings may await you Shall ever be the fervent wish Wish [sic] and Prayer of your Most Obeadant Ser[van]t   ANA CHEETWOOD.

This was presumably not Cibber's granddaughter Jenny, said to have married that William Rufus Chetwood who wrote a history of the stage.

28. Conversation seemed then to count for much. Little John Wilkes, who knew enough as a result of tireless research to write a successful *Essay on Women* ⟨1763⟩, claimed that though he was ugly all he needed to outdistance any handsome man was a half-hour's start in conversation.

29. Quoted by Miss Senior, *op. cit.*, p. 150.

30. Cibber contemptuously called Garrick "the completest little doll of a figure—the prettiest little creature." Peg Woffington lived with Garrick for two years—paying her own way, for Garrick was stingy—and then she took off for France with Cibber's old friend, Owen Swiney.

31. *Correspondence*, II, 206.

32. "But once," Richardson recalled, "I faced the laureate squatted on one of the benches, with a face more wrinkled than ordinary with disappointment. 'I thought,' said I, 'that you were of the party of the tea-treats—Miss Chudleigh is gone to the tea-room.' 'Pshaw!' said he, 'there is no coming at her, she is so surrounded by the toupees.' And I left him to fret. But he was called to soon after; and in he flew, and his face shone again and looked smooth."

33. Mrs. Pilkington married while still in her teens, but before she had been a wife a year she had met Jonathan Swift in St. Patrick's Cathedral (where he was dean) and moved into his house as a sort of secretary-companion. Then scandal wrecked her comfortable existence there. Her husband surprised her with still another man in her bedroom. (She said he had come about a book she had borrowed from him.) Swift could not countenance such immorality in his deanery. He threw her out —and wrote (*Correspondence*, VI, 69) that Matthew Pilkington was "the falsest rogue and [his wife] . . . the most profligate whore in either kingdom. She was taken in the fact by her own husband."

34. She made Cibber's acquaintance, she said, by sending him some poetry and inquiring if a poor, unattached woman who wrote like this had any prospects in London. Cibber came to call and ended up listening, rapt, to the story of her colorful life. Some gossips insinuated that she had stolen the poetry from her husband, who also wrote, but who could doubt that a woman so attractive was also honest?

35. It was claimed that sixteen dukes contributed a guinea each.

36. Quoted by Barker, *op. cit.*, p. 251.

37. Thomas Gray, writing to Horace Walpole: Cibber "seems to me full as pert and as dull as usual. There are whole pages of common-place stuff, that for stupidity might have been wrote by Dr. [Daniel] Waterland [the Master of Magdalene College, Cambridge], or any other grave divine, did not the flirting saucy phrase give them at a distance an air of youth and gaiety." Surely this was Cibber's talent as a playwright too—the morality of a grave divine presented with an air of youth and gaiety.

38. *Correspondence*, II, 174.

39. Not to be confused with James Ralph's play of this title, the one parodied in John Gay's *The What D'Ye Call It.*

40. Chesterfield, though known to us today for his letters to his bastard son (and married to an illegitimate daughter of George

I), had to keep up some standards.

41. Such bets were not unusual. The same Montfort bet Lord Leicester a hundred guineas that a dozen members of Parliament would die within a year. Bucks wagered on when they would inherit family fortunes. By the end of the century as much as £ 300,000 was hazarded by various people as to whether the transvestite Charles de Beaumont, Chevalier d'Éon was a man or a woman. The wager on Cibber's life contained no malice. Such bets were so frequently made that in 1774 Parliament was forced to declare wagers invalid unless it could be proved that the person insuring the "policy" had a legitimate interest in the person or thing on which he bet. Since 1845, when English law made it impossible to go to court to collect winnings on a wager, such bets as Mountfort's have been rare.

42. "Colley, we are told, had the honour to be a member of the great club at White's; and so, I suppose, might any other man, not quite unknown, who wore good cloaths, and paid his money when he lost it. But on what terms did Cibber live with this society? Why, he feasted most sumptuously, as I have heard his friend Victor say with an air of triumphant exultation, with Mr. Arthur and his wife, and gave eighteen pence for his dinner. After he had dined, when the clubroom door was opened, and the laureate was introduced, he was saluted with the loud and joyous acclamation of 'O King Coll! Come in, King Coll! Welcome, welcome, King Colley!' And this kind of gratulation, Mr. Victor thought, was very gracious and honourable." *Memoirs of David Garrick,* (London, 1780), II, 353. For *The History of White's* see Algernon Bourke, 2 vols., London, 1892.

43. The *Dictionary of National Biography* states that the place of Cibber's death is uncertain: "According to one account, Cibber died in Berkeley Square, where he had for some time resided, having previously lived (1711-14) near the Bull's Head Tavern in old Spring Gardens at Charing Cross. . . . Another statement is that Cibber died in a house next the Castle Tavern, Islington." I am inclined to believe that the Islington story is incorrect, as was Dr. Doran's statement that Cibber was buried in Westminster Abbey. Perhaps as Laureate he was entitled to that honor, but it was not claimed for him.

44. R. W. Lowe's edition of the *Apology* (II, 292) gives the text of a letter from the Reverend Daniel Greatorex, Vicar of St. Paul's parish, who tells of his part in the removal of the bodies when the Danish Church was torn down: "When the church was removed, the coffins were all removed carefully into the crypt under the apse, and then bricked up. So the bodies are still there. The Danish consul was with me when I moved the bodies. The coffins had perished except the bottoms. I carefully removed them myself, personally, and laid them side by side at the back of the crypt, and covered them with earth."

Selected Bibliography

PRIMARY SOURCES

1. Plays

Love's Last Shift, or the Fool in Fashion. London, 1696. Text revised 1721. Comedy.

Womans Wit, or the Lady in Fashion. London, 1697. Comedy.

Xerxes, London, 1699. Tragedy.

The Tragical History of King Richard III. London, 1700. Text revised in 1721. Tragedy.

Love Makes a Man, or the Fop's Fortune. London, 1701. Comedy.

She Wou'd and She Wou'd Not, or the Kind Impostor. London, 1702. Comedy.

The Careless Husband. London, 1704. Comedy.

Perolla and Izadora. London, 1706. Tragedy.

The School-Boy, or the Comical Rival. London, 1707. Comedy.

The Double Gallant, or the Sick Lady's Cure. London, 1707. Comedy.

The Comical Lovers. London, 1707. Comedy.

The Lady's Last Stake, or the Wife's Resentment. London, 1707. Comedy.

The Rival Fools. London, 1709. Comedy.

Venus and Adonis. A Masque. Written by Mr. Cibber and set to Musick by Dr. Pepusch. London, 1715. "A printed book of the masque will be given to each person that pays in the pit or boxes."—*Advertisement*

Myrtillo. A Pastoral Interlude. Written by Mr. Cibber and Set to Musick by Dr. Pepusch. London, 1716. Actually published November 5, 1715.

The Non-Juror. London, 1718. Comedy. First edition January 2, second edition January 3, third edition January 7.

Ximena, or the Heroick Daughter. London, 1719. Tragedy.

The Refusal, or the Ladies Philosophy. London, 1721. Comedy.

Plays Written by Mr. Cibber. 2 vols. London, 1721. Contains: *Love's Last Shift, Richard III, Love Makes a Man, She Wou'd and She Wou'd Not, The Careless Husband, The Lady's Last Stake, The Rival Fools, Ximena, The Non-Juror, The Refusal.*

Caesar in Aegypt. London, 1725. Actually published December 15, 1724. Tragedy.

The Provok'd Husband, or a Journey to London. "Written by the Late Sir John Vanbrugh and Mr. Cibber." London, 1728. Comedy.

The Rival Queans, With the Humours of Alexander the Great. Dublin, 1729. "A Comical-Tragedy."

Love in a Riddle. A Pastoral. London, 1719 (misprint for 1729). "Pastoral."

Damon and Phillida. A Ballad Opera. London, 1729. This is the subplot of *Love in a Riddle* as presented separately.

Polypheme. An Opera. By Paul Rolli, F.R.S. Composed by Nicholas Porpora, for the English Nobility. London, 1734. Translated into English by Cibber. Libretto.

Papal Tyranny in the Reign of King John. London, 1745. Tragedy.

The Dramatic Works of Colley Cibber, Esq. London, 1760. Four 12mo. vols.

The Dramatic Works of Colley Cibber, Esq. London, 1777. Five 12mo vols. Contains the following not in the 1760 edition: *Perolla and Izadora, Caesar in Egypt* [sic], *The School-Boy, Xerxes, Venus and Adonis, Myrtillo, Damon and Phillida.* Cibber's *The Rival Queans, with the Humours of Alexander the Great* in the 1760 edition is replaced in the 1777 edition by *The Contre Temps, or Rival Queans.* Also *Flora, or Hob in the Well* (not by Cibber) appears instead of *Hob, or the Country Wake* (which may be by Cibber).

2. Plays Attributed to Cibber

Cinna's Conspiracy. London, 1713. Tragedy.

Hob, or the Country Wake. A Farce. By Mr. Doggett. London, 1715. Farce.

Chuck. London, 1736. Opera.

The Temple of Dullness. With the Humours of Signor Capochio and Signora Dorinna. A Comic Opera in Two Acts. The Music by Mr. Arne. London, 1745. Comic Opera.

Capochio and Dorinna. An Interlude for Music of Two Acts. Translated from an Italian Intermezzo of That Title, by the Late Colley Cibber, Esq., Poet Laureat. The Music Composed by Dr. Arne. London, n.d. [1759 or later]. Comic Opera.

The Devil to Pay; or, The wives metamorphosed: a comic opera in two acts, by Charles Coffey. Revised by Colley Cibber. London, 1838 (?). Comic Opera.

3. Dramatic Prologues and Epilogues.

Prologue for the reopening of the Theatre-Royal in Drury Lane. March 25, 1695.

Prologue to Mrs. Aphra Behn's *Abdelazer, or the Moor's Revenge.* Drury Lane. April, 1695.

"Prologue spoken at Her Majesty's theatre in the Haymarket, on Saturday the 8th of November, by I. B., Esq. Written by Mr. Cibber." In *The Muses Mercury, or the Monthly Miscellany*. October, 1707.

Epilogue (spoken by Mrs. Oldfield) to Mrs. Centlivre's *The Man's Bewitch'd, or the Devil to Do About Her*. Drury Lane. December 12, 1709.

Epilogue (spoken by Mrs. Oldfield) to Mr. Johnson's *The Victim*. Drury Lane. January 5, 1714.

Epilogue (spoken by Mrs. Oldfield) to Mr. Dennis' *The Invader of his Country, or the Fatal Resentment*. Drury Lane. November 11, 1719.

Epilogue (spoken by Mr. and Mrs. Theophilus Cibber) to Theophilus Cibber's *The Lover*. Drury Lane. January 20, 1731.

Epilogue (spoken by Theophilus Cibber) to Mr. Lillo's *The London Merchant, or the History of George Barnwell*. Drury Lane. June 22, 1731.

Epilogue (spoken by Mrs. Heron) to Mr. Fielding's *The Modern Husband*. Drury Lane. February 14, 1732. Printed before the play. Acknowledged as Cibber's in the second edition.

Epilogue (spoken by Mrs. Raftor) to Mr. Fielding's *The Miser*. Drury Lane. February 17, 1733.

Epilogue (spoken by Theophilus Cibber) to Mr. Hill's *The Tragedy of Zara*. Drury Lane. January 12, 1736.

4. Dramatic Epilogue Attributed to Cibber

Epilogue to Philip Francis' *Eugenia*, 1752. The Earl of Chesterfield wrote to his son that it was "old Cibber's, but corrected, though not enough, by [Philip] Francis," February 20, 1752.

5. Non-Dramatic Works

A Poem on the Death of Our Late Soveraign Lady Queen Mary. London, 1695.

An Ode to His Majesty, for the New Year 1730/31. "By Mr. Cibber, Servant to His Majesty." London, 1730. (As Poet Laureate Cibber wrote annual odes hereafter.)

An Ode for His Majesty's Birth-Day, October 30, 1731. London, 1731. (Later productions of Cibber as Poet Laureate were published by the singers themselves who wished to hold him up to ridicule and gave the texts to *The Gentleman's Magazine* and other periodicals.)

To Miss Eger[to]n singing in the Long Room. By C[olle]y C[ibbe]r. Verses "wrote on a window in the Long Room at Scarborough. By the Poet Laureate." In *The Scarborough*

Miscellany for the Year 1734. (A fair example of Cibber's occasional verse of the sort that appeared in *The British Musical Miscellany,* 1734; *Tunbridgalia,* 1740; *Poems on Several Occasions,* 1749; etc.)

The Blind Boy. London, c. 1735. Poem in broadside.

An Apology for the Life of Mr. Colley Cibber, Comedian, and Late Patentee of the Theatre-Royal. With an Historical View of the Stage during His Own Time. Written by Himself. London, 1740. Autobiography. First edition April 7, second (cheaper) edition May 14. Other editions throughout the eighteenth century. "A new edition with many critical and explanatory notices" by Edmund Bellchambers, London (W. Simpkin and R. Marshall), 1822. "A new edition with notes and supplement" in 2 vols., limited (510 copies), by R. W. Lowe, London (Nimmo), 1889. "Connoisseur edition" (150 copies) in 2 vols., by R. W. Lowe, London (The Grolier Society), 190-?. The 1756 edition "with modern modifications of spelling and punctuation" reprinted in 2 vols., London (Golden Cockerel Press), 1925.

A Letter from Mr. Cibber to Mr. Pope, Inquiring into the Motives that Might Induce Him in His Satyrical Works, to be so Frequently Fond of Mr. Cibber's Name. London, 1742.

The Egoist, or Colley upon Cibber. Being His Own Picture Retouch'd to so Plain a Likeness That No One Now Would Have the Face to Own it but Himself. London, 1743.

A Second Letter from Mr. Cibber to Mr. Pope. In Reply to Some Additional Verses in His Dunciad, Which He Has not yet Published. London, 1743.

Another Occasional Letter from Mr. Cibber to Mr. Pope. Wherein the New Hero's Preferment to His Throne in the Dunciad Seems not to be Accepted. And the Author of That Poem His More Rightful Claim to it is Asserted. With an Expostulatory Address to the Reverend Mr. W[arburto]n, Author of the New Preface and Adviser in the Curious Improvements of That Satire. London, 1744.

The Character and Conduct of Cicero, Considered from the History of His Life by the Reverend Dr. Middleton. With Occasional Essays and Observations upon the Most Memorable Facts and Persons during that Period. London, 1747.

The Lady's Lecture, a Theatrical Dialogue between Sir Charles Easy and His Marriageable Daughter. Being an Attempt to Engage Obedience by Filial Liberty, and to Give the Maiden Conduct of Virtue, Chearfulness. London, 1748.

A Rhapsody upon the Marvellous, Arising from the First Odes of Horace and Pindar. Being a Scrutiny into Ancient Poetical Fame Demanded by Modern Common Sense. By Colley Cibber, Esq., P[oet]. L[aureate]. London, 1751.

Verses to the Memory of Mr. Pelham. Addressed to His Grace the Duke of Newcastle. London, n.d. [1754?]

6. Non-Dramatic Work Attributed to Cibber

Mr COLLEY CIBBER's EPITAPH *on Mr* POPE. *The Gentleman's Magazine,* XIV (June, 1744), 330. "It is Cibberian in thought and style and may possibly be genuine."—R. H. Barker.

SECONDARY SOURCES

1. Books

Aston, Anthony. *A Brief Supplement to Colley Cibber, Esq.* London, [1748]. To be read in connection with Cibber's autobiography. Reprinted in R. W. Lowe's edition of the *Apology* for the Grolier Society.

Ault, Norman. *New Light on Pope* . . . London: Methuen, 1949. The Cibber-Pope controversy in the hands of a very just critic.

Avery, E. L. *The London Stage 1700-1729.* Part of the series *The London Stage 1600-1800.* Carbondale: Southern Illinois University Press, 1960. Lists of performances, etc. Use with Allardyce Nicoll, *below.*

Ayre, William. *Memoirs of* . . . *Alexander Pope.* London, 1745. The second volume has some information relative to Cibber.

Baker, D. E. *Biographia Dramatica, or, A Companion to the Playhouse* . . . London: Printed for Longmans, Hurst; enlarged (3 vols.), 1812. A dictionary of playwrights, plays, and actors. Antiquated but still useful.

Barker, R. H. *Mr. Cibber of Drury Lane.* New York: Columbia University Press, 1939. The definitive and comprehensive study, scrupulously documented from original sources, originally a doctoral dissertation.

Bateson, F. W. *English Comic Drama, 1700-1750.* Oxford: The Clarendon Press, 1929. A standard book.

Beljame, A. O. *Men of Letters and the English Public in the Eighteenth Century.* E. O. Lorimer, trans., Bonamy Dobrée, ed., London: Kegan Paul, [1948]. A major book by a French critic of English letters.

Bell, John. *Bell's British Theatre, Consisting of the Most Esteemed English Plays.* 36 vols. London: J. Bell, 1791-1802. A convenient source of the texts of a great many plays of the period, famous and obscure.

Bernbaum, Ernest. *The Drama of Sensibility.* Cambridge: Harvard University Press, 1915. Still the most important book on sentimental drama.

Broadus, E. K. *The Laureateship: A Study of the Office of Poet Laureate in England.* Oxford: The Clarendon Press, 1921. Cibber as Poet Laureate.

Burton, E. J. *The British Theatre: Its Repertory and Practice.* London: Jenkins, 1960. Period plays, their backgrounds and their production problems.

Carlson, C. L. *The First Magazine: A History of the Gentleman's*

Magazine. Brown University Studies, IV. Providence, 1938. Cibber was sometimes mentioned or quoted in *The Gentleman's Magazine.*

Charke, Charlotte Cibber. *A Narrative of the Life of Mrs. Charlotte Charke* . . . London, 1755. The incredible tale of Cibber's madcap daughter, reprinted 1829. (A play, *The Wild Girl,* by George Gravely [Edwards] was based on this, 1949.)

Cibber, Susannah Maria Arne. *An Account of the Life of that Celebrated Actress Mrs. Susannah Maria Cibber* . . . London, 1887. The lifestory of Colley Cibber's daughter-in-law, Theophilus Cibber's wife.

Cibber, Theophilus. *A Lick at a Liar* . . . London, [1752]. Colley's rambunctious son in a controversy again.

—— *The Lives and Characters of the Most Eminent Actors and Actresses.* London, 1753. A hackwork history of the stage.

—— *An Account of the Lives of the Poets* . . . 5 vols. London, 1753. Theophilus got about thirty guineas (to pay his debts) out of this but most of the credit should go, says Dr. Johnson, to his former secretary, Robert Shiels, a Scotsman.

—— *Memoirs of the Life of Barton Booth.* London, 1753. A life of Colley Cibber's partner, founder of the famous acting family.

Collier, Jeremy. *A Short View of the Immorality and Profaneness of the English Stage.* London, 1738. The first edition (1698) made Dryden repentant, Vanbrugh more insolent, but little affected the stage.

Crane, R. S. *et al. English Literature 1600-1800. A Bibliography* . . . 4 vols. Princeton: Princeton University Press, 1950-1962. Students may also consult bibliographies by F. W. Bateson (in *Cambridge Bibliography of English Literature*), R. W. Lowe (*Bibliographical Account of English Theatrical Literature*), Blanch M. Baker (*Theatre and Allied Arts*), and others.

Cross, W. L. *The History of Henry Fielding.* 3 vols. New Haven: Yale University Press, 1918. Fielding satirized Cibber in his novels, in the press, and on the stage.

Davies, Thomas. *Dramatic Miscellanies.* 3 vols. London, 1783-1784. Theatrical news and gossip by the author of *Memoirs of . . . David Garrick,* London, 1780.

Dennis, John. *The Critical Works.* E. N. Hooker, ed. 2 vols. Baltimore: The Johns Hopkins Press, 1939-1943. Cibber was attacked by this shrewd critic and perennial malcontent.

Dent, E. J. *Foundations of English Opera.* Cambridge: Cambridge University Press, 1928. Cibber's theater had always to contend with the competition of opera, ballad opera, etc.

Dobrée, Bonamy and Wilson, F. P., eds. *English Literature in the Early Eighteenth Century.* Vol. II. Oxford: The Clarendon Press, 1959. Survey.

Doran, John. *Their Majesties' Servants.* 2 vols. London: W. H. Allen, 1864.

Downes, John. *Roscius Anglicanus.* Montague Summers, ed. London: Fortune Press, 1926. Stage history by the prompter of Drury Lane who began in D'Avenant's theater in Lincoln's Inn Fields (1662). He retired in 1706.

Dudden, F. H. *Henry Fielding: His Life, Work, and Times.* 2 vols. Oxford: The Clarendon Press, 1952. More recent than W. L. Cross' study, *above.* Reliable.

Egerton, William. *Faithful Memoirs of the Life, Amours, and Performances of . . . Mrs. Anne Oldfield.* London, 1731. During her acting career (1704-1730) she created sixty-five roles, including such gems of genteel comedy as Lady Betty Modish, Lady Townly, Sylvia, and Mrs. Sullen.

Faber, Harald. *Caius Gabriel Cibber, 1630-1700.* London: Oxford University Press, 1926. The standard biography of Cibber's sculptor father.

Fisher, Dorothy Canfield. *Corneille and Racine in England.* New York: Columbia University Press, 1904. French influences on the English drama. See Chapter 11.

Fujimura, T. H. *The Restoration Comedy of Wit.* Princeton: Princeton University Press, 1952. The plays, and immorality, of Wycherley, Congreve, Etherege, etc., discussed.

Gagey, E. McA. *Ballad Opera.* New York: Columbia University Press, 1937. Having rejected *The Beggar's Opera,* Cibber found himself forced to bow to the public taste and produce ballad opera himself.

Galt, John. *The Lives of the Players.* London: Hamilton, Adams, 1886. Theatrical biographies.

Genest, John. *Some Account of the English Stage from the Restoration in 1660 to 1830.* 10 vols. Bath: H. E. Carrington, 1832. Early records of actors, plays, casts, playwrights, by a clergyman who loved the stage. Not always accurate.

Gray, C. H. *Theatrical Criticism in London to 1795.* New York: Columbia University Press, 1931. Criticism published in contemporary newspapers and periodicals handled with dissertation thoroughness.

Grove, Sir George. *Dictionary of Music and Musicians.* H. C. Colles, ed. New York: Macmillan, 1940. For information about Händel, Dr. Pepusch, the Arnes, etc.

Habbema, D. M. E. *An Appreciation of Colley Cibber, Actor and Dramatist.* Amsterdam: H. J. Paris, 1928. The drama before Cibber; Cibber's life and work; the text of *The Careless Husband*; and appendices on the theater of the Commonwealth, Cibber and Collier, Cibber and Pope.

Hillhouse, J. T. *The Grub-Street Journal.* Durham, N. C.: Duke University Press, 1928. A study of one of the most influential periodicals of Cibber's time.

Hotson, Leslie. *The Commonwealth and Restoration Stage.* Cambridge: Harvard University Press, 1928. The theater whose traditions Cibber inherited.

Hughes, Leo and Scouten, A. H., eds. *Ten English Farces.* Austin: University of Texas Press, 1948. Contains *Hob: Or The Country Wake* (by Thomas Doggett?) which Chetwood ascribed to Cibber. Barker says it must be ascribed to Cibber because Chetwood is "too good an authority to be set aside on *a priori* grounds."

Johnson, Edgar. *One Mighty Torrent: The Drama of Biography.* New York: Macmillan, 1955. Includes a discussion of Cibber's *Apology.*

Krutch, J. W. *Comedy and Conscience after the Restoration.* New York: Columbia University Press, 1924. The comic tradition of the Restoration and the growth of sentimental comedy.

Langbaine, Gerard. *Lives and Characters of the English Dramatick Poets.* London, 1698-1699? Langbaine's "exact account of all the plays that were ever yet printed in the English tongue; their double titles, the places where acted, the dates when printed, and the persons to whom dedicated; with remarks and observations on most of the said plays" was continued to 1698 by "a careful hand" (Charles Gildon). William Oldys' manuscript notes (British Museum) might be consulted by the advanced student using this book.

Lecky, W. E. H. *A History of England in the Eighteenth Century.* 8 vols. London, 1878-1890. Irish historian of Rationalism and European morals, who was offered an Oxford professorship and declined it. Use the newer edition (7 vols.), New York: D. Appleton, 1892-1893.

Lewis, D. B. W. and Lee, Charles, eds. *The Stuffed Owl.* New York: Coward, 1930. An anthology of bad verse in which Cibber has an honored place beside Wordsworth and others of the British Pantheon.

Loftis, John. *Steele at Drury Lane.* Berkeley: University of California Press, 1952. The complex story of the famous essayist's career in the theater as governor, dramatist, etc. "I am busy about the main chance."—Steele in a letter, 1708.

Macdonald, W. L. *Pope and his Critics.* London: Dent, 1951. "Some judge of authors' names, not works, and then/Nor praise nor blame the writings, but the men."—Pope, *Essay on Criticism, Part II.*

MacQueen-Pope, W. J. *Theatre-Royal, Drury Lane.* London: W. H. Allen, 1946. The theater from its opening (1663) to the present, profusely illustrated with anecdotes and pictures. By the author of *Pillars of Drury Lane,* London, 1955.

MacMillan, Dougald and Jones, H. Mumford, eds. *Plays of the Restoration and Eighteenth Century.* New York: Henry Holt,

1931. A convenient collection of the texts of the most important plays, with good notes.

Miles, D. H. *The Influence of Molière on the Restoration Comedy.* New York: Columbia University Press, 1910. Molière's influence was felt by Cibber too. *Cf. The Non-Juror.*

Nettleton, G. H. *English Drama of the Restoration and Eighteenth Century* . . . New York: Macmillan, 1914. Based on original texts and documents, this survey of dramatists picks up where Sir Alphonsus William Ward (*see below*) stops and continues to Sheridan.

Nicoll, Allardyce. *A History of Early Eighteenth Century Drama, 1700-1750.* London: Cambridge University Press, 1929. Continuing the 1660-1700 volume (*below*), Professor Nicoll meticulously examines the theaters, the companies, and the various forms of tragedy, comedy, farce, pastorals, pantomimes, masques, political plays, burlesques. Lists of theaters and plays 1700-1750, documents illustrating the history of the stage, etc. Standard work.

—— *A History of Restoration Drama, 1660-1700.* London: Cambridge University Press, 1928. The first of the five volumes that make up Nicoll's monumental history of the English drama, 1660-1900. Not scintillating but authoritative survey of theater and stage conditions, tragedy and comedy. Lists of playhouses and plays 1660-1700, select documents, etc. Standard work.

Odell, G. C. D. *Annals of the New York Stage.* 15 vols. New York: Columbia University Press, 1927-1949. Odell's magpie approach preserved every tiny fact, even a notice of Mrs. Catherine Maud Harman (who was on the stage and died in New York at age 43), one of Colley Cibber's granddaughters.

—— *Shakespeare from Betterton to Irving.* New York: Scribner, 1920. An exhaustive study of the tides of taste in relation to productions of Shakespeare, including Cibber's, from 1660 to 1902.

Palmer, J. L. *The Comedy of Manners.* London: G. Bell, 1913. The beginnings (Etherege and Wycherley), the zenith (Congreve), and the decline (Vanbrugh and Farquhar) of the comedy of manners. For a bibliography on the *Comedy of Manners 1660-1700,* see C. S. Paine's Bulletin of Bibliography pamphlet, 36. Boston, 1951.

Paul, H. G. *John Dennis, His Life and Criticism.* New York, 1911. Cibber had some clashes with this contrary character.

Pope, Alexander. *Correspondence.* George Sherburn, ed. 5 vols. Oxford: The Clarendon Press, 1956. As one might expect from one of the greatest satirists in all of world literature, the letters are lively. Some concern Cibber, one of the many people with whom Pope quarreled.

—— *The Dunciad.* James Sutherland, ed. Twickenham Edition, Vol. V. London: Methuen, [1943]. Cibber became the "hero" of this poem, which was written in 1728 and revised in 1743.

—— *Prose Works.* Norman Ault, ed. Twickenham Edition, Vol. I. Oxford: The Clarendon Press, 1936. Replaces Elwin and Courthope (*below*) as far as the prose works are concerned.

—— *Works.* Whitwell Elwin and W. J. Courthope, eds. 10 vols. London: J. Murray, 1871-1889. A complete edition.

Schultz, W. E. *Gay's Beggar's Opera.* New Haven: Yale University Press, 1923. When Cibber refused to produce it, Gay took his ballad opera to John Rich. It made Rich gay and Gay rich. Cibber was forced to imitate it.

Senior, F. Dorothy. *The Life and Times of Colley Cibber.* New York: Rae D. Henkle, [1925]. Too much of the times and not enough of the life. Swelled out with a reprint of *The Careless Husband* and extracts from *The Tryal of Colley Cibber,* studies of Nance Oldfield and Peg Woffington, etc.

Smith, D. F. *Plays about the Theatre in England . . . 1671 . . . 1737 . . .* London and New York: Oxford University Press, 1936. Cibber was frequently satirized on the stage by such men as Fielding.

Smith, J. H. *The Gay Couple in Restoration Comedy.* Cambridge: Harvard University Press, 1948. The sprightly wit of the author of *All the King's Ladies* (Restoration actresses) and *Court Wits of the Restoration* is here put to good use in a scholarly and entertaining book about one of the staples of English comedy in the seventeenth century. See pp. 168-73.

Spencer, Hazelton. *Shakespeare Improved.* Cambridge: Harvard University Press, 1927. Performances of Shakespeare 1660-1710 and discussions of the adaptations then so popular, including Cibber's.

Sprague, A. C. *Beaumont and Fletcher on the Restoration Stage.* Cambridge: Harvard University Press, 1926. Exhaustive discussion of performances of their plays 1660-1710 and of a score or more adaptations.

Steele, Sir Richard. *Correspondence.* Rae Blanchard, ed. London: Oxford University Press, 1941. "I was going home two hours ago, but was met by Mr. Griffith, who has kept me ever since. I will be home within a pint of wine." Letter to his wife Prue, 11 p.m., January 5, 1708. Cibber was one of his many business acquaintances. He was "no undelightful companion."

—— *Dramatic Works.* G. A. Aitken, ed. London: T. F. Unwin, 1894. Cibber gave advice on writing *The Conscious Lovers.*

—— and Addison, Joseph. When Steele appointed himself unofficial "Censor of Great Britain" and began to publish *The Tatler* (April 12, 1709-January 2, 1711) a couple of times a week, Joseph Addison occasionally contributed. Later they collaborated on *The Spectator* (daily, March 1, 1711-December

6, 1712). It was revived by Addison for eighty numbers in 1714. *The Tatler* was edited by G. A. Aitken. 4 vols. London, 1898-1899, who also edited *The Spectator,* 8 vols. London, 1898. More convenient is G. Gregory Smith's edition of *The Spectator* (8 vols., 1897-1898) as reprinted in Everyman's Library (4 vols.).

Summers, Montague. *The Playhouse of Pepys.* New York: Macmillan, 1935. The major and minor dramatists, 1660-1682, with the history of the stage up to the union of the companies of D'Avenant and Killigrew (1682), omitting rhymed heroic drama.

—— *The Restoration Theatre.* New York: Macmillan, 1934. Emphasis on the scenes, machines, costume, etc. Full details of modern revivals (by The Phoenix Society) of plays of this period.

Swift, Jonathan. *Correspondence.* F. E. Ball, ed. 6 vols. London: Bell, 1910-1914. Both Cibber and Swift were involved with the notorious Mrs. Pilkington. Harold Williams is now reediting the *Correspondence* for The Oxford University Press, 1963-

—— *Poems.* Sir Herbert Davis, ed. London: Oxford University Press, 1937. Swift wrote verses that comment on the Laureate Cibber.

—— *Prose Works,* Sir Herbert Davis, ed. London: Oxford University Press, 1939 *ff.* The definitive edition is in progress.

—— *Works.* Sir Walter Scott, ed. 19 vols. Edinburgh, 1824. A complete edition. Convenient in the second edition, London: Bickers, 1883-1884.

Thaler, Alwin. *Shakespeare to Sheridan.* Cambridge: Harvard University Press, 1922. A survey replete with documents, illustrations, statistics.

Thorndike, A. H. *English Comedy.* New York and London: Macmillan, 1929. A survey of comedy from birth (medieval) to "new birth" (1890-1900) by the author of a standard book on tragedy (1908). In the volume on tragedy, only representative plays are covered after 1600 but the volume on comedy deals with all principal playwrights.

Turberville, A. S. *English Men and Manners in the Eighteenth Century.* London and New York: Oxford University Press, 1926. The backgrounds of literature.

Victor, Benjamin. *The History of the Theatres of London and Dublin from the Year 1730 to the Present Time.* 2 vols. London, [1761]. A selective bibliography has to omit many good books—Bonamy Dobrée's on *Restoration Comedy* and *Restoration Tragedy,* for example—but this antiquated study by a man who was "sub-manager and treasurer, first at Dublin, then at Drury Lane" (R. W. Lowe) must be included, for it is virtually a supplement to Cibber's *Apology.* (Moreover, Cibber was one of Victor's correspondents in his last years.) A third volume, covering 1760-1771, was printed in the latter year. W. C. Oulton then continued the history 1771-1817 in five more volumes.

Voorde, F. P. van de. *Henry Fielding: Critic and Satirist.* 'S Gravenhage, 1931. Fielding was highly critical of Cibber in *Joseph Andrews* and elsewhere. See his *Works.* William Ernest Henley, ed. 16 vols. London, 1903. He even used a variant of Cibber's name as a pen name for *An Apology for the Life of Mrs. Shamela Andrews. By Mr. Conny Keyber.*

Walpole, Horace (Earl of Orford). *Letters.* Mrs. Paget Toynbee, ed. 16 vols. Oxford: The Clarendon Press, 1903-1905. There is a *Supplement to the Letters.* Paget Toynbee, ed. 3 vols. Oxford: The Clarendon Press, 1918-1925. When there was any gossip worth hearing in the eighteenth century, the Sage of Strawberry Hill heard it—and wrote it to his friends, brilliantly. He heard some about Colley Cibber, of course.

Ward, Sir Alphonsus William. *A History of English Dramatic Literature to the Death of Queen Anne.* 2 vols. London: Macmillan, 1875. Revised, 1899, 3 vols. The development of the English drama and the works of its chief dramatists from the beginnings to "Later Stuart drama." Standard and sound.

——— and Waller, A. R., eds. *The Cambridge History of English Literature.* 15 vols. Cambridge University Press. First edition, 1907-1916. Reprinted 1952-1953. It is indeed "the full story of English literature," told by many scholars and authorities, each an expert in his field. Of particular interest here are Volume VIII (The Age of Dryden), chapters 1, 5, 6, and 7; Volume IX (From Steele and Addison to Pope and Swift); and Volume X (The Age of Johnson), chapter 4.

Whistler, L. *Sir John Vanbrugh, Architect and Dramatist.* London: Cobden-Sanderson, 1938. Cibber's friend, critic, and collaborator. Pronounce the name VAN BROOK.

Wiley, A. N. *Rare Prologues and Epilogues 1642-1700.* London: W. H. Allen, 1940. Many of these contain useful sidelights on the drama.

Williams, A. L. *Pope's Dunciad, A Study of its Meaning.* Baton Rouge: Louisiana State University Press, 1955. "Is impudence in prose made wit by rhyme?"—Cibber.

Wright, James. *Historia Histrionica: an Historical Account of the English-Stage . . . In a Dialogue, of Plays and Players.* London, 1699. This is most conveniently found prefaced to Robert William Lowe's edition of Cibber's *Apology* for the Grolier Society, 2 vols., London, 190-?.

2. Anonymous Pamphlets

The Age of Dullness. A Satire By a Natural Son of Mr. Pope. London, 1757.

The Bays Miscellany, or Colley Triumphant. London, 1730, [Thomas Cooke].

A Blast upon Bays; or, A New Lick at the Laureat. London, 1742. [Pope rebutting, August 3, Cibber's letter of July.]

Blast upon Blast and Lick for Lick, or a New Lesson for P[ope]. London, 1742.

The Case of the Present Theatrical Dispute Fairly Stated. London, 1743.

A Congratulatory Poem; Inscribed to Mr. [Joseph] Gay, on his Valour and Success behind Drury Lane Scenes. London, 1717. Printed with *The Confederates: A Farce* by "Joseph Gay" [John Durant Bevel], 1717.

Cibber and Sheridan: Or, The Dublin Miscellany. London, 1743.

Colley Cibber's Jests: Or, The Diverting witty Companion. Newcastle, 1761.

A Lash for the Laureate: or An Address . . . to . . . Mr. Rowe. . . . London, 1718.

The Laureat: or, The Right Side of Colley Cibber, Esq. London, 1740.

The New Sessions of the Poets. In the *Universal Spectator,* February 6, 1731.

The Scribleriad, Being an Epistle to the Dunces, On Renewing their Attack upon Mr. Pope . . . London, 1742.

The Theatre-Royal Turn'd into a Mountebank's Stage . . . By a Non-Juror. London, 1718.

The Tryal of Colley Cibber, Comedian . . . London, 1740. ["T. Johnson."]

To Diabebouloumenon: or, The Proceedings at the Theatre-Royal in Drury Lane. London, 1742.

Sawney and Colley. London, 1742.

The Tryals of the Two Causes. London, 1740.

3. Other Pamphlets

"Gay, Joseph." *A Complete Key to the Non-Juror.* London, 1718.

"H. S." *Some Cursory Remarks on the Play Call'd The Non-Juror.* London, 1718.

Hervey of Ickworth, Baron (John Hervey). *The Difference between Verbal and Practical Virtue, with a Prefatory Epistle from Mr. C[ib]b[e]r to Mr. P[ope].* London, 1742.

—— *A Letter to Mr. C[ib]b[e]r on His Letter to Mr. P[ope].* London, 1742.

Parker, E. *A Complete Key To The New Farce, call'd Three Hours after Marriage.* London, 1717.

Pope, Alexander. *The Plot Discover'd; or, A Clue to the Comedy of The Non-Juror.* London, 1718.

"Scriblerus Tertius." *The Battle of the Poets, or the Contention for the Laurel.* London, 1731. [Thomas Cooke.]

4. Unpublished Manuscripts

Colley Cibber's Last Will and Testament. Somerset House, London.
"Mr Swiney's Case, humbly Offerd to ye Consideration of my
Lord Chamberlain." Harvard Theatre Collection.
Documents in The Public Record Office, London, relating to
Patents, Licenses, etc. Many catalogued in Allardyce Nicoll's *History of Restoration Drama, 1660-1700* and his *History of Early
Eighteenth Century Drama, 1700-1750.*
Documents relating to the management of the Theatre Royal in
Drury Lane. In the British Museum, the Folger Shakespeare
Library, the Huntington Library, the Berg Collection (New
York Public Library), and elsewhere. Cataloged in L. R. N.
Ashley's "The Management of The Theatre-Royal in Drury
Lane under Cibber, Booth and Wilks", Doctoral Dissertation,
Princeton University, 1956.

5. Periodicals

Fog's Weekly Journal. September 1728-October 1737.
The Gentleman's Magazine. January 1731-December 1757.
The Grub-Street Journal. January 1730-December 1737.
Mist's Weekly Journal. December 1716-April 1725.

6. Theses and Dissertations

Ashley, L. R. N. "The Management of The Theatre-Royal in
Drury Lane under Cibber, Booth and Wilks." Doctoral Dissertation, Princeton University, 1956.
Kenion, A. L. "The Influence of Criticism upon English Tragedy,
1700-1750." Doctoral Dissertation, Duke University, 1963.
Miles, D. H. "The Relation of *The Non-Juror* to *Le Tartuffe.*"
Master's Thesis, University of Chicago, 1908.
Morse, A. S. "Satire on Literary Topics in the Drama of Henry
Fielding." Master's Thesis, University of Chicago, 1904.
Peavy, Charles D. "Cibber's *Crown of Dulness*: a Reexamination
of the Pope–Cibber Controversy." Doctoral Dissertation, Tulane
University, 1963.

7. Biographical and Critical Essays

Anonymous. "A Cibber Puff," *Notes and Queries,* CCI (1956),
388-91.
Anonymous. "Our Old Actors—The Cibbers," *Temple Bar,* LIII
(May, 1898), 60-70.
Avery, Emmett L. "Cibber, *King John,* and the Students of the
Law," *Modern Language Notes,* LIII (1938), 272-75.
——— "*The Craftsman* of July 2, 1737, and Colley Cibber,"

Research Studies of the State College of Washington, VII (1939), 91-103.

——— "Dancing and Pantomime on the English Stage, 1700-1737," *Studies in Philology*, XXXI (1934), 417-52.

——— "Foreign Performers in the London Theatres in the Early Eighteenth Century," *Philological Quarterly*, XVI (1937), 105-23.

Bateson, F. W. "The *Double Gallant* of Colley Cibber," *Review of English Studies*, I (1925), 343-46.

Croissant, DeWitt C. "Studies in the Work of Colley Cibber," *Bulletin of the University of Kansas, Humanistic Studies*, Vol. I, No. 1., Lawrence, Kansas, 1912.

Downer, Alan S. "Nature to Advantage Dressed: Eighteenth-Century Acting," *Publications of the Modern Language Association*, LVIII (1943), 1002-37.

Fagan, L. A. "Caius Gabriel Cibber," *Dictionary of National Biography*.

Gardner, W. B. "George Hicks and the Origin of the Bangorian Controversy," *Studies in Philology*, XXXIX (1942), 65-78. (*Re: The Non-Juror.*)

Glicksman, Harry. "The Stage History of Colley Cibber's *The Careless Husband*," *Publications of the Modern Language Association*, XXXVI (1921), 244-50.

Griffith, R. H. "A 'Wildfrau Story' in a Cibber Play," *Philological Quarterly*, XII (1933), 298-302.

Highet, Gilbert, "*The Dunciad*," *Modern Language Review*, XXXVI (1941), 320-43.

Kalson, Albert E. "The Chronicles in Cibber's *Richard III*," *Studies in English Literature, 1500-1900*, XIV (1963), 253-57.

Knight, Joseph. "Colley Cibber," *Dictionary of National Biography*.

Lynch, K. M. "Thomas D'Urfey's Contributions to Sentimental Comedy," *Philological Quarterly*, IX (1930), 249-59.

MacMillan, Dougald. "The Text of *Love's Last Shift*," *Modern Language Notes*, XLVI (1931), 518-19.

Miles, D. H. "A Forgotten Hit: *The Non-Juror*," *Studies in Philology*, XVI (1919), 67-77.

——— "The Original of *The Non-Juror*," *Publications of the Modern Language Association*, XXIII (1915), 195-214.

——— "The Political Satire of *The Non-Juror*," *Modern Philology*, XIII (1915), 281-304.

Nichols, C. W. "Fielding and the Cibbers," *Philological Quarterly*, I (1922), 278-89.

Nicholson, Watson. "Colley Cibber's 'Apology,' " *Notes and Queries*, Eleventh Series, Number III (January-June, 1911), 266.

Parnell, P. E. "An Incorrectly Attributed Speech-Prefix in 'Love's Last Shift,' " *Notes and Queries*, CCIV (1959), 212-13.

Peterson, W. M. "Cibber's *She Wou'd, and She Wou'd Not* and Vanbrugh's *Aesop*," *Philological Quarterly*, XXXV (1956), 429-35.

—— "Cibber's 'The Rival Queans,'" *Notes and Queries,* CCIV (1959), 164-68.

—— "The Text of Cibber's *She Wou'd, and She Wou'd Not,*" *Modern Language Notes,* LXXI (1956), 258-62.

—— "Pope and Cibber's *The Non-Juror,*" *Modern Language Notes,* LXX (1955), 332-35.

Prosser, Eleanor. "Colley Cibber at San Diego," *Shakespeare Quarterly,* XIV (1963), 253-61.

Ross, J. L. "Dramatist versus Audience in the Early Eighteenth Century," *Philological Quarterly,* XII (1933), 73-81.

Sherburn, George. "The Fortunes and Misfortunes of *Three Hours after Marriage,*" *Modern Philology,* XXIV (1926), 91-109.

Sprague, A. C. "A New Scene in Colley Cibber's *Richard III,*" *Modern Language Notes,* XLII (1927), 29-32.

Taylor, H. W. "Fielding upon Cibber," *Modern Philology,* XXIX (1931), 73-90.

Tucker, S. I. "A Note on Colley Cibber's Name," *Notes and Queries,* CCIV (1959), 400.

Tupper, F. S. "Colley and Caius Cibber," *Modern Language Notes,* LV (1940), 393-96.

Vincent, H. P. "Two Letters of Colley Cibber," *Notes and Queries,* CLXVIII (1935), 3-4.

Waddell, Helen. "Eccentric Englishwomen: viii Mrs. Charke," *Spectator,* June 4, 1937, 1047-48.

Waterhouse, Osborn. "The Development of English Sentimental Comedy in the Eighteenth Century," *Anglia* XXX (1907), 137-72, 269-305.

Whiting, G. W. "Colley Cibber and 'Paradise Lost,'" *Notes and Queries,* CLXIV (1933), 171-72.

—— "*The Temple of Dullness* and Other Interludes," *Review of English Studies,* X (1934), 206-11.

Wingfield, Hon. Lewis. "Queens of the Trump," *The Theatre,* Series 3, II (July, 1880), 43-48.

Wood, F. T. "A Letter of Colley Cibber," *Notes and Queries,* CXCI (1946), 15.

Woods, C. B. "Fielding and the Authorship of *Shamela,*" *Philological Quarterly,* XXV (1946), 248-72.

Index

PRINTED IN U.S.A.

GAYLORD